Beyond Epistemology

Beyond Epistemology

NEW STUDIES

IN THE PHILOSOPHY OF HEGEL

Edited by

FREDERICK G. WEISS

MARTINUS NIJHOFF / THE HAGUE / 1974

ISBN 90 247 1584 9

PRINTED IN THE NETHERLANDS

TO
ALL TRUE LOVERS OF HEGEL, QUICK AND DEAD,
AND IN PARTICULAR TO
GEOFFREY MURE

Io veggio ben, che giammai non si sazia
Nostro intelletto, se'l *Ver* no lo illustra
Di fuor dal qual nessun vero si spazia.

Dante, *Paradiso* IV, 124–6

FOREWORD

This book approaches Hegel from the standpoint of what we might call the question of knowledge. Hegel, of course, had no "theory of knowledge" in the narrow and abstract sense in which it has come to be understood since Locke and Kant. "The examination of knowledge," he holds, "can only be carried out by an act of knowledge," and "to seek to know before we know is as absurd as the wise resolution of Scholasticus, not to venture into the water until he had learned to swim."* While Hegel wrote no treatise exclusively devoted to epistemology, his entire philosophy is nonetheless a many-faceted theory of *truth*, and thus our title – *Beyond Epistemology* – is meant to suggest a return to the classical meaning and relation of the terms *epistēmē* and *logos*.

I had originally planned to include a lengthy introduction for these essays, setting out Hegel's general view of philosophic truth. But as the papers came in, it became clear that I had chosen my contributors too well; indeed, they have all but put me out of business. In any case, it gives me great pleasure to have been able to gather this symposium of outstanding Hegel scholars, to provide for them a forum on a common theme of great importance, and especially, thanks to Arnold Miller, to have Hegel himself among them.

Frederick G. Weiss

Charlottesville, Va.

---

* *The Logic of Hegel*, trans. from the *Encyclopaedia* by William Wallace. 2nd ed. (London: Oxford University Press, 1892), p. 17.

TABLE OF CONTENTS

HEGEL:
HOW, AND HOW FAR, IS PHILOSOPHY POSSIBLE?

G. R. G. MURE

Oxford University

1) David Hume, the gifted amateur, woke Kant from his dogmatic slumber, and Kant, being a professional physicist as well as a professional philosopher, proceeded to ask himself how pure physics and pure mathematics are possible. With his a priori categories and forms of sensuous intuition (*Anschauung*) he provided an answer. Whether he provided any positive answer to the question how the critical philosophy is itself possible is more doubtful. He confined human knowledge to the deliverance of the understanding (*Verstand*) in cooperation with sense; to phenomenal objects, that is, which we know to be the appearances only of things forever unknown to us as they are in themselves. We know that these objects are only phenomenal, because they present themselves everywhere and always as conditioned *ab extra* and not as self-subsistent, as terms in, e.g., an endless causal series in which every term is an effect and, in its turn, a cause. It is true that human reason (*Vernunft*) has Ideas (*Ideen*) of the unconditioned, but these are mere thoughts which do not yield us knowledge of any object. Their function is at once to stimulate *Verstand* and to restrict it to its proper cognitive function in cooperation with sensuous intuition. They merely regulate: they cannot, since we have no faculty of intellectual intuition, constitute any object of knowledge. This is the human condition.

2) Despite this cautious attitude, the critical philosophy, once stated, is a claim to knowledge which is not mere knowledge of phenomenal objects but knowledge of what phenomena are, of what *Verstand* and *Vernunft* are, and ultimately of what the allegedly unknowable things in themselves are. To show that knowledge is confined to phenomena Kant has tacitly to contradict himself and assume knowledge where he cannot admit it. So in general Hegel criticizes the critical philosophy, on which, none the less, his own speculation was

so largely based that he is constantly adapting and reinterpreting Kant's terminology.

3) If we ask how, on Hegel's showing, his own absolute objective idealism is possible, we get a fairly straight short answer in the opening sections 1–18, of the *Encyclopaedia*, Part I. The gist of it is this:[1] Philosophy is "a thinking study of things," and the novice cannot learn to swim before he enters the water. He may be presumed to have some acquintance with the objects which philosophy studies, and some interest in them; for they are in general the same as the objects of religion, namely the finite worlds of Nature and the human spirit (*Geist*), and the relation of these to each other and to God, who is their truth (*Wahrheit*). He will know something of mathematics and the empirical sciences, of history and of art, and he is already a moral agent and a citizen. Now, desiring to philosophize, he must reflect thoughtfully (thought is his innermost self, that which distinguishes man from brute) upon his cognitive empirical experience (*Erfahrung*) as a finite thinker who lives ordinarily at the level of common sense.

4) In *Erfahrung* thought is only *Verstand*, not yet *Vernunft*.[2] It is an activity which develops out of a relatively passive sentience, but is forced to accept the cooperation of a partner which it tries to supersede, and this is a contradiction. In *Erfahrung* the immediate object on which thought works is sensuous, a percept, a cognitive image, or an imagined end of volition. The subject in *Verstand* assumes that his thinking, like his sensing, is merely adjectival to himself as one singular experient subject among others, and that the deliverance of his senses, even if it is, as Kant said, blind without thought, is nevertheless a communication from without, a "given" content of at least potential knowledge from a separate source. His unreflective assumption is not simply false, but it is an inadequate insight which involves contradiction. The function of *Verstand* is to elicit from sensuous contents which come to the experient as contingently given, as indubitably "there" but not understood, a universal and necessary essence which shall be what they really and necessarily are. That is what the empirical scientist[3] is trying to do when he first observes and classifies his

---

[1] In what follows I have both omitted and expanded.

[2] These are not separate faculties, as Kant tended to view them, but phases through which thought logically develops. We shall see later that Hegel extends thought further downwards, too, labelling it *Intelligenz*, to cover all that is articulate in sense experience; see §§ 8 and 13 below.

[3] See *Enc.* §§ 9 and 16. All references to Hegel's works are to the Jubilee Edition (JE) of Glockner (Stuttgart 1928) unless otherwise stated.

subject matter, and then attempts to establish necessary laws – ultimately a unitary system of laws – governing its behaviour. His procedure thus debases his initial sensuous data to the status of appearances. They become endlessly multiple phenomena which in comparison and contrast to the inward essence fail to present the truth. But here the contradiction emerges. Because his thought is only *Verstand*, only aware of itself as adjectival to a singular finite subject, his elicited universal essences and laws cannot fully transform and/or supersede the sensuous content. As they first emerge from sense they are "essences" only as purely general concepts, mere identities abstracted from indefinitely multiple particulars, bare common characters which ignore difference and patently demand to be completed and "verified" in sensuous instantiation.[4] Indeed, it is largely the seeming authority of the senses as importers of knowledge from without which convinces (if they reflect at all) most ordinary men and most special scientists that the object-world they experience, whatever subjective mistakes they may make about it, is real independently and apart from their experiencing. This sub-philosophical realism is the distinctive attitude of *Verstand*. Doubtless the special scientist comes to see these merely general concepts as not only self-specifying up to a point but also as developing necessary universal connections, but the necessity is always compulsive *ab extra* necessitation, causal series in particular, which he can on reflection only think as endless regress, as series which must have, and yet cannot have, a first term, so that the necessity in his thinking remains always hypothetical.

5) Out of these contradictions have sprung, both before and after Hegel, endless controversies about the status of universals, the fierce battles of variously assorted rationalists, empiricists, positivists and phenomenalists, and in our own day the attempt to distinguish from logic and psychology a questionable science called epistemology. In Hegel's view, all such disputants, even Kant, have been endeavouring to philosophize without transcending the level of *Verstand*.

The contradictions in his thinking which arise from its ambiguous relation to sense do not seriously trouble the progress of the empirical scientist. He has perhaps a vague ideal of an all-embracing kingdom of scientific laws, but he has his own garden to cultivate. His primary

---

[4] Between *Verstand* and immediate sensuous intuition imagery (*Vorstellung*) is a mediating phase. So close is the tie at this level between thought and the sensuous content which it is struggling to supersede but must still rely on for support, that Hegel frequently uses the term *Vorstellung* to cover together both *Verstand* and its habitual accompaniment of images. It may then be conveniently rendered as "pictorial thinking." See § 18 below.

aim is a limited truth which is not philosophical. The novice, whom
Hegel in the early sections of the *Encyclopaedia* is introducing to
philosophy through logic, must, on the other hand, reflect self-
consciously on the contradictions which *Verstand* generates and on
nothing else. By virtue of a craving, a nisus in thought's own nature
(and therefore in himself),[5] he may find himself able to solve these
contradictions, not by rejecting one side or the other but by a continuous dialectical ascent. Kant had taken a negative and depreciatory
view of dialectic. He had seen it as no more than the helpless and
illusive oscillation of human reason when confronted by humanly
insoluble dilemmas such as (a) the necessity and (b) the impossibility
of thinking a primary cause into causal series. Under Hegel's guidance
the novice will recognize that *Vernunft* has categories in which the
stark oppositions of *Verstand* emerge as half-truths reconciled through
their very opposition at levels above the world of phenomena to which
Kant had restricted human knowledge. He will see that dialectic is not
illusory but is everywhere the genuine and concrete self-development
of thought.

6) Philosophy, then, is possible by virtue of an inherent dialectical
nisus of thought. But that is a very short answer. We must try to
expand it, though at first in terms which may seem obscure. This nisus
in the individual thinker is itself possible because, in Hegel's view, the
universe is the single dialectical activity of Absolute Spirit, and the
individual thinker is an integral element, a constituent phase, of its
self-developing activity. It constitutes him, and he goes to constitute
it. From this reciprocity Hegel concludes that a man's philosophizing
will be a coming to comprehend the universe through and as a growing
comprehension of his own real nature, so that his philosophizing will
not be a comment *ab extra* on the universe but a pulse of its activity.
Thus in the whole of Hegel's tripartite system, but more and more
conspicuously in the *Philosophy of Spirit* in Part III of the *Encyclopaedia*, which offers a dialectical ascent through all the levels of human
experience up to philosophy, the subject of Hegel's discourse will
at least seem to be ambivalent as between man and Absolute Spirit.
On how far Hegel succeeds in making intelligible this ambivalence,
this dual-centred nature of spirit, depends the answer to the second
part of our question. Before we can try to formulate it, something
must be said later of Hegel's Absolute *eo nomine*,[6] but it may be useful

[5] Cf. *Enc.* §§ 11–12.
[6] See §§ 21–29 below.

first to glimpse this ambivalence in the early stages of the *Philosophy of Spirit*, and this may also help to amplify and elucidate what has already been said of sense and *Verstand*.

7) In *Encyclopaedia* III, §§ 440–468,[7] Hegel traces, under the title of Theoretical Mind (*Geist*),[8] a development through sensuous intuition (*Anschauung*), through presentation in imagery (*Vorstellung*), to thinking as *Verstand*. The dialectical treatment may be described in formal terms as follows. A first immediate and affirmative phase is, as it stands, contradicted by a second phase. But this second phase, or "moment," is not the mere rejection and discarding of it as a false start. It is a mediating and determining of its nature,[9] whereby in a third phase the contradiction *qua* mere negative rejection, which Hegel calls "first negation," is cancelled by what Hegel calls "second negation," and the subject of development survives to emerge more fully developed: it is sublated, *aufgehoben*, cancelled-and-preserved,[10] in the third phase. This process continues by the breaking out of new contradictive determination, fresh mediation, in the re-immediated third phase, and thereby, as before, the developing subject is further developed. Thus each phase – conspicuously, so long as we dissect the movement in this formal analytic manner, each third phase – is an interim result which contains and is constituted by its own process, and the real and full nature of the developing subject is always still to come. Hence the ordered movement of the dialectic, whatever the terminology in which we may have to describe it, is not temporal but logical.[11] It must be remembered, however, when we examine Hegel's account of the development from sense to *Verstand*, that the dialectic is conceived by Hegel as objective and immanent in the human subject of development, but as at best only dimly apparent to that subject. Only the reflecting philosopher sees it clearly, and the empirical psychologist who assumes the detached, realist attitude of *Verstand* does not see it at all. What he does see is a hard question.

8) Hegel uses for pedagogic purposes a triadic notation in all his

---

[7] These should be read with the *Zusätze*.

[8] "Mind" has seemed to most translators more natural English than "spirit" at the lower levels of human experience, but *Geist* covers all manifestation of intelligence.

[9] Cf. *Enc.* § 12.

[10] *Aufheben* in ordinary German has both these alternative meanings. Hegel delightedly synthesizes them. See *Enc.* § 96, *Zusatz*, and *Science of Logic*, JE 4, p. 120; A. V. Miller trans., *Hegel's Science of Logic* (New York: Humanities Press, 1969), pp. 106–7.

[11] Any process of development – the passage, e.g., from the acorn to the oak, or from the zygote to the adult animal – has this logical movement in it, although time is its measure. That is why Aristotle insisted on a final as well as an efficient cause in all change.

mature works to indicate the dialectical movement in detail. It is often highly obscure, and the transitions often fail to convince the most sympathetic reader that no alternative was possible, whether the fault be the reader's or Hegel's. It is indispensable as a rough guide to direction, especially in respect to the main triads which mark the large-scale pattern of the development, but in attempting a brief outline of Hegel's doctrine we shall make no effort to observe it strictly.

The sections with which we are concerned have a long dialectical ancestry. *Geist* in this context, where it is often given the less exalted title of *Intelligenz*, has emerged as the higher level to which soul (*Seele*) has developed its fuller nature through becoming determined as consciousness (*Bewusstsein*). Soul is not an immaterial entity detachable from a mortal body. It is a result containing as its constituent process a developing series of barely differentiable psycho-physical levels, and it now achieves a truer, more determinate nature in consciousness. [12] If we look back, so to say, instead of forward, we find Hegel calling soul "the universal immateriality of Nature," [13] and later he says, "*Geist* is the existent truth of matter, the truth that matter has no truth." [14] Thus *Geist* as *Seele* has emerged as a contradiction of Nature. Yet Nature itself is, for the philosopher but not for the natural scientist, a dumb prefiguration of spirit. Nature is spirit in self-alienation. It exhibits multifarious contingency side by side with external necessitation, and Hegel speaks accordingly of its "impotence." [15] The dialectic of Nature (such rationality as it reveals to the philosopher) is, as it were, rough and embryonic, and Hegel sees Nature as stages of "developedness" rather than as developing phases. These present to the philosopher a scale rising from space and time through what in his *Philosophy of Nature, Encyclopaedia* Part II, he labels Mechanics, Physics, and Organics. Despite, however, the dumb unconsciousness of inanimate Nature, this passage of the dialectic from the inanimate through organic life is continuous. It is a gradual logical passage from the sheer dispersedness or, as Hegel calls it, "self-externality" (*Aussersichsein*), of space and time towards concentrated individuality and self-subsistence.

9) The sections of Theoretical Mind which we are to outline only concern (as in the main does this whole essay) cognitive development.

---

[12] Hegel's *Seele* is much more Aristotelian than Christian.
[13] *Enc.* § 389.
[14] *Ibid.*
[15] Cf. *Science of Logic*, J E 5, pp. 45–6; Miller, pp. 607–8.

They are followed by Practical Mind, in which the will emerges. The germ of volition was present in consciousness, but Theoretical Mind is a purely cognitive determining of spirit, and so far as we think of the subject of our discourse as a typical human experient, Theoretical Mind is an abstraction from his full experience. For that reason intuition, presentation in imagery, and thought will appear only as modes or forms of experience.[16] Certainly in each phase a content or object of the mode will emerge – one could not attempt to specify a mode of experiencing without any reference to its object –, and each mode-with-its-object will become object to the subject in the mode which succeeds it; but there will be complete abstraction from any empirical content. The object will be no more than the bare promise of an objective world. Theoretical Mind, indeed, falls under the broader heading, the larger-scale triad, of Subjective Mind, and mind remains subjective until Theoretical Mind has been contradictively determined as Practical Mind and thereby become concrete as Free Mind. Only then do we pass from mere modes to Objective Mind, which is spirit (it is natural here to change the word) developing as intelligent will into a truly objective world, moral, social, and historical in Hegel's sense of world-history as the march of spirit in time, the progress of successive national civilizations. The supreme large-scale phase of the dialectic is Absolute Spirit. Here Subjective Mind, fully determined through Objective Mind, is reinstated at a level at which the distinction is unified, and the three phases of Absolute Spirit are Art, Religion, and Philosophy. Thus Philosophy is set down at the close of the *Philosophy of Spirit* as the supreme result containing, cancelled but preserved, the whole preceding dialectical process of itself. But at the risk of anticipating a doctrine which we cannot yet attempt to justify, we must add that "the whole preceding dialectical process of itself" is not to be imaged as a rectilinear (or even zigzag) ascent, nor as making an absolute beginning in spatio-temporal Nature. The continuous dialectic of the whole system begins, so far as that term is applicable,[17] with a logic of the categories of pure thought, and the total content of Philosophy, the process of itself which, as result, it contains, is the whole triad of "pure" thought, Nature, and the increasingly explicit activity of spirit which Hegel presents in the *Philosophy of Spirit*, and in a rather different and not wholly congruent shape in the *Phenomenology of Spirit*. The dialectic may be imagined, says Hegel, making a rare

[16] Cf. *Enc.* § 440.
[17] It applies only to the beginner in philosophy; cf. *Enc.* § 17.

concession to pictorial thinking, not as a straight line but as an endless circle;[18] but if we choose to use Hegel's circle image we must remember that this "circularity" symbolizes not only the dialectic of the system as a whole but equally the return upon itself, through determining negation, of the first phase in the third phase of every triad on every scale.

10) This glance at Hegel's giant system has perhaps served only to accentuate the seeming ambivalence as between man and the Absolute. We may hope that it will become clearer as we proceed. Meanwhile it is to be noted that Hegel, when he is about to introduce Theoretical Mind, says "*Geist* starts only from its own being and relates itself only to its own determinations (*Bestimmungen*)."[19] This means that, as the philosopher sees it, the determining of soul through consciousness has resulted in self-consciousness. All the phases of *Geist* from sensuous intuition onwards will be, for philosophical insight, phases of self-consciousness.

11) Intuition (*Anschauung*) is begotten out of feeling (*Empfindung*) by attention (*Aufmerksamkeit*). In simple immediate feeling there is no distinction of feeler and felt.[20] The sheer feeling of hardness, e.g., no more determines a subject than it does an object. Feeling as such is a mere neutral, though richly potential, stuff. Attention divides it into a rudimentary subject which distinguishes itself from an objective this-here-and-now, and the union of the two sides is spatio-temporal intuition.[21] The subject is unquestioningly certain of this object and accords it self-subsistent being, but only because it finds in it its other self. Here is the germ of self-consciousness.

12) Space and time, the forms of sensuous intuition, are sheerly self-external and therefore endlessly continuous and endlessly discrete. Thus both the subject and the object of sensuous intuition have a formal, abstract and empty, universality.[22] "This-here-and-now" is

---

[18] Cf. *Enc.* §§ 15 and 17.
[19] *Enc.* § 440.
[20] Cf. *Enc.* § 446.
[21] Cf. *Enc.* § 448.
[22] Cf. *Enc.* § 448, *Zusatz* penultimate paragraph. Yet this empty universality is not mere empty generality. Intuition is for Hegel, as it was for Kant, a form of wholeness. We intuit space and time, for all their indefinitely regressive and therefore ultimately self-contradictory nature, as wholes, or at any rate as quasi-wholes, not as merely general "spatiality" and "temporality." Hegel, abandoning Kant, here implies his own doctrine that the universal as such is concrete: the general particularizing itself to the fully individual (see § 28 below), not depending for implementation on sense as a separate faculty. As against Kant's view that *Vernunft* is purely regulative, and that *Verstand* is purely discursive and requires supplementation by sensuous intuition to constitute an object of knowledge (cf. §§ 1-2

really a too determinate description of the immediately intuited object. Placing and dating only become explicit as *Anschauung* develops into *Vorstellung*. For the first phase of *Vorstellung* is *Erinnerung*, recollection. The subject arrests, as it were, the vague and fugitive "here-and-now," placing and grasping it as a present containing a past.[23] Hegel's *Erinnerung* preserves the literal meaning of the German word. This beginning of memory is a "making inward" of the intuition, which thereby loses some of its self-externality and is "taken up into the universality of the ego."[24] It is thus freed from its first immediacy and the space and time in which it was intuited. It becomes an image placed and dated in the ego's own space and time.

Images lapse from the ego's direct and conscious possession into a subconscious state of merely formal and potential universality, a store house, as it were, or a mine.[25] But the image is recollected (in the ordinary sense of the term) when a fresh intuition occurs and is recognized as identical in content with the reproduced past image. The latter is the formal universal under which the fresh intuition is subsumed.

13) The content of *Vorstellung* as it now develops is more and more surely possessed and mastered by the subject, or ego, as its own self. *Vorstellung* is on the way to be sublated into thought as *Verstand*, and it is to be noted that Hegel treats this whole ascent from its beginning in feeling as the work of *Intelligenz*.[26] For Hegel, though not for the ordinary man, not for the special scientist, not for the empiricist thinker, sense is only the germ of thought, not a complementary source of knowledge, not the medium of some message from any realistically preconceived ready-made thing in itself. The intuition and the image must never be thought of as copies.[27]

14) The further development of *Vorstellung* from reproduction,

---

above), Hegel absorbs intuition into thought as its moment of immediacy (cf. § 7 above), and that is how he constructs his rational dialectic.

[23] For Hegel the verb "to have," when used to express the perfect tense, retains the meaning of possession. What I have seen I experience in my present seeing (cf. *Enc.* § 450, *Zusatz*, and § 125). The transition might have been expressed as the object acquiring extension and duration – Hegel warns us not (as Kant had) to take space and time as merely subjective –, but his point here is that mind is developing *itself* in and as its object.

[24] *Enc.* § 452.

[25] Cf. *Enc.* §§ 453–4.

[26] Cf. § 4, Note 2, and § 8 above.

[27] It is easier to avoid this error if we remember that intuition and imagery involve all the senses and not, as psychologists tend to forget, vision alone. "Intuition" and "*Anschauung*" both suggest sight only, and "image" (perhaps also *Vorstellung*) is apt to suggest a copy or replica.

through *Erinnerung* to productive imagination (*Einbildungskraft*)[28] may seem to suggest that Hegel, rejecting realism, has lapsed into subjective idealism, but productive imagination, even as *Phantasie*, the "free" imagination of the day-dreamer, of the artist who "creates" with it, and of the religious man who experiences truth in the form of allegory and myth, is still the according of subsistence to another *self*; to a world of the ego's own making, but a world which genuinely *is*, whatever the degree of depth and coherence it may or may not reveal.[29] Here and in factual cognition alike the *Vorstellung* is a quasi-universal which roughly associates and orders the manifold particularity of upsurging sensuous intuitions.

15) The image next begins to approximate yet more nearly to a universal of thought. It is now grasped first as a sensible symbol which means something else. It represents something which differs in import from itself but is still recognizably akin, as, for example, the eagle represents the strength of Jupiter.[30] Then the symbolic *Vorstellung* becomes intellectualized. The sensuous tie attenuates as the image becomes an arbitrary sign, namely the linguistic symbol. Imagery has developed into language. The factor of remembrance in this process towards thinking has become *Gedächtnis*, purely mechanical verbal memory in which the words come by habit (which originated in soul) and demand no effort from the speaker, who is thus freed to think. More precisely, images become names. Names are at first meanings of things, but the distinction between name, meaning, and thing is "inwardized" in the now explicit universality of the *thinking* subject, which arranges and orders the named things comprising its whole content. "We think in names," says Hegel, and he regards it as absurd to suppose that a man can think without words.[31]

16) Thought now emerges as *Verstand*. The ego "knows that what is thought (*gedacht*) *is*, and that what *is* only *is* in so far as it is a thought."[32] The finite thinker, the subject in *Verstand*, is truly universal to the extent that it is the unity of itself and its "other,"

[28] Cf. *Enc.* § 457.
[29] Does a painter paint what he sees, or does he paint in order to see? Does he "explore" colour and shape, or does he "create" them? In art these are not mutually exclusive disjunctions. Cf. Wordsworth, *Tintern Abbey*: –
            "All the mighty world
            Of eye, and ear, – both what they half create,
            And what perceive."
[30] Cf. *Enc.* § 457, *Zusatz*.
[31] *Enc.* § 462, *Zusatz*.
[32] *Enc.* § 465.

viz. being, which it overlaps and includes. But this unity still falls within the mind as subjective, and the universality is still only formal: the objects which it thinks as general concepts, working them up into species, genera, forces, laws, in general into categories, are still *given*, remembered, *Vorstellungen*. These remain a stuff on which (though it is for philosophic insight its other self) the thinking subject of *Verstand* can only impose those forms which it possesses as implicitly *Vernunft*, namely the forms of judgement and syllogism. Hegel means, I think, that in inference at the level of *Verstand*, everyday inference and even inference in the special sciences, the point at which inference begins is contingent. It is arbitrarily selected from possible starting points which are manifold and contingent as sensed objects are manifold and contingent. [33] The premiss taken as primary is always in fact borrowed from empirical experience. Hence formal and material truth do not coalesce. If the conclusion is to be fully true it must be (a) valid, conformable to the rules of syllogism, and this validity is all of pure thought that the inference contains. But (b) it must also be materially true as fact in an empirically experienced and therefore contingent world. Thus the necessity of inference in *Verstand* is definite and rigorous only at the cost of being hypothetical and external. Yet this syllogistic inference is the nearest approach to *Vernunft* in Theoretical Mind, and Hegel then begins Practical Mind with the remark, *"Geist* as will knows itself as the author of its own conclusions, the origin of its self-fulfilment." [34]

17) It may be well to summarize and a little amplify what we have learned about thought as *Verstand*. The thinker, to the extent of his minimal self-consciousness, assumes himself to be no less a singular subject among other such subjects in his thinking than in his sense perception. In both he takes his object to be real independently and apart from his awareness of it. This independence of his object seems to him the guarantee that his thinking can be true in the sense that it can, though in varying degree, correctly reflect its object. His cognitive attitude is that of an observer trying to record as faithfully as he can. He may recognize that what he records is only the appearance of an independently real, but so far as he fails to achieve correct correspondence he blames his own thinking and perceiving. For him there are degrees of correctness in the appearance as it approaches truth, but the real which appears does not itself admit degrees of reality.

[33] Cf. *Enc.* § 9.
[34] *Enc.* § 469.

18) He thinks in universals, but these are general concepts and there are many of them. They are "essences" only as identities elicited from their multiple instantiation, lowest common characters which ignore difference. They retain the multiplicity of the sensuous objects of which they are meant to be the superseding essences, because they are not fully emerged from *Vorstellungen*, and between the image and the thought there is a contradiction which is only dialectically intelligible. The image is imperfectly sublated in the thought, and Hegel frequently means by *Vorstellung* "imaging-and-thinking," or as it is often rendered, "pictorial thinking."[35] *Verstand*, however, for all that rigidity of its logical movement by virtue of which it claims the title of scientific precision, is itself a developing phase of thought. As his thinking struggles to transcend sense, the finite thinker's general concepts begin to exhibit necessary interconnexion. Whiteness, sweetness, and cubic shape are still highly sensuous universals, barely raised above *Vorstellungen*. They all characterize a lump of sugar, but only as the conjoint *de facto* predicates of a contingent sensible "thing." But to comprehend the causal relation between the compression of steam in a cylinder and the movement of a piston, or the reciprocal relations between the organs of an organism, is to have insight into universal and necessary connection (however hypothetical) within a system. *Verstand* can even, as Kant had shown, establish causation and other principles as a priori categories, exceptionless laws which govern the nature and behaviour of all phenomena in the object-world apparent to *Verstand*. Without them that world would be an unintelligible chaos, although they are not derivable, as whiteness, sweetness, and cubic shape seem to be, from the deliverance of sense. Furthermore, the perceiving and thinking subject in *Verstand* has a vague ideal of an overall subjective unity of all his own actual and possible experiencings, a unity which is at the same time objective in that it is correlated necessarily with an overall unity of his phenomenal object-world. Kant had called it "the transcendental unity of apperception," and he had regarded it as somehow explicated in his categories.

19) In this a priori unity explicit in categories Kant, whom on the whole Hegel regards as attempting to philosophize within the limits of pictorial thinking, has an inkling of reason (*Vernunft*) as more than merely regulative. But Hegel objects that this Kantian unity is not

---

[35] Cf. § 4, Note, above.

systematically coherent, which means for Hegel not dialectically ordered. These categories of *Verstand*, though not empirically derivable from sense, refer only to sensuous objects and are empty without a sensuous filling. Each is a more or less separate principle of self-contradictory necessitation (as in cause and effect), which reflection reveals as indefinite regress. Kant retains the observer attitude of *Verstand*. The subject of his discourse is the generalized finite experient and no more. Despite his unity of apperception he fails to grasp the true significance of self-consciousness. He does not tackle the obvious problem of how a singular finite thinker can possess and move in universals when he thinks, and yet somehow share sweetness and whiteness and the category of cause and effect with other finite thinkers. And yet, Hegel points out, though any man can say "I" and mean to indicate himself and nobody else, it is nevertheless a universal "I," since any man can say it, which he has despite himself asserted.[36] He has shown a dim inkling that self-consciousness is universal.

Despite its shortcomings, or what one might call its semi-rationality, *Verstand* is a necessary phase or, as Hegel calls it, "moment" of thought.[37] It is "first negation," the contradictive determining which is there to be cancelled but preserved in the dialectic of reason. Without it there would be no definiteness in men and things, no first negation for second negation to cancel.

20) Before we pass on, there is a point to be made which bears importantly on our enquiry. We have seen that the modes of experience from *Empfindung* to *Verstand* constitute a dialectical *Stufenleiter*, a series such that form and content at each stage are the transformation and development of the preceding stage. But so far as the ambivalent subject of the development is a human being, his position on the ladder can vary. Content which is normally and properly experienced in a higher form can in the individual man exist in a lower form. A man may philosophize but be unable fully to sublate pictorial thinking, an error – or was it dialectically inevitable immaturity? – which Hegel in different degrees imputes to most of those predecessors whose thought he professes to sublate in his own system, and also to the religious man (at any rate to the theologian) whose faith rests stubbornly in the form of mere devotional feeling and anthropomorphic imagination. Again, there is feeling to the intensity and all-embracingness of passion (*Leidenschaft*) in the thought and action of the best

---

[36] Cf. *Enc.* § 20, last paragraph and § 24, *Zusatz* 1, paragraph 3.
[37] Cf. *Enc.* § 80 and *Zusatz*.

and greatest of men, but it is passion sublated, preserved but transformed.[38] But a man's nisus and the world of his activity may sink
disastrously towards the form of mere feeling.[39] The result may be a
conflict between two selves within a man's self, a lapse into irre-
soluble contradiction which can become madness. If the lower form
dominates the content proper to the higher, the issue can be, not mere
ignorance and innocence but the twin perversions of cognitive error
and moral evil.

21) It may help us to a better insight into that ambivalence of spirit
on which the possibility of philosophizing seems to depend, if we here
make a fresh start and consider certain formal attributes of Hegel's
Absolute Spirit. Hegel has warned us that we must enter the water
before we can learn to swim, and that to expound philosophy not
dialectically but, as Spinoza did, by deduction from allegedly primary
premisses is to misapply a method proper only to *Verstand*.[40] We shall
not, however, be trying to lay down primary premisses from which
the detail of the system can be deduced, but a few provisional abstractions. These can only be thought, not imaged – *Vorstellung* in this
context can hopelessly mislead –, but they cannot even be intelligibly
stated except (a) through contrast with the relative and finite which
a monistic Absolute must *ex vi termini* contain within itself, and (b)
in words often precariously metaphorized to signify beyond the field
of their everyday application. In philosophy a metaphor – to speak
metaphorically – is like an overdraft: indispensable at the time but
difficult to repay. The philosopher must suppress imagery and make
language his servant, but words he must use, and he rarely achieves
the *mot juste*. Hegel takes important terms from his predecessors, and
when he shapes them to his own use they often seem almost synonymous
because of his concern to reinterpret them all as exhibiting the triple
rhythm of his dialectic.

A direct attack on the Absolute is justified also as a protest against
a current tendency to push Hegel's Absolute under the carpet, to praise
only his empirical acumen, and to emasculate his ethical writings into
sociology.

22) Hegel's absolute monism is the assertion that the Absolute is
one, but single and not singular; not a unit but a unity, and not a
finite unity nor an indefinite multiplicity of unities, but a single

[38] A fair answer, incidentally, to absurdly dichotomous emotivist doctrines of value.
[39] Cf. *Enc.* § 447.
[40] Cf. *Enc.* § 231.

infinite totality. Only by metaphor can it be counted as one. By the same token it is actual, *wirklich*, not as the actualization of one of many possible universes, but as containing within itself all possibility. [41]

23) Being infinite unity, the universe is no more spatio-temporal than it is countable, for space and time are emphatically not unity but dispersion: they have only the bastard ambiguous infinity of the indefinite regress which must have, but cannot have, an end and a beginning. Yet one is forced to say in spatial metaphor that "outside it" is nothing, nothing which it is not, nothing which is other than it or different from it and would by such otherness or difference determine it from outside and so destroy its absolute nature. Otherness lies only "within it," and this entails what is stark paradox for *Verstand*: it must be other than itself. Hence springs Hegel's supremely important doctrine of negation. We have had a glimpse of it at work, and for the moment we need only say that it equates negation, otherness, difference, and contradiction with determining (*Bestimmung* and *Bestimmtheit*). Spinoza, though he did not confuse true infinity with the indefinite regress, had said, "*determinatio est negatio*," a dictum which tends to obliterate finitude as an illusion; Kant had seen no purpose in the negative judgement except to ward off error; Hegel says, "*negatio est determinatio*." If to these terms we add "mediation" (of the immediate) we may sum their significance as "negativity," a term which has the advantage of suggesting movement. [42]

24) Viewed in provisional abstract contrast with an absolute and infinite universe, any finite entity, any object of *Verstand* and sense, is in a degree determined *ab extra* by what it is not, by what is in one way or another different from it; determined *de facto* so far as it is sensed, and by no more than external necessity so far as it is thought by *Verstand*. Thus the being of any given finite entity, the answer to the question what it is, lies not only within it by virtue of such individuality as it has in its immediately presented "reality," but also beyond it. One cannot cut with a knife between these two aspects or moments of its unstable being, and the extent of the "beyond" which determines it cannot itself be determined. *Verstand* may judge a finite thing, but the series of concepts predicable of it as qualities or relations is inexhaustible, and the characterization can never be complete.

[41] Cf. § 36 below.
[42] In equating negation with determination Hegel does not exclude negation in the sense of annihilation. The death of living beings is an essential determining of their finitude.

Hegel calls this reaching beyond itself for its truth the finite's "ideality," which thus contrasts with its *Realität*, its mere existence or, as
Hegel prefers to put it, its mere "being-there" (*Dasein*). It is not so
much on the object's non-independence of the subject as on this
relation of ideal to "real" (a relation incomprehensible to *Verstand*)
that Hegel's philosophical idealism is founded. "This ideality of the
finite," he says, "is the chief maxim of philosophy; and for that reason
every genuine philosophy is idealism." [43] In a man his ideality shows
as a clear nisus towards self-completion; perhaps, though he may not
know it, towards absolute totality. He grows up, he acts and thinks.
His grasp may become more and more nearly commensurate with his
reach, until he finds a fuller truth and more genuine reality as a
statesman, an artist, a saint, or a philosopher. But any finite entity,
even a man, stands either less or more passively in endless negative
relations which determine it from without. It is what it is always to
some not finally determinable extent by external necessitation; that
is, from its own standpoint, contingently. If it is a man he may fail by
what seems mischance, or his nisus may become perverted. Like all
things finite, he comes to be and passes away, and while he exists his
imperfect self-subsistence subjects him to change in space and time,
which are the very media of self-externality.

On the other side of this abstract contrast, the Absolute, we have
seen, must be other than itself. Since it has no "beyond," its negativity
must fall "inside" it. It must be self-negating, self-mediating, self-
determining. We might be tempted to try to think it as a purely
positive immediate self-identity, but it would then turn out to be not
just empty but simply null. We should in fact have reintroduced the
negation which we were trying to exclude and precisely demonstrated
the first step in Hegel's own logic of categories, the "first negation"
of pure being as pure not-being or nothing. [44]

25) If the Absolute is self-determining it must be absolute self-
conscious spirit. Hegel takes that for granted. He was endeavouring
to consummate a rationalist tradition as old as Plato, and he was also
a decidedly unorthodox Lutheran theist. Indeed the novice, having
been told that the objects of religion and philosophy are in general the
same, [45] might incline to identify Hegel's Absolute Spirit with the God
of Protestant Christianity. In that he would be both right and wrong.

[43] *Enc.* § 95, last paragraph. Cf. also § 96 *Zusatz*.
[44] Cf. § 35 below.
[45] See § 3 above.

Religious experience has, according to Hegel, the same rational content as philosophy, but comprehended inadequately in the form of pictorial thinking. The Creation, the fall of Adam and Eve, the incarnation and atonement by death and resurrection of Christ, and the immortality of the singular individual soul are *Vorstellungen*, symbolic myths of highly significant rational import, but neither actual historic fact nor *Vernunft* in its supreme form. In art, which for Hegel is identical with aesthetic experience and is primarily religious art, rational content has a directly sensuous form. Thus it looks as if religion and art were supreme cases of a content lapsing to a lower form in an individual man, [46] but the problem of Hegel's precise meaning is too difficult to discuss here. Be it only said that on the whole Hegel remains firmly rationalist; yet he certainly finds man's most significant pain and joy in religious experience, and he frequently uses Christian allegory to throw light by analogy on his Absolute, pushing it beyond orthodoxy for the purpose. He sees the Creation, for instance, as symbolizing no arbitrary act. God created the world unreservedly as his total other self, and only in his union through contradictive opposition with it is God perfect.

26) Absolute self-conscious spirit is *Vernunft*, the single rationally thinking subject which determines timelessly as its other self the being which it thinks and knows. Hegel strives thus to supersede the partial truth of realism which persists in the attitude of *Verstand* and presupposes as its object a being self-subsistent apart from thought and knowledge, and of subjective idealism which, having already tacitly defined thought by contrast with being, would reduce being to thought. He unites these half-truths by virtue of his doctrine of negativity. Thought and being are contradictory opposites (A and not-A), because absolute difference is not merely contrary but contradictory opposition. But *negatio est determinatio*. The contradiction of thought by being is sublated, doubly negated, in the absolute concrete self-determining of thought in and as being, in the explication of what Hegel calls the "original" identity on which the opposition is based. Here is, as it were, the fundamental original pattern and source of the dialectic, which is neither subjective argumentation nor, as the stultifying thesis of "dialectical materialism" suggests, contradiction somehow at work in matter upon which thought supervenes as an epiphenomenal consequence. For *Verstand* A and not-A, since they divide between them all that is,

[46] Cf. § 20 above.

cannot both be predicated of the same logical subject. But for *Verstand* the logical subject is a flatly real finite entity which does not transcend itself. [47] Being only contradicts thought because it is that as which thought determines itself.

27) This concrete unity, in which thought, as Hegel puts it, "overlaps and grasps" (*übergreift*) being, demands from the novice in philosophy a new conception of truth and reality. [48] For *Verstand* truth is mere correctness. It belongs to subjective thinking in so far as that corresponds accurately to a being taken as apart from and independent of thought. Truth can be no more than that for thought which is merely adjectival to a singular thinker. But absolute thought *qua* true – and indeed all thought so far as it achieves any degree of rationality – is, for Hegel, the truth not "about" but "of" being. [49] Being is real not apart from but in and as thought, and only thereby is thought itself real. Hence for Hegel *das Wahre* comes to mean "genuine," "authentic," "veritable." [50] Moreover, absolute pure thought, which Hegel entitles "Absolute Idea" (*Idee*), is the supreme category not simply of theoretical thinking. It is not only thought as cognition idealizing a real self but also will, volition realizing an ideal self. It is the unity of the distinction, as God in religious *Vorstellung* is at once omniscient and omnipotent. Hegel was a rationalist but not an intellectualist. His absolute reason is conceived as transcending and unifying the uncomfortable Kantian duality of pure (in the sense of theoretical) reason and practical reason. Consequently *das Wahre qua* true-and-real is *eo ipso* the good. Truth of fact and truth of value are no more ultimately separable than they were for Plato.

28) This absolute thought can also be expressed as "the universal." For *Verstand* the universal is not one but many, an indefinite multiplicity of general concepts. Such a general concept can be specified to a

---

[47] Cf. § 24 above.

[48] "Reality," that is, not in the sense of *Realität* as mere existence or *Dasein*, (see § 24 above) but of "the really real" (the Platonic ὄντως ὄν), which is a commoner usage of the term in English philosophy than in Hegel, who prefers, being an objective idealist, to express "the really real" as *das Wahre* "the true-and-real."

[49] Cf. Hegel's letter to Duboc, Hoffmeister's ed., Vol. III, p. 13. I translate the immediately relevant passage of the letter as follows: "When I mean the philosophical absolute I define the true as that which is in itself *concrete*, i.e. as unity in itself of *opposed* definitions (*Bestimmungen*) such that this opposition remains preserved in the unity. In other words, I view truth not as what stands still and rigid (not as abstract identity, abstract being) but as in itself movement, life; as indifference only as having a mere show of indifference in it, or as having a difference in it which *qua* within it, within the unity, is at the same time not a difference, a *sublated* (i.e. cancelled and preserved) difference which, because it is mere show, *is* not."

[50] Cf. *Enc.* § 24, *Zusatz* 2, paragraph 5.

certain point, but it can never touch objective being save in logically indiscriminable singular instances, which are nevertheless, but contradictorily, taken as the inessential and contingent. For Hegel rational thought is *the* universal, the universe as thinking subject. In its absolute form it is *Idee*. At lower levels where philosophic insight is beginning to grasp it, it is the notion, the *Begriff*.[51] As *Begriff*, and more explicitly as *Idee*, the universal does not remain subjective, abstract, and general, but particularizes itself to total concrete individual. It determines itself fully, not defectively and contradictorily by the support of endless instantiation. It is the concrete universal, the universal becoming logically the individual. It is the thinking subject which, negating, determining, mediating its empty self-identical generality, regains logically its self-identity as concrete individual unity – once again the triadic dialectical pattern. It is in this sense of individual which is not singular that Hegel's universe is one, is infinite, is actual (*wirklich*).[52] Hegel calls *wirklich* any content in which philosophic insight can grasp the indwelling notion. Hence the scandal to pictorial thought when Hegel proclaimed the identity of the real (*das Wirkliche*) and the rational.[53] And the notion, naturally, connotes value, too. Hegel talks of a finite entity which fails to be what it ought to be, a sick man, e.g., or a criminal, as not conforming to *its* notion.

In abstract contrast with this absolute, self-concentrated individuality, not only sick men and criminals but all finite entities fail of individuality in some degree. They are contradictory unities of general and singular, essential and contingent. Their unstable being lies in large measure beyond them, and to the extent that it does so they are self-external, not inwardly concentrated and self-possessing. Individuality lessens as we descend in Hegel's system from man, through organic and inanimate Nature to time and lastly to space, the vanishing point of the individual in the sheerly self-external.

29) The Absolute neither rests nor changes. It is the eternal, not everlasting but timeless, self-conscious activity wherein spirit severs itself as thinking subject from being and reconciles this contradictive self-alienation in concrete objective self-unity. It is a timeless logical process at once self-fulfilling and self-fulfilled, a process constituting the result which contains it.

[51] Cf. § 38 below. Hegel thus gives a special sense to *Begriff*, the ordinary German word for a concept.
[52] Cf. § 22 above.
[53] Cf. *Enc.* § 6.

Here we can begin to put together our two provisional abstractions. This activity, this driving force of negativity, is free, which means for Hegel that it is neither capricious nor necessitated by external compulsion but self-determining – as, so far as it is free, is the human will. Absolute Spirit is not the transcendent God of Aristotle. Since "outside it" is nothing and "within it" all is finite, it can constitute itself only in the finite and all that is finite. Its timeless process of self-alienation and self-reconstitution must embrace all finitude, and at the human level it must even negate itself in error, evil, and pain. In Hegel's religious *Vorstellung* God determines himself freely and totally in the Creation without which he would not be, and with the same freedom he suffers, dies, and atones in the person of Christ.

Thus Hegel's Absolute Spirit is the active immanent totality of all finite approximations to its own perfection, and apart from them it would be nothing. His system is their dialectical ordering, and the one among them with which we are concerned is man struggling to fulfill the immanent nisus in him to philosophize. How far does it now seem that he can succeed?

30) To judge fairly the success or failure of Hegel one must read his major works and make up one's own mind. A critic can of course assume that there is no rationality save in the thinking of *Verstand* and demonstrate from this external standpoint that the whole dialectic is nonsense. But he has no claim to be taken seriously unless he can first prove that sense is a source of knowledge which provides true data in independence of thought; and secondly that the inferences of *Verstand* have anywhere a more than hypothetical necessity. Until he can do this – and, despite many vehement but logically self-defeating appeals to direct intuition, it has never been done – he is attempting to apply to Hegel's dialectical system a criterion which is not valid. It is a futile *ignoratio elenchi* to complain that the dialectic never exhibits the cogency of mathematical deduction. Hegel conceives it as the free movement of *Vernunft* coming to find its other self in and as being, and freedom for Hegel, as has been said, means neither arbitrary caprice nor the external necessitation of *Verstand* but self-determination. That is why we must provisionally accept Hegel's view that the criterion of thought is immanent in thought itself and read him from beginning to end. We must, however, read him critically. The difficulty is to decide, when we have mastered the general direction of his thought, what is a fair standpoint for criticism which shall not be merely external and question-begging. We can here do no more than offer a

few points which the student might bear in mind as he struggles to swim.

31) If in spite of their identity as mutually constituent human thinking is a finite approximation to Absolute Spirit,[54] then it would be absurd to believe that human philosophy either was perfected by Hegel or is perfectible. The ambivalent nature which we noted in the subject of Hegel's discourse is not to be conjured into plain equivalence. There are passages in Hegel where he may seem to imply that philosophy has reached its final consummation in his own thinking, but he never explicitly asserts anything so ridiculous, and there are passages which point in the other direction. We may ask, then, what are the inevitable defects in a system such as his, whether he recognized them or not.

32) If Hegel's free self-determining dialectic fails, it is plausible to argue that it fails because Hegel himself has failed fully to transcend *Verstand*. Freedom will then have sunk into caprice and pseudo-cogency. The moment of contradiction will have become mere difference. The overall unity of spirit will have faded and broken into contexts not clearly connected, and within them the necessity of the movement will have become hypothetical. Hegel's most sympathetic critics have commonly confessed that many of his transitions admit of an alternative direction, and some have accused him of often imposing the triadic formula quite artificially.

33) To this line of attack Hegel might possibly have replied that if the dialectic fails in this way its failure is not mere lapse into capricious thinking but also a lapse, on the other side, of the object and content into contingency. The failure must be a failure of *Wahrheit*, not merely of incorrect subjective thought. Dialectic is the only true philosophic method because in it form and content are one.[55] Hence if form fails content fails too. If Absolute Spirit constitutes itself in a circle of approximating phases of finitude, these, to remain distinct from one another and not vanish in the night of an Absolute wherein all cows are black,[56] must possess a degree of *Wahrheit* which dwindles as the approximation grows more distant. That is why Nature may be called "impotent."[57] The lack of individuality, the dispersedness and

---

[54] Cf. § 29 above.

[55] Cf. *Science of Logic*, JE 4, pp. 51–2; Miller, p. 54.

[56] So Hegel unkindly describes the Absolute of Schelling (see *Phenomenology of Spirit*, JE 2, p. 22; Baillie trans., 2nd ed., p. 79) whom he heavily attacks for the caprice and artificiality of his dialectic.

[57] Cf. § 8 above.

contingency of Nature do not betoken the inadequacy of subjective thinking: they are its inseparable correlate. Thought and being are here concomitantly defective. The defect attaches to both sides, because "impotent" Nature and the thought of it (which consists in the constructions of natural science and the merely rough dialectic in which reason sublates them) together constitute a logically indispensable phase of approximation to Absolute Spirit, but a phase in which spirit is only beginning to reconcile the opposition of thought and being in its return from self-alienation.

If this be Hegel's answer, it follows that the dialectic, as unity of form and content, was bound to remain a degree approximative, failing of full freedom, throughout the system and not merely in Nature. The conclusion seems obvious, but it was perhaps worth stating, because Hegel seems sometimes unready to accept it, and his commentators often seem uncertain of the proper grounds on which to find fault with his dialectic.

34) This inherent and inescapable defect in Hegel's system – for such it surely is – raises the kindred problem of time, for one may fairly describe Hegel's enterprise in one aspect as an effort to show time and eternity as mutually constituent. It may be urged – and this, again, is obviously true and explicitly accepted by Hegel himself[58] – that Hegel's dialectic everywhere presupposes the deliverance of *Verstand* which it claims to sublate, notably the natural sciences but also the work of ordinary historians in every sphere; and that in the endless course of time this suffers both obsolescence and actual increment. Civilization may or may not progress, but it does not stand still, and any philosophy which does not disdainfully ignore the finite in its pursuit of the infinite must itself grow perpetually more obsolete.

One can here imagine Hegel offering a partial but not a complete defence. He would have conceded that a man can no more leap out of his own epoch than out of his own skin,[59] but he would have pointed out that (a) the present as he sees it is the sublation and consummation of the past[60] (Hegel virtually anticipates Croce's dictum that all history is contemporary history), and (b) that the future is the subject of hope and fear but not of knowledge, because, as such, it *is* not.[61] Certainly time is "vanishingness," and all that is finite must perish.

[58] Cf. *Enc.* § 9.
[59] Cf. *Philosophy of Right*, JE 7, p. 35; Knox trans., p. 11.
[60] Cf. § 12 above.
[61] Cf. *Enc.* § 259.

But the idea of time reaching back and forward endlessly from the present is a mere *Vorstellung* in which reflective thought at once finds contradiction. Doubtless it faintly symbolizes the all-inclusiveness of the Absolute, but time without change to measure has no meaning, and so far as the finite in its little lifetime is self-transcending, its temporality and death are of small importance.

35) Where is Hegel's dialectic at its best? Where is its movement nearest to a convincingly self-demonstrating freedom? Certainly in the larger rather than in the small scale triads, but fitfully everywhere, perhaps particularly in the magnificently adventurous *Phenomenology of Spirit*. Hegel himself was probably best satisfied with his dialectic of pure thought, his logic of categories. We have no space to discuss the vexed question of the transition from pure thought to Nature, but a word must be said of the logic itself, though we can here present no more than a dim telescopic view of it.

The categories are an enormous expansion and transformation of the Kantian categories supplemented from many other sources. They constitute a series of more and more full and concrete definitions of the Absolute, and Hegel insists strongly that, whereas Kant's categories lack any systematic interconnection and are empty without sensuous filling, his own interrelate dialectically and are form and content in one. Thus we may say that in the Logic the ambivalent subject of discourse is Absolute Spirit rather than man, or at least that the categories are man's nearest approach to grasping the self-manifestation of absolute thought in him. The Logic may be symbolized in religious *Vorstellung* as the eternal essence of God before the Creation,[62] but the reference to human thought is always present. The first main section of the Logic covers the categories of Being, which operate in human sensuous experience in so far as it is intelligent but below the level of *Verstand*. One could call them the categories of *Intelligenz* conceived as the first and relatively immediate stage of *Vernunft*. The Absolute is first minimally defined as Pure Being, being as the utterly indeterminate potentiality (or privation, if we prefer to look at it that way) of the concrete universal-individual,[63] so indeterminate that the first dialectical negation is Pure Not-being,[64] and as doubly negated it is Becoming, the bare thought of the coming-to-be and passing away

---

[62] Cf. *Science of Logic*, JE 4, p. 46; Miller, p. 50.

[63] Every category, however rudimentary and undeveloped, prefigures the universal in the sense of universal-individual, not of merely general. Cf. § 28 above.

[64] Cf. § 24 above.

which is the destiny of all things finite. But what becomes is at any
rate Somewhat (*Etwas*), though it is not yet some*thing*. Somewhat is
quality as yet devoid even of quantity, and when quantitative determinations emerge to characterize our ambivalent subject of discourse they "contradict" it, because they hold true of it irrespective
of its quality: a pint is a pint whatever the liquid it measures. In the
third section of Being Quality and Quantity merge as the relatively
concrete unity of Measure (in the sense of proportion), in which
quality and quantity are mutually relevant in a sensuous world, a
world which is as intelligible as it can be until it develops the conscious
reflection of *Verstand* upon it. Contradiction in these categories is not
acute. The movement is fluid, and the transitions wherein the higher
category supervenes are almost mere supersession without logical
conflict, because no opposition between essence and necessity on the
one hand and appearance and contingency on the other has yet arisen
for the experient subject.

36) The categories of Essence are the categories of *Verstand*. They
are more and more explicitly contradictory couplings of essence with
contingent being. Essence begins with the thought of identity-in-
difference. This first reflection of *Verstand* disturbs the naïve innocence,
so to say, of intelligence in the categories of Being, of thought, that
is, which had taken its object for granted *wie es geht und steht*. That
proportioned being is self-identical in difference is a new thought
which leads to the concept of Thing-and-properties, Thing and constituent materials, and so Matter-and-form. Then the distinctive
character of *Verstand*, the coupled opposition of Essence and its
contingent appearance, deepens through Whole-and-parts, Force and
its phenomenal expression, Inner-and-outer. After the inclusion of
Spinoza's concept of attribute and mode (which indicates that Hegel
did not regard Spinoza's thought as wholly transcending *Verstand*),
we pass through categories in which the Possible is sublated in the
Actual (*das Wirkliche*) – a criticism of Leibniz – and contingency is
sublated in the necessity of Substance and accident, Cause and effect
(the relation between accidents of substance), and then Reciprocity
(action and reaction). But this necessity, seen by Kant as the only
necessity which man can know, is not freedom but the rigid *ab extra*
necessitation of *Verstand* in which contradiction reaches its sharpest.
When natural science elicits the truth of phenomena in terms of cause
and effect and reciprocity it has done its utmost. In Reciprocity
Verstand is on the threshold of grasping the true, notional nature of

das Wirkliche, but the universal of its thought is still not concrete, and its necessity is still external and hypothetical.[65]

37) The categories of Being and Essence are reason's criticism and continuous development of the lower forms in which it is logically first manifested, *viz.* (a) in the *Intelligenz* which is all the truth that sensuous experience has, and (b) in *Verstand*. The dialectic is often obscure and perhaps sometimes capricious, but the general direction of the movement is clear, and it is an uniquely brilliant constructive critique of the disconnected categories in which the ordinary man in general and the special scientist in particular find themselves thinking without logical self-criticism. If Hegel's effort was inevitably a partial failure it was at least successful enough to show that, unless the philosophical nisus is sheer illusion, Kant, Fichte, and Schelling had left open a field in which the philosopher must labour and can at any rate produce some sort of order out of anarchy. It is enough, too, to fill one with apprehension at the present undisciplined proliferation of special sciences, especially "social sciences," which are being accorded the dignity of inclusion in our university curricula without much questioning of their logical status.

38) The categories of Being were below the distinction of universal and individual save for the prescient philosopher. In the categories of Essence the essential moment is generality contradictively coupled with a relatively contingent moment of individuality which does not adequately implement it. The first category of the notion is the concrete universal as the simple unity of its three moments: universal, particular (or specific), and individual.[66] In all the notional categories this triunity abides and develops perspicuously without the sharp clash of contradiction which marked the conflicting duality of the categories of Essence. These triune categories are all actual and rational, and the sublation of each is preservation rather then cancellation.[67] They are reason recognizing its other self in Being, self-conscious thought which characterizes only what is explicitly spirit.

The concrete universal is Hegel's rational substitute for the "simple concept" of formal logic, which he sees as having produced at the level of *Verstand* a sort of natural history of thought-forms merely classified *de facto*. He proceeds, under the broad heading of Subjective Notion,

---

[65] Cf. *Enc.* § 156 and *Zusatz*.

[66] Cf. § 28 above.

[67] Thus Hegel, even if he does not openly admit the inevitable presence in some degree everywhere of contingency, does not see the rhythm of the dialectic as everywhere precisely uniform.

to shape the forms of judgement and syllogism into a dialectical series.[68] This culminates in Disjunctive Syllogism, and we pass to Objective Notion, in which the subject has an explicit object, a world which it thinks and knows as itself. The dialectic of these *Weltanschauungen*, as we might call them, leads somewhat obscurely through Mechanism and Chemism to Teleology, the detail of which is both subtle and intelligible and very well repays close study.

Subjective Notion, become determinate in Objective Notion, passes into the final main triad of the Logic, the Idea (*Idee*). Here it is hard to be sure that one follows Hegel's thought. A teleological world is still finite, though spirit is very clearly immanent in it. End and means cannot be thought as fully conforming and coalescing. Hegel accordingly begins Idea with a category of Life, having in mind as an illustration of this thought the reciprocal relation of a living individual's members as both ends and means to one another. He then picks up again his rationalizing of formal logic. Life becomes (somewhat obscurely) determinate as, first, Cognition (*Erkennen*), the Idea of the True, which Hegel explicates by dialectizing the logical methods of scientific thinking; secondly as will, the Idea of the Good. These unite – indeed the whole series of categories coalesces and culminates – in Absolute Idea: Absolute Spirit *qua* fully and timelessly thinking-and-knowing its own thinking-and-knowing, which was Aristotle's definition of God. But we must note, recalling the ambivalence inherent in the subject of Hegel's discourse, that (a) there is absolutely nothing to be said of Absolute Idea over and above the ascending *Stufenleiter* of humanly thinkable categories in which it constitutes itself, and which is the only philosophical "proof" of it; and that (b) the categories are intended to comprise all thinkable shapes of finitude. They are all equally phases of Absolute Spirit's self-manifestation and of the ideality of the finite, whereas the self-consciousness of Aristotle's remote God excludes any consciousness of the finite world.

39) We could do no more than faintly adumbrate the general direction of Hegel's Logic, and we have evaded its tortuous detail. Yet if Hegel is often obscure and dubious, and if the material which he dialecticizes has often grown obsolete (though where it is least important), he yet does visible justice throughout the Logic in his sustained attack on the gulfs and disconnections which sever men's various ways of thinking the world they live in and themselves. And if this is not the task of

[68] Cf. § 16 above. The logic of Bradley and Bosanquet draws largely on Subjective Notion.

philosophy, what is? [69] Hegel's transition from pure thought in its own element to Nature and the human spirit may be something of a puzzle, but it is indispensable to the system, and it shows Hegel's determination to do full justice to being within the unity of thought and being. Without it he could have made no sense of error, evil, and pain, and he is always acutely conscious of their presence in human life. As a rationalist who does not confine reason to *Verstand*, he is able to deny, as *Verstand* cannot, that sense is an independent source of knowledge, but in attempting to accord everywhere its due degree of *Wahrheit* to the empirical deliverances of *Verstand* in its struggle to elicit the essence from the blindness of sense he is indefatigable and often marvellously perceptive. And, though you may praise his empirical acumen, his brilliant insights in nearly every field which he enters spring from his basic philosophic attitude. They bear powerful witness to his conviction that sense is no independent source of knowledge. "Even if Hegel's construction has failed," wrote Bradley in 1894, "Hegel's criticism is still on our hands. And whatever proceeds by ignoring this is likely, I will suggest, to be mere waste of time." [70] It is true, and millions of philosophical man-hours have since been wasted. But it is no less true that criticism has no effective criterion without positive construction, and that a great deal of Hegel's construction remains sounder than much new building.

40) How far, then, on Hegel's showing, is philosophy possible? For all that has been said, there is no serious answer until we have plunged into the Hegelian ocean and learned to swim, and whatever progress we make we shall only be able to measure the distance we have swum by looking back at the shore from which we started, because the problem is not simply finite. We may perhaps helpfully close this too desultory essay by trying to consider what, on Hegel's account, an individual philosopher really is. He repeatedly insists that a man is what he achieves. A man, that is to say, has *Wahrheit*, is truly real and individual, in proportion to the degree of his self-transcendence, his realized ideality. Hegel himself, then, is not more than minimally real in his own sense of *wahr* in so far as he possessed a singular individual body which was born at Stuttgart in 1770 and died of cholera in Berlin in 1831; not even in so far as during the interval he experienced himself in a fairly stable empirical content of organic feelings, sights,

[69] Philosophies of *Verstand*, committed to catch-as-catch-can pluralism, cannot attempt it, and if some kind of dialectic is not the proper method, once again, what is?
[70] *Collected Essays*, p. 687.

sounds, and contacts. Yet that is how most of us, vividly if not intelligently, experience ourselves, content to accept "the weights of becoming" as normal ballast and convinced that here and now is our abiding personality, our persisting self-identity; and when pain or the fear of death contracts and depresses us to our narrowest and lowest, most of us feel that we really are mere lonely singular individuals, whose deeds and thoughts, loves and hates, are fading from us into nothingness. But if, as Hegel holds, a man really is what he is in his intelligent action, in his aesthetic, religious, and speculative adventure, then the real Hegel is bounded by the range of his mind, by the degree to which spirit is immanent in him. But in that case to set any precise limit to what he really is becomes quite arbitrary, because we are dealing with the ideality of a self-conscious finite and we cannot resolve the ambivalence of spirit by cutting with a knife. We must in some sense include in him the thought of his predecessors, out of which, re-thinking it, he so largely constituted his own mind. Yet they, too, from Parmenides to Schelling all remain for us real individuals. Bradley in *"What is the real Julius Caesar?"* remarks, "We must treat the individual as real so far as anywhere for any purpose his being is appreciable."[71] Can we, then, exclude from the real Hegel his presence in the subsequent sympathetic thinkers, even in the bitter opponents, whom he influenced?

41) This overlap of minds might *prima facie* suggest a complete obliteration of human individuality in thought, a truth as merely general, impersonal, and independent *qua* true of this or that particular thinker as the truth of natural science, and even more so of mathematics, appears to be. But mathematics and natural science belong to *Verstand*. They present the inevitable impersonality of truth about an independently real and value-free object-world confronting singular observers. Hegel's thought does not fade into abstract generality because it overlaps the thought of his predecessors and successors. Equally a great artist (or a great saint) is universal *in* his individuality and not in abstraction from it.[72] The overlap of philosophic thinkers does not reveal a bare generality of philosophic thought but the differencing of its identity in this thinker and in that. And yet, if the infinite must of its own nature constitute itself in finite approximations to itself, the

---

[71] *Essays on Truth and Reality*, p. 427.
[72] That is why nothing is gained and a great deal is lost by playing Shakespeare in modern dress and with contemporary colloquialized diction, presumably in order to emphasize his "universality."

self-transcendence and reality of any philosophical thinker must fall short in principle as well as in fact. Without a residue of unreality and finitude, without a singular idiosyncratic tinge in his individuality, one thinker would not differ from another either for himself or for us. We need the biographer as well as the philosophical commentator, and even his valet's comment on a great man may be evidence. The nisus to think is an urge to self-criticism as well as to the conquest of contradiction. It guarantees the possibility of philosophic thinking, but it brings home *eo ipso* to the thinker that he suffers from an inherent ignorance which he can neither at any point measure nor finally conquer. He must pay for his certainty that Absolute Spirit constitutes him and therein constitutes itself, by recognizing that at his best he is not fully real. But this applies equally to his critics.

HEGEL'S THEORY OF RELIGIOUS KNOWLEDGE

MEROLD WESTPHAL

Yale University

Just as Augustine's proof of the existence of God has been described as "neither an argument nor a series of arguments, but a complete metaphysics plus an ethics and a mysticism which crowns it,"[1] so Hegel's *Lectures on the Proofs of the Existence of God* are a microcosm of his systematic thought. Delivered in the summer semester of 1829, just two years before his death, and apparently intended for publication, they represent a mature statement of themes Hegel had worked on since Bern, Frankfurt, and Jena. Although they are by no means self sufficient, due to Hegel's tendency to summarize at times what he had worked out in detail elsewhere and to the fact that only the cosmological argument gets discussed, they remain, properly supplemented, the best guide to a systematic statement of his theory of religious knowledge.

For Hegel such a theory concerns two questions, corresponding to the distinction between natural and revealed theology: Can we know God? and Can reason relate constructively to the positive (historically particular) elements of religion?[2] Since his university education at the Tübingen Seminary was in the atmosphere of conflict between Enlightenment rationalism and orthodox supernaturalism, it is not surprising that he was concerned with "The Positivity of the Christian Religion."[3] In the earliest section of this essay he sketches a theology of reason drawn from Lessing, Rousseau, and Kant. He then speculates

---

[1] Etienne Gilson, *The Christian Philosophy of Saint Augustine*, New York, 1967, p. 23.

[2] *Lectures on the Philosophy of Religion* (henceforth PR), trans. Speirs and Sanderson, New York, 1962, I, 48–52. For the German text see *Sämtliche Werke*, Jubiläumsausgabe, 15:65–69. I have modified the standard English translations where I felt it might be helpful. Once the German text consulted has been identified, it will in each case be referred to with a lower case g.

[3] This is the title given to an essay published in 1907 by Nohl in *Hegels Theologische Jugendschriften*. The English translation of some of these materials is by T. M. Knox in *On Christianity: Early Theological Writings* (henceforth ETW), New York, 1961.

on how this religion, which he attributes to Jesus, became the positive religion about Jesus which orthodoxy upholds. But he soon came to view both parties to this dispute as one sided and sterile, [4] and he went on to develop a mediating position. By the time he published the *Phenomenology*, about ten years later, he not only had solved the problem theoretically to his permanent satisfaction, but had provided concrete speculative reinterpretations of the doctrines of the trinity, the incarnation, the atonement, reconciliation, the church, and the Holy Spirit.

The *Lectures on the Proofs of the Existence of God*, however, are devoted to the prior question, Can we know God? Its significance also relates directly to the theological situation of the time. In the first place, Enlightenment deism, whose view of reason as criticism allowed only a negative relation to the positivity of Christianity, had so limited the content of what reason could affirm that deism and materialism became indistinguishable. To be sure, it was intended that there should be a difference between "Supreme Being" and "matter," but if asked to specify the respect in which they differ, they more and more reveal themselves, like "Being" and "Nothing" at the beginning of Hegel's Logic, to be the same. [5]

In the second place, even the truncated knowledge of God which deism certified came under fire in the Humean-Kantian critique of the traditional proofs. Not only did it become "a sin against the good society of the philosophers of our time to continue to mention those proofs," but even the theologians came to view them as "a barren desert of arid understanding" and "rotten props" for belief in God. [6] Thus Hegel regularly complains that both philosophy and religion have made it a dogma that man cannot know God. When he tries to take God as the starting point in order that "we may discuss the relation in which He stands to the human spirit," he is met with the assumption that "we do not know God; that even in believing in Him we do not know what He is, and therefore cannot start from Him. To take God

---

[4] *Lectures on the Proofs of the Existence of God* (henceforth LP), p. 161. *Vorlesungen über die Beweise vom Dasein Gottes*, hrsg. Lasson, Hamburg, 1966, S. 9-10. The English translation appears as the last half of volume III of PR, although the two sets of lectures are quite distinct and were not given together. See also *The Phenomenology of Mind* (henceforth PS), trans. Baillie, New York, 1949, pp. 549-98 and *Phänomenologie des Geistes*, hrsg. Hoffmeister, Hamburg, 1952, S. 376-413.

[5] PS, 576-94, g397-410. Cf. *Lectures on the History of Philosophy* (henceforth HP), trans. Haldane and Simson, New York, 1963, III, 420 and *Sämtliche Werke*, 19:546.

[6] LP, 239 and 156, g137 and 2-3. The first of these references is not from the lectures proper but from a separate discussion of Kant's critique of the proofs found among Hegel's papers and included with the lectures by the German and English editors.

as the starting point would be to presuppose that we know how to
state and had stated, what God is in Himself as the preeminent object.
The previous assumption, however, permits us to speak merely of our
relation to Him, to speak of religion and not of God Himself. It does
not permit a theology, a doctrine of God, though it certainly does
allow a doctrine of religion. ... We at least hear much talk ... about
religion, and therefore all the less about God Himself."[7]

Hegel sees these assumptions as leaving theology two alternatives.
It can turn to history, making theology into the history of doctrine or
the history of religions; or it can turn to ethical, psychologiocal, and
existential translations of religious affirmations, a phenomenon Hegel
was able clearly to observe in Kant and Schleiermacher. The former
alternative treats theology as descriptive anthropology, while the
latter treats it as normative anthropology; but in either case, theology
is reduced to anthropology. In short, Hegel foresees Feuerbach on the
scene. "If, in fact, we are to understand by religion nothing more than
a relation between ourselves and God, then God is left without any
independent existence. God would exist in religion only. He would be
something posited, something produced by us."[8] It can be argued that
Hegel has his own theory of religion as projection and that his theory
of the incarnation as expressing the unity of divine and human natures
universally is distinguishable (again like "Being" and "Nothing") only
in intention from Feuerbach's theory of the ultimacy of human species
being. But at least the intention is fundamental to Hegel's project.[9]
His early enthusiasm for the slogan of autonomy is considerably
tempered as he sees it destroy the objective content of religion as the
knowledge of God. He sees that "since the firm standpoint which the
almighty age and its culture have fixed for philosophy is one of reason
dependent upon sensibility, it follows that such philosophy can

---

[7] LP, 191–92, g45–46. In the light of statements like this it is clear that the problem of
religious knowledge for Hegel is the problem of the *knowledge of God* (as well as the problem
of positive religion). But there is an ambiguity here. Hegel distinguishes a religious and a
philosophical form in which God is known. Were he to use the phrase "religious knowledge"
he might well intend only the former. As used in the title and body of this essay, however,
the phrase refers generically to the knowledge of God within which such a distinction could
be made.

[8] *Idem.*

[9] In this regard Hegel's relation to Schleiermacher parallels Tillich's to Bultmann in our
day. Against the failure of Schleiermacher and Bultmann to articulate a systematic theory
of God and their tendency to reduce theology to normative expressions of pious self-concious-
ness and human existence respectively, Hegel and Tillich insist that theology must first and
foremost be ontological, and only then existential. The real target, however, is Kant, who
is the starting point both for Schleiermacher and (via Heidegger) for Bultmann. It was indeed Kant who insisted that we know God not as He is in Himself, but only in relation to us.

proceed to knowing, not God, but what one calls Man." Consequently, his own theory, in an unexpected parallel with Kierkegaard's, begins with a critique of the present age. [10]

I. THE POSSIBILITY OF RELIGIOUS KNOWLEDGE

Hegel's early declaration of war on the present age describes its culture in a number of ways. It is the culmination of Protestantism, the principle of the north, of subjectivity; it is a culture of reflection and a culture of "healthy human reason." But above all it is the fulfillment of Locke's and Hume's empiricism; it is "Lockean and Humean culture." [11] In the *Proofs* he sees it expressed in two mutually implicative forms: the one denying knowledge, by making the understanding with its finitude absolute, the other making room for faith, by seeking in immediacy what discursive knowledge cannot provide. As Hegel interprets these two sides of his day's cultural coin they parallel almost exactly what, in the language of twentieth century logical positivism, are the elimination of metaphysics and the emotive or non-cognitive interpretation of ethical and religious language. Thus his argument for the *possibility* of religious knowledge, i.e., knowledge of God, not just of religion, takes the unexpectedly contemporary form of a critique of positivism. [12] Only when this is accomplished can he proceed to an analysis of *actual* religious knowledge in his discussion of the proofs and how they should be understood.

---

[10] *Glauben und Wissen*, in *Gesammelte Werke*, Deutschen Forschungsgemeinschaft Ausgabe, IV, 323. Modernity is not always a reproach on Hegel's lips. See PS, 85–86, g24 and PR, I, 253 and III, 111, g15:263 and 16:319. But in PR and LP references to "the present standpoint," "the culture of the age," "our age," etc., normally carry strongly negative implications. When combined with Hegel's frequent statements that philosophy cannot transcend its age, the problem of historicism in Hegel emerges. By historicism I mean the view that reality is an historical process and that knowledge arising within it is so conditioned by its immediate horizon as never to be simply true but only true for such and such a period. If the "almighty age and its culture" are to be surpassed as limited historical perspectives, what assurance can be given that Hegel does not replace it with another, different, but equally limited point of view? Marx and Kierkegaard make this question central to their critiques of Hegel.

[11] *Ibid.*, IV, 388.

[12] The deliberately anachronistic description of Hegel's opposition as positivistic is designed to underscore the deep affinities between what he saw in the prevalent temper of his times and what has since become known as positivism. Similarly, the frequent comparisons of Hegel with other thinkers is designed neither to reduce him to his sources nor to suggest that he must have been a very bright fellow (since he anticipated what some twentieth century thinker said). Rather, it is assumed that some students of philosophy and theology who are trying to overcome the hurdles of getting into Hegel will be more familiar with some of these other thinkers than with Hegel, and that the comparisons will serve to illumine the unknown by the known.

The procedure of positivism, then as now, involves three steps: 1) analysing the structure of formal-deductive knowledge in logic and mathematics[13] and the method of its application to empirical data in the natural sciences, 2) calling attention to the fact that knowledge of this sort can never be the knowledge of God, and 3) asserting that there is no other knowledge. Hegel methodically considers each step.

1) Kant interpreted the methodological breakthrough of the scientific revolution as the discovery that "objects must conform to our knowledge" and not the other way around. The leaders of the revolution "learned that reason has insight only into that which it produces after a plan of its own, and that it must not allow itself to be kept, as it were, in nature's leading strings, but must [constrain] nature to give answer to questions of reason's own determining."[14]

Although he doesn't mention this Kantian formula explicitly, it lies at the heart of Hegel's analysis of that knowing which positivism countenances. He interprets this knowing as "controlling knowledge" (Scheler, Tillich) and its method as the "logic of domination." (Marcuse)[15] It is guided, not by the inner life of the object, but by the interest of the subject, whose project is environmental control and whose slogan is "knowledge is power."

This is even true in mathematics. The process of knowing is determined by *our* aim, e.g., discovering whether a certain proposition is a theorem of Euclidian geometry. *We* extend the base of the triangle, and *we* construct a line parallel to the opposite side, etc. This whole activity is ours and not the object's, though the relations we discover are really there.[16]

Such a procedure may be adequate to mathematics, whose objects it exhausts only because of their original lack of content. But the empirical sciences seek to apply it to the whole of nature and spirit. The point is not that they try to proceed deductively, but rather that their inductive procedure parallels the external and subjective method of the formal sciences. Again the material is not left to itself, but

---

[13] Hegel is fully aware of the close link of logic to mathematics. See LP, 171–72, 822 and *Science of Logic*, (henceforth SL) trans. Johnston and Struthers, New York, 1929, I, 63–64 and II, 342, and *Wissenschaft der Logik*, hrsg. Lasson, Leipzig, 1932, I, 34 and II, 333.

[14] *Critique of Pure Reason*, B xvi and xiii.

[15] Hegel would have applauded Tillich's description of "controlling knowledge" as knowledge which "unites subject and object for the sake of the control of the object by the subject. It transforms the object into a completely conditioned and calculable 'thing.' It deprives it of any subjective qualities. [It] looks upon its object as something which cannot return its look ... [It] 'objectifies' not only logically (which is unavoidable) but also ontologically and ethically." *Systematic Theology*, Chicago, 1951, I, 97.

[16] PS, 100–03, 835–38.

abstracting consciousness, guided by the criterion of usefulness, seeks to discover laws, forces, etc., by selecting some features of its object as essential and dismissing as unessential those which do not yield useful correlations. Locke described this process as the search for nominal essences. More recently this view has come to expression in Dewey's *Logic: The Theory of Inquiry.*[17]

It is important properly to locate the point of polemic in this analysis. Many of Hegel's empiricist opponents would accept Hegel's account as both descriptive and normative for the natural sciences. Further, Hegel does not deny that this knowledge is power or that it has its proper place. In an early critique of the Enlightenment's utilitarian intellectualism, he grants that "their wares are useful if it is a matter of building a house," but in relation to human feeling, imagination, and religious needs, "their mistake is to offer stones to the child who asks for bread."[18] Consequently he stresses the limits of this knowledge, its externality and its subjectivity.

It is external in that "it remains in its own forms, and does not reach the qualities of the object. ... Real knowledge ... must be immanent in the object, the proper movement of its nature."[19] This externality is that of form to matter. The knowing subject is conceived in a formal way as a set of formal calculi and categories. It confronts an object inherently unstructured, a brute fact. But the relation of these leaves knowledge itself unintelligible. Either it is the passive matter which becomes something only through the activity of the formal ego, or the object is the agent, and knowledge is its effect in the subject. But why either of these causal relations should be called knowledge, while, e.g., the sun's warming of the stone is not, who can tell?[20]

Hegel never tires of criticizing the metaphor which sees knowledge as a tool or instrument, precisely because it demands conceiving of the subject and object in such an external relation that the language and images of the master-slave dialectic become the foundations of epistemology. The essential foreignness of subject and object is presupposed from the outset. Rather, says Hegel, than thinking of the categories of

---

[17] LP, 167–71, 817–21.
[18] ETW, 171 g142. Today one might make the same point by noting that our technological rationality is useful if it is a matter of getting to the moon, but it offers nothing but moon rocks to a world starving for food, justice, and peace.
[19] LP, 163, g12–13.
[20] *Glauben und Wissen, Gesammelte Werke*, IV, 331. For a helpful discussion of this same issue as developed in the introductory materials to the Lesser Logic, see John Smith, "The Relation of Thought and Being: Some Lessons from Hegel's *Encyclopedia*," *The New Scholasticism*, XXXVIII (January, 1964).

thought serving us and our interest, we should think of serving them, for only then are we truly free. A hard and puzzling saying, to be sure, but one indicative of Hegel's passion on this point. "These prejudices [unless kept to their proper limits] are errors, the refutation of which throughout all departments of the spiritual and natural world is philosophy itself; or rather, since these errors bar the way, they must be renounced at the very threshold of philosophy."[21]

Essentially the same point can be put in terms of the subjectivity of this knowledge. Since the product results from a process guided by "the subjective purpose of isolating properties for our use,"[22] there is no reason to think that this product is really knowledge of the object. It consists of abstractions guided by subjective aim, and to treat these as what is essential in the object itself would be, to put Hegel's point in Whitehead's language, a fallacy of misplaced concreteness.

In summary, "this method has its own characteristics and procedure which are quite different from the characteristics and processes of the object in itself. ... It is seen to be a movement of thought which is outside the object and different from the development of the object itself. ... In the opposition of the process of knowledge to the object to be known lies the finiteness of knowledge."[23]

2) If it be said that this finite knowledge knows only appearances or phenomena, Hegel will immediately agree. And since it is not even an adequate knowledge of nature and finite spirit, outside the limits of technological usefulness, it is obvious that it cannot know God. It neither needs God nor allows for Him. Like La Place, it can get along without that hypothesis. "In this manner science forms a universe of knowledge to which God is not necessary. ... Consistent connection of what is determinate belongs to the side of knowledge, which is at home in the finite ... but can only create a system which is without absolute substantiality – without God."[24]

This comes as no surprise to those who consider the "general character of the age," for which "the more the knowledge of finite things has increased – and the increase is so great that the extension of the sciences has become almost boundless ... – so much the more has the sphere of the knowledge of God become contracted. There was a time when all knowledge was knowledge of God. Our own age, on the

[21] SL, I, 43–45, 55, gI, 13–16, 25. Cf. PS. 131–36, g63–68.
[22] LP, 168, g19.
[23] LP, 169–70, g20–21.
[24] PR, I, 15, g15:32–33.

contrary, has the distinction of knowing about all and everything, about an infinite number of subjects, but nothing at all of God. Formerly the mind found its supreme interest in knowing God ... it found no rest except in thus occupying itself with God ... Our own age has put this need, with all its toils and conflicts, to silence. We have done with all this, and got rid of it." [25]

3) In this analysis of the instrumental and finite character of what Hegel calls the understanding and we would call common sense and scientific knowledge, and in the immediate corollary that it does not and cannot know God, Hegel is basically at one with the spirit of his age and is merely articulating it. The break comes, not when he affirms that "in the opposition of the process of knowledge to the object to be known lies the finiteness of knowledge," but only when he continues, "but this opposition is not on that account to be regarded as itself infinite and absolute." Hegel keeps repeating that it would be arbitrary to take positivism's third step and deny the possibility of any other kind of knowledge. He promises "to show by facts that there exists another kind of knowledge than that which is given out as the only kind." [26]

Both Kant and Spinoza knew well enough that this latter method of knowing yields only a world of mechanism and efficient causality (*natura naturata*). But while the former, in the spirit of the times, insisted that any other mode of knowing transcended human powers, Spinoza went out and showed, however imperfectly, that beyond the finite modes there is an infinite mode of knowledge in which man can know God (*natura naturans*). This is why "thought must place itself at the standpoint of Spinozism; that is the essential beginning of all philosophizing." [27] While Hegel accepts the challenge to show constructively that such knowledge is possible by actualizing it, he simultaneously challenges positivism to show why we should assume from the start that this cannot be done. Later positivism was to face the same challenge in the discussion of the status of the verifiability criterion.

Hegel's own position is that the critique of knowledge carried out by modern philosophy, culminating in Kant, reveals, not the limits of knowledge, but the limits of the understanding, of natural science and

---

[25] PR, I, 35–36, g15;52–53. Cf. PS. 73, g14.
[26] LP, 173, g24.
[27] HP, III, 257, g19:376, *Glauben und Wissen, Gesammelte Werke*, IV, 342. This contrast presupposes that one either ignores or rejects Kant's repeated claim in the second Critique that we do achieve *knowledge* of God.

that philosophy which restricts itself to analysis of scientific method. But if one holds to the opposite conclusion, that "thought is capable of comprehending only one thing, its incapacity to grasp the truth ... with the result that suicide is its highest vocation," [28] what happens to whatever gets left outside the pale of knowledge, religion in particular? Lacking even the curious objectivity (public acceptance) of that knowledge which knows only appearances, it can find its home only in subjectivity. Jacobi's philosophy of faith as immediate or intuitional certainty was the form which this obvious conclusion took in Hegel's time. It represents the other side of the positivist coin.[29] Hegel's attitude toward this standpoint is the same as Kant's toward those Scottish critics of Hume whose appeal to common sense, "taking for granted whatever he doubted," was their "method of being defiant without insight." [30] He makes no attempt to hide his contempt.

"The human heart will not allow itself to be deprived of [its elevation to God.] In so far as the human heart has been checked in this matter of elevation to God by the understanding, faith has, on the one hand, appealed to it to hold fast to this elevation, and not trouble itself with the fault-finding of the understanding; but it has, on the other hand, told itself not to trouble about proof at all, in order that it may reach the surest foundation." [31] To the demand for certainty about the divine in the face of discursive thought turned critical and negative, faith presents itself as immediate knowledge, towering above the misty flats of criticism and doubt like the Cartesian *cogito* (one example of the kind of awareness Jacobi calls faith).

Hegel takes faith's profession seriously. Is it immediate? Really? Then it is devoid of content. Since all determinations are negations, the introduction of any determination involves the mediating act of thought distinguishing something from something else. Faith is the affirmation of – mere being, the emptiest of abstractions. Like sense certainty in the *Phenomenology*, it presents itself as full of the richest content, but reveals itself as the emptiest emptiness. By its own

[28] LP, 161, 910.

[29] This position can be called fideism only if it is remembered that it has absolutely nothing to do with another way of elevating faith above reason as in Augustine, Luther, Kierkegaard, Barth, and, with well known qualifications, Aquinas. According to these thinkers special, divine revelation in history and scripture and not reason as a universal human capacity, whether intuitive or discursive, is the final norm for the knowledge of God.

[30] *Prolegomena, Werke*, Akademie Textausgabe, IV, 258–59.

[31] LP, 232, 983.

confession it knows for certain *that* God exists, but does not know *what* He is. [32]

This certainty, purchased at the price of content, shows itself generous to a fault in relation to any determinate content. It rests on the Cartesian criterion of subjective certainty. "Only that which I know and know as certain is true; what I know as certain is true just because I know it as certain." Consequently it is hospitable to any and every content. Men have known for certain that the sun goes around the earth and that the Dalai-Lama is God. With such examples Hegel gently invokes the distinction between certainty and truth. [33]

The same immediacy which first presents itself as intuitive certainty also presents itself as feeling. And the same dialectic ensues. Feeling is an abstraction receptive to all contents and "just as little is religion true because it exists in our feelings or hearts, as because it is believed and known immediately and for certain. All religions, even the most false and unworthy, exist in our feelings. . . . There are feelings which are immoral . . . Out of the heart proceed evil thoughts, murder, adultery, backbiting, and so forth." Both modes of immediacy, intuitive certainty and feeling "reduce the divine content, be it the religious as such or the legal and moral, to a minimum, to what is most abstract. With this the determination of the content becomes arbitrary." [34]

The philosophy of faith thus turns out to be an all out attack on the concept of truth, not only in the religious realm but also (as in contemporary positivism) in the ethical. "If immediate knowledge is to be allowed, everyone will be responsible merely to himself. Then everything is justified. This man knows this, another that, and consequently everything is sanctioned, however contrary to right and religion." [35] For just this reason there is a practical as well as a theoretical consequence. Faith is a threat to community as well as to truth, or rather a threat to community because a threat to truth. "The man who betakes himself to feeling, to immediate knowledge, to his own ideas or to his own thoughts, shuts himself up, as I have already said, in his own particularity, and breaks off any fellowship or community with others – one must leave him alone." Romanticism with its irony, its subjective yearning, its ontological anarchism, comes to life,

[32] LP, 174–77, g25–29.
[33] LP, 178, g30.
[34] LP, 181–83, g33–35. Cf. PR, I, 129–30, g15:141–42.
[35] HP, III, 421, g19:547.

and in the laboratory of Jacobi's alchemy the humility of finitude (Kant) is transformed into that pride in which the finite subject posits itself as absolute. Philosophically this "apotheosis of the subject culminates in Fichte, religiously in Schleiermacher's *Speeches on Religion*.[36]

What follows this apotheosis of the subject like its shadow is the Feuerbachian critique of religion. If God is removed from the realm of knowledge and assigned to accidental subjectivity and feeling, "it may well be a subject of wonder that objectivity is ascribed to God at all. In this respect materialistic views ... have been at least more consistent, in that they have taken spirit and thought for something material, and imagine they have traced the matter back to sensations, even taking God to be a product of feeling, and denying him objectivity. The result has in this case been atheism. God would thus be an historical product of weakness, of fear, of joy, or of interested hopes, cupidity, and lust of power. What has its root only in my feelings exists only for me. It is mine, but not its own. It has no independent existence in and for itself."[37]

It thus appears that Hegel would scarcely be a stranger to our present situation. Since he was able to see Werther and Novalis as the natural offspring of the same spirit which produced the *Critique of Pure Reason*, he might find it less puzzling than we do to find springing up in the midst of a society heady with the advances of its technological rationality not only the theoretical subjectivism of positivistic non-cognitivism, but also the practical subjectivism of a neo-romantic and neo-anarchist pop culture. He would be saddened but not surprised to see the way in which Marxist, Freudian, and Nietzschean atheism are welcomed by theologians on behalf of mankind come of age, as if the first step toward religious renewal were to get rid of God. He would again be saddened, but not surprised to find a new Schleiermacher who, though he understands the powerful Christian message of the forgiveness of sins and beautifully portrays faith as the "courage to accept acceptance," takes his stand instead with an "absolute faith" which avoids the problems of doubt and uncertainty about the implications of that message and that faith by surrendering all content.[38] And he would be heartened to find another theologian who

---

[36] LP, 183–86, g36–40, PR I, 131, 188–89, g15:143, 199–200, *Glauben und Wissen, Gesammelte Werke*, IV, 385.

[37] PR, I, 51, g15:68.

[38] Paul Tillich in Chapter Six of *The Courage to Be*.

recognized in every absolute theism, i.e., one which affirms God *simpliciter* without specifying what he is not and thereby what he is, the open invitation to idolatry. [39] Could he awake to the present like Rip Van Winckle, he might not detect his long nap for some time, if a few names could be changed.

In the light of the disastrous theoretical and practical implications which Hegel sees in positivism, his references to "another kind of knowledge" become crucial. If one asks where he proves its reality and displays its nature, the answer would have to be that his system (Logic, Philosophy of Nature, and Philosophy of Spirit) and the *Phenomenology* (originally published as the introduction to the system) together constitute his demonstration (proving by showing). Since an exposition of these is obviously out of the question here, a brief general account will have to suffice as background to an account of how God is known in this "true" knowledge.

To begin with, the externality of knowledge to its object must be overcome. "True" knowledge differs from "untrue" knowledge as "the knowledge which does not remain outside of its object, but which, without introducing any of its own qualities, simply follows the course of the object." This calls for a new logic, one which will surpass the formalism of both deductive calculi and categorial systems drawn exclusively from mechanistic physics. The new logic must be more radically empirical than the logic of the empiricists. Rather than being an unpacking of the Cartesian or Newtonian "I think," cut off from the rest of the world, it must reflect all the forms and processes of the real, not just those of the abstract thinker. Rather than coming to the world as a master with tools for inducing nature to do its bidding, the new logic comes to the world as a lover, confident that the beloved will reveal herself to one who is patient and open. "True scientific knowledge ... demands abandonment to the very life of the object." [40]

This new logic implies a new ontology in so far as the object to be known is no longer conceived as a brute and formless facticity but as having an inherent intelligibility which it will share with a lover. But

[39] Leslie Dewart in Chapter Two of *The Future of Belief*.

[40] LP, 189, g43, PS, 112, g45. Among the commentators Findlay, Haym, and Fackenheim are particularly sensitive to the Hegelian empiricism. The latter two stress its connection with the problem of historicism. If the subject matter to which knowledge abandons itself is an historical subject matter, that knowledge will be relative to and valid only for the epoch which it chooses or is given as its beloved. Thus when Hegel complains that "there are no traces in Logic of the new spirit which has arisen both in learning and in life," and when he describes his own Logic as a work "pertaining to the modern world," he seems to be all but confessing that his own Logic is ideology. See SL, I, 35 and 51, gI, 5 and 22.

there is an even more important demand of the new knowledge for a new ontology. It will be objected that the knower, whether master or lover, is, after all, only finite, and that his knowledge, whether more or less formal, more or less genuinely empirical, remains incorrigibly finite and imperfect, especially when the object is the infinite, God. There can be only one solution. Knowledge of God cannot be a merely human activity. God himself must be actively involved and present in the knowing process. The classical notion of supernatural divine revelation attested to by the inner witness of the Holy Spirit addresses this problem. Hegel's solution, on the other hand, takes its starting point from the Greeks, for whom the soul, as reason, is itself divine; from Lessing, for whom the witness of the Spirit is reason, and from Spinoza – "That man knows God implies, in accordance with the essential idea of community, that there is a common knowledge; that is to say, man knows God only in so far as God himself knows himself in man. This knowledge is God's self-consciousness, but it is at the same time a knowledge of God on man's part, and this knowledge of God by man is a knowledge of man by God. The spirit of man, whereby he knows God, is simply the Spirit of God Himself." [41] Again we see why one must first be a Spinozist if one is to be a(n Hegelian) philosopher.

II. THE STRUCTURE OF RELIGIOUS KNOWLEDGE

It now appears that the theory of religious knowledge presupposes a theory of God, that we can come to a rational comprehension of the proofs for God's existence only on the basis of a prior knowledge of God. Hegel is entirely untroubled by the circularity involved here for he thinks that theorizing about knowing independently of and prior to actual knowing is "inherently absurd," [42] rather like refusing to enter the water until one knows how to swim. Nor does the logic of the theological or hermeneutical circle lead him, as it has led others, to use the language of the "leap" or other symbols of cognitive and existential discontinuity. This is why his treatment of religion, both in the *Proofs* and in the *Philosophy of Religion*, constantly and overtly presupposes his entire philosophical system, especially the Logic. [43]

---

[41] LP, 158 and 303–04, g5 and 117. Cf. pp. 195 and 283, g49 and 102.

[42] LP, 163, g12.

[43] A student manuscript of LP begins with the sentence, "These lectures may be viewed as a supplement to the Logic." Hegel's own manuscript reads, in the opening paragraph: "I have therefore chosen a subject which is connected with the other set of lectures which I gave on logic, and constitutes, not in substance, but in form, a kind of supplement to that set,

Why the Logic in particular? Do not the *Phenomenology* and the *Philosophy of Spirit* contain the Hegelian ontology in so far as it is a theory of God and his relation to man? They do. But the former has a preliminary and introductory character, while the latter has something of an applied character. The heart of the matter is the Logic, and it too, or rather it above all, expresses the Hegelian ontology. Our puzzlement over his insistence that his Logic is his Metaphysics or Ontology disappears when we remember that it is not so much a theory of inference as a theory of categories. It is to be compared, not with the *Prior* and *Posterior Analytics*, but with the *Metaphysics*; not with *Principia Mathematica*, but with *Process and Reality*. Like Aristotle and Whitehead, Hegel develops a categorial scheme which culminates in a doctrine of God integral to the whole. His scheme, like theirs, is revisionary and not descriptive. It is developed in critical interaction with the categorial practices of earlier science, theology, and philosophy. One could even read Hegel's Logic fruitfully through the eyes of the Whiteheadean criteria of consistency, coherence, applicability, and adequacy.

Such an ontological logic is to guide our reflection on the proofs. Religion is the elevation of the human spirit (subjective, thinking spirit) to God. In the proofs this elevation is understood, expressed, and explained. Since the question is whether this is correctly done and "in accordance with the old belief that what is substantial and true can be reached only by reflection, we effect the purification of this act of elevation ... by explaining it in terms of thought," i.e., of Hegelian logic. [44]

As traditionally conceived, the proofs represent an either-or confrontation of theism and atheism. This is obviously incompatible with the Spinozistic features of Hegel's ontology, and he sees it as a defect due to the way in which the understanding grasps the proofs. But they are not to be merely dismissed. For example, "the so-called cosmological proof is of use solely in connection with the effort to bring into consciousness what the inner life, the pure rational element of the inner movement, is in itself ... If this movement, when it appears in that form of the understanding in which we have seen it, is not understood

inasmuch as it is concerned with only a particular aspect of the fundamental conceptions of logic. These lectures are therefore chiefly meant for those of my hearers who were present at the others, and to them they will be most easily intelligible."

[44] LP, 202, g56. Elsewhere Hegel describes the task as "reconstructing their true significance, thus restoring their fundamental ideas to their worth and dignity." SL, II, 346, gII, 356.

as it is in and for itself, still the substantial element which forms its basis does not lose anything in consequence. It is this substantial element which penetrates the imperfection of the form and exercises its power. ... The religious elevation of the soul to God consequently recognizes itself in that expression, imperfect as it is, and is aware of its inner and true meaning, and so protects itself against the syllogism of the understanding."[45]

Hegel is operating on what might be called the Durkheim principle. "It is an essential postulate of sociology that a human institution cannot rest upon an error and a lie, without which it could not exist. ... One must know how to go underneath the symbol to the reality which it represents and which gives it meaning. The most barbarous and the most fantastic rites and the strangest myths translate some human need, some aspect of life, either individual or social. The reasons with which the faithful justify them may be, and generally are, erroneous; but the true reasons do not cease to exist, and it is the duty of science to discover them. In reality, then, there are no religions which are false. All are true in their own fashion."[46] If it is far from clear that Hegel's own Logic permits such a loose relation of form and content or substance, at least the thrust of the "purification" he has in mind becomes clearer. We might say that he plans to vindicate the proofs by demythologizing them.

A. The Cosmological Proof

After devoting nine lectures to general considerations, including the critique of positivism, Hegel devotes the last seven lectures to "purification" of the cosmological argument. Hume and Kant, in their critiques of this and the teleological argument, had launched a devastating, double-barreled assault, first questioning the legitimacy of the inferences involved, then suggesting that even if the inferences were impeccable, the result achieved was far from being the God of the religious interest which motivated the proofs. Hegel addresses himself to both considerations.

[45] LP, 264–65, g157. This is from the supplement on Kant. See note 6 above.
[46] Emile Durkheim, *The Elementary Forms of the Religious Life*, New York, 1965, pp. 14–15. It was Hegel's adoption of this principle around 1800 which constituted his break with Enlightenment criticism. He called for a theology that "would derive that now discarded theology from what we now know as a need of human nature and would thus exhibit its naturalness and inevitability. An attempt to do this presupposes the belief that the convictions of many centuries, regarded as sacrosanct, true, and obligatory by the millions who lived and died by them in those centuries, were not, at least on their subjective side, downright folly or plain immorality." ETW, 172, g143. Cf. PS 569–70, g391–92.

To begin with he not only grants but insists upon the fact that the cosmological argument yields an abstract and inadequate concept of God. But his "even if" argument runs as follows: even if this way of showing *that* God exists inadequately reveals *what* He is, and even if He is more than the Infinite and the Absolutely Necessary Essence, He is not less than that – indeed, He only is infinite and absolutely necessary. Besides, this is only the first form of the elevation to God, the general basis of religion. There are other proofs which employ richer categories and supply what is lacking here. The task of philosophy is not to complain about what the proof doesn't do, but to state clearly what it does. [47]

Examination of the inference or movement of thought expressed in the proof is more complex. Thought begins with the world as finite and contingent and moves to the Infinite or Absolutely Necessary Essence. The starting point is the world conceived as an aggregate of visible things, limited by one another, which can "equally well either be or not be." [48] An element of necessity is introduced into this mass of contingency with the discovery that the particulars do not behave capriciously but in accordance with laws. But these laws themselves share the same contingency as the particulars at first seemed to possess, and they remain unexplained explainers. The contingency of the world is unmitigated by natural science, by conceiving it as *natura naturata*.

The proof articulates the act in which the human spirit "raises itself above this crowd of contingent things, above the merely outward and relative necessity involved in them," i.e., denies the ultimacy of the world as portrayed by the natural sciences. "Spirit rises above contingency and external necessity, just because these thoughts are in themselves insufficient and unsatisfying. It finds satisfaction in the thought of absolute necessity, because this latter represents something at peace with itself ... Thus all aspiration, all striving, all longing after an other have passed away, for in [the Absolutely Necessary] the other has disappeared. There is no finitude in it. It is absolutely complete in itself. It is infinite and present in itself. There is nothing outside of it." [49]

---

[47] LP, 229 and 313, g80–81 and 124.

[48] LP, 267, g89.

[49] LP, 269 and 276–77, g90 and 96. Marx and Kierkegaard both complain that Hegel talks as if thinking could replace existence; as if conceiving the ideal were identical with realizing it. Hegel explicitly denies that here, for he goes on to add: "It is not the act of rising to this necessity on the part of spirit which in itself produces satisfaction. The satisfaction has reference to the goal spirit tries to reach and is in proportion to its reaching this goal."

In concert with a tradition which includes Descartes and Aquinas as well as Augustine and Pascal, Hegel is presenting the question of God as the question of human happiness, the satisfaction of man's deepest and innermost longings. To see the everyday world even in the glory which science gives it as the place where the restless human spirit cannot be at home and at peace is to see it as finite and contingent. From this we do not need to infer the Infinite in the sense of some new reality. To see the world as finite is already to have made the move to the Infinite, for it is only in the light of the latter that the former reveals itself as such. "Furthermore, this elevation is essentially rooted in the nature of our spirit. It is necessary to it ... and the setting forth of this necessity itself is nothing else than what we call proof."[50]

It will immediately be asked whether what is already present in recognizing the world as contingent is the reality of the Infinite, or only the idea. Post-Hegelian atheism (Feuerbach, Marx, Nietzsche, and Freud) argues that just because the issue at stake is human happiness the presumption is in the direction of wish-fulfilling projection, opiates, lies, and illusions. Further, the fact that the movement of thought in question is "natural" or even "necessary" to our spirit leads to no final conclusion. Humeans and Kantians are going to ask why we should assume that the natural (Hume) and necessary (Kant) movement of human thought inevitably unveils reality, that in moving beyond the sciences to dialectic we get a logic of truth and not a logic of illusion. From the side of religion itself will come, in addition, the claim that human thought is not merely finite, but also corrupted by sinfulness, making it an even less trustworthy guide to the truth than if it were merely finite.[51]

These questions evoke the contrast between human knowledge as finite or sinful and divine knowledge as void of defect. In granting that the understanding and its knowledge are finite, Hegel seemed to agree with Kant and others who employ this contrast, but the important difference between their conclusions now appears. For Hegel that knowledge is finite because of its method and inherent purpose, not because of the ontological or moral deficiencies of its possessor. But as we have already seen, Hegel is working in the context of an

---

[50] LP, 164, 814.

[51] Had he remembered his Luther or been able to foresee Kierkegaard, Hegel might have examined this latter point of view as the fourth attitude of thought toward objectivity in the introduction to his Lesser Logic.

ontology which so relates God to man that God's infinite and perfect
knowledge resides in man. Accordingly the distinction between finite
and infinite knowledge is one between two modes of human knowing.
From this perspective it seems entirely arbitrary to represent a
knowledge adequate to grasping God as a knowledge transcending
finite human powers. "A gulf is simply fixed between them."[52]

Among those for whom the contrast between human and divine
knowledge is most explicit the response will be immediate. To call the
distinction arbitrary is to invite repayment in kind. For Hegel, it will
be said, "A bridge is simply fixed between them." Hegel's protest that
his theory of knowledge has a foundation in a systematic ontology
and is therefore not arbitrary will be of no help, for the finitist position itself (at least sometimes) rests on another systematic ontology,
a creationist ontology for which God and man stand in an asymmetrical
dependence relation, quite distinct from one another. Spinoza knew
this well and began his effort to establish an ontology and epistemology
similar to Hegel's with a careful attempt to dismantle the creationist
ontology (*Ethics*, Bk. I). If Hegel's purpose is to suggest that this
ontology is itself arbitrary, merely a set of axioms or meaning postulates whose theorems have no necessary relation to reality, is he not
inviting the same evaluation of his own ontology and Spinoza's, which
even looks the part? Kierkegaard thought so when he said the Hegelian
system was a great thought experiment. Once inside the basic framework things fall nicely in place, but for the existing individual who
needs something to live and die by, the problem of getting in may be
of overwhelming importance and difficulty. Kierkegaard thought so
when he ironically used the terms "Fragments" and "Postscript" to
entitle his discussions of just this problem.

Hegel, of course, does not permit himself to be drawn outside of his
own ontology to discuss these questions. He is eager to get on with the
task of purifying the proof under examination by giving it its proper
interpretation. Since it is essentially a denial of the ultimacy of the
world as seen by the understanding, it is to be expected that the
understanding will misinterpret the proof, distorting its truth. It treats
the proof as a causal inference, whereas, in fact, it concerns the category
of substance.[53] Thus instead of seeing the move from the finitude of

---

[52] LP, 290–92, g107–08. Hegel's language here evokes the picture of Luke 16:26 (Luther's
translation) in which Lazarus in Abraham's bosom and the rich man in Hades are separated
by a gulf fixed between them.
[53] LP, 315–17, g125–27. Cf. pp. 247–48, g143–44 in the supplement on Kant (see note 6).

the world to the infinity of God as the move to Absolute Substance from its accidents and manifestations, it sees the inference as moving from one reality, the world, to another reality, its cause. This is evident in the language used by the understanding. It says, "Because contingent being exists, therefore absolutely necessary being exists." But "the contingent is in this way retained on its own account separately from the Absolutely Necessary," even when it is explained that the conditioned is the condition of the necessary only in the order of knowing. The contingent "remains standing on the one side confronting the other side, the Eternal, the Necessary in and for itself, in the form of a world above which is heaven. Still the real point is not the fact that a double world has actually been conceived, but the value which is to be attached to such a conception. This value is expressed when it is said that the one world is the world of appearance or illusion, and the other the world of truth." Corrected by Hegelian logic, the proof would look like this: "Not because the contingent is, but on the contrary, because it is non-being, merely phenomenal, because its being is not true actuality, the Absolutely Necessary is. This latter is its being and truth." Or, "The being of the contingent is not its own being, but merely the being of an other, and in a definite sense it is the being of its own other, the Absolutely Necessary." [54]

Hegel is trying to steer clear of a theistic interpretation of the proof which portrays God as creator, a being sufficient to himself and distinct from the world He freely creates. Overlooking the fact that such an ontology places the world in an asymmetrical dependence relation to God, Hegel sees it only as a kind of Manichean dualism. [55]

Over and above this theoretical deficiency relative to the Hegelian system, there is a practical problem. If finite and infinite are conceived as separate and unrelated realities, i.e., dualistically, the actions by which we relate to them are also separate and unrelated. The sacred and secular fall hopelessly apart in experience. "When spirit occupied itself with the finite it would in turn do this in an absolute way and be entirely confined to the finite as such." But a true relation to the finite is possible, whether theoretical or practical, "only in so far as the finite is not taken for itself, but is known, recognized, and its existence affirmed in terms of its relation to the Infinite." Instead of this the

[54] LP, 285–90, g103–07.
[55] LP, 297, g112. Tillich has said that since "pantheism" has become a "heresy label" it "should be defined before it is applied aggresively." *op. cit.*, I, 233. Whether the usage is aggressive or otherwise, one could do worse than defining as pantheistic those systems which view classical theism as dualistic. In this sense the label fits both Hegel and Tillich.

"religious element in the form of devotion, contrition of heart and spirit, and the giving of offerings, comes to be regarded as a matter apart with which we can occupy ourselves and then have done with; while the secular life, the sphere of finitude, exists along-side of it, and gives itself up to the pursuit of its own ends, and is left to its own interests without any influence being exercised upon it by the Infinite, the Eternal, and the True."[56]

This criticism reveals one of the most basic elements of the Hegelian project. His secondary and university education between 1780 and 1793 exposed him to the militant secularism of the Enlightenment and to the enormous gulf between it and the supposedly official Christianity of Europe. During this period his favorite reading (excepting Rousseau) was the Greek poets, especially Sophocles. Through this reading and his reading of Goethe and Schiller he developed a fervent admiration for Greek culture, especially its folk religion, which he saw as permeating all of life with a sense of the presence of the Divine. In romantic reaction against the cultural dualism of his own day, he plaintively concludes one of his early essays with this lament: "between these extremes which occur within the opposition between God and the world, between the divine and life, the Christian church has oscillated to and fro, but it is contrary to its essential character to find peace ... And it is its fate that church and state, worship and life, piety and virtue, spiritual and worldly action can never dissolve into one."[57]

The task of overcoming this sacred-secular dualism is the inner, driving spirit of all of Hegel's thought. Its purpose is to provide the conceptual tools for freeing Christianity from this fate, for recovering in a post-pagan world the harmony of divine and human which paganism had enjoyed but lost. Thus, rather than saying (as above) that Hegel's practical objection to a theistic interpretation of the cosmological proof is "over and above" his theoretical objection, we should say that the latter is possible only in a systematic framework ultimately motivated by the former. The two objections are really the same. To say from a logical point of view that the categories of finite and infinite are improperly conceived is to say in an Hegelian way that from an existential point of view the dimensions of the secular and the sacred are improperly experienced.

This does not conclude Hegel's purification, however. The truth of the cosmological proof, totally missed by the understanding, is grasped

[56] LP, 298–99, g113.
[57] ETW, 301, g342.

by those systems which might be called pantheistic, or, as Hegel prefers, "systems of substantiality." Oriental religion, especially Hindu, the Greek view of Fate as supreme, the Eleatic doctrine of being, and the Spinozistic movement from *natura naturata* to *natura naturans* – all of these have avoided the pitfalls of the understanding and conceived the proof in its true form. By now we are prepared for this. Since the cosmological proof is not a causal argument, but one pertaining to substance, we should not be surprised to find that Spinozism is its truth.

But its truth is not the truth, and Hegel's criticism of these systems is that they do not get beyond it. Their conception of the Absolutely Necessary, while free from all suspicion of dualism, turns out to be a one-sided monism. The Stoic's renunciation and the tragic hero's repose in the face of Fate are not the satisfaction which the human heart longs for in longing for God.[58] Absolute necessity is here conceived so as to leave no hope for the individual beyond the internal freedom of acquiescence. "They start from actual existence, treat it as a nullity, and recognize the Absolute One as the truth of this existence. They start with a presupposition, they negate it in the absolute unity, but they don't get out of this unity back to the presupposition ... Everything passes into this unity as into a kind of eternal night, while this unity is not characterized as a principle which moves itself to its manifestation or produces it." "The souls of the eastern poets dive into this ocean and drown in it all the necessities, the aims, the cares of this petty, circumscribed life, and revel in the enjoyment of this freedom." "We rise above finiteness, we forget it. But yet it is not truly transcended simply because we have forgotten it."[59]

Hegel is criticizing the Spinozism which is his own starting point, not for its so-called pantheism, but for not getting beyond the category of substance in describing the Absolute. The teleological argument, for example, while it does not yet conceive of God as Spirit, does view Him as living substance. All the categories of Hegel's Logic are attributes of God, but the richer ones are more adequate. Thus it is true that God is the Absolute Substance, but truer that He is living, i.e., that this substance is internally purposive in the mode of finite organisms. To reach the category of spirit we need only to add the

---

[58]   Bertrand Russell's essay, "A Free Man's Worship," is a classical modern expression both of the view of the world which is supposed to be transcended in the cosmological proof and of the inadequate way of doing so which Hegel is here criticizing.

[59]   LP, 318–20, g128–29, PR, I, 109, g15:122. Cf. PS 79 and 110, g19 and 43.

concept of self-consciousness to this notion of a purposive development of substance, and the ontological argument provides this further enrichment. These conceptions begin the movement back from the Infinite to the finite starting point. With the ideas of purposiveness and self-consciousness Hegel believes the finite individual is restored to a place of meaning and importance which he seemed to be losing in the movement toward the Absolute Substance. This is why it is so crucial, from the Hegelian point of view, to conceive substance as subject (as in the Preface to the *Phenomenology*).

B. The Ontological Proof

Though Hegel clearly intended to discuss all three of the classical arguments in the *Proofs*, he did not complete his project. But because of the importance of the ontological argument in his thinking and because of the contemporary revival of interest in it, it would be inappropriate not to summarize briefly what he says elsewhere about it.

In spite of his special fondness for "the great theologian Anselm of Canterbury" and his proof, it is important to recognize that it is not his contention that "all arguments must ultimately be reduced to the ontological argument and thus share its validity as a description of the human spirit's elevation to God." [60] Following Kant, he distinguishes the cosmological and teleological proofs, whose starting points are experienced reality, from the ontological proof, whose starting point is the concept of God. But since both directions which thought can take are one-sided, both are equally necessary. Just as the denial of the ontological proof absolutizes an "untrue concept," so the denial of the others would be the absolutizing of an "untrue reality." [61] It is true that the two historically prominent arguments of the former kind, even when "purified," compare unfavorably with the properly understood ontological argument, since the latter alone grasps the Absolute as Spirit. But this superiority is accidental. There are potentially any number of proofs which start from the world as experienced, and there is nothing in principle to keep them from coming to understand God as Spirit. In fact, Hegel's own *Realphilosophie* (Philosophy of Nature and Spirit) is just as much such an argument as his Logic is a complex version of the ontological proof. Since, as we have seen, Hegel does not permit any wedge to be driven between (human) thought and

---

[60] Quentin Lauer, "Hegel on Proofs of God's Existence," *Kant-Studien*, 55/4, 1964, p. 444. The constant reiteration of this thesis mars this otherwise helpful essay.

[61] LP, 215–22, g69–75, SL II, 345 and 225–26, gII, 356 and 229–30.

being, the real is rational and the rational is real. It does not matter whether one begins with the necessities of thought which express themselves in actuality, or with given reality, which shows itself to be fully intelligible, as long as neither movement of thought is left out.

With regard to the proof itself, the same two points are to be considered as before, the adequacy of the result and the legitimacy of the inference. With regard to the first the question arises why it should be the ontological argument alone, of the classical proofs properly interpreted, which yields an adequate concept of God as Spirit. The reason is simply that it begins with the concept of God. Like all the proofs, according to Hegel, this one expresses the intelligiblity of a certain kind of religious experience, but since it starts with the concept of God, each version of the proof will begin with its author's answer to the question, What is worthy of worship? [62]

Just because Anselm's formula for perfection, "that than which a greater cannot be conceived" is an entirely formal one, it has lent itself to many different concepts of perfection. The ontological proof has been used to express such widely different views of God as Anselm's, Spinoza's, Hegel's, Tillich's, and Hartshorne's. This means that Hegel must purify the proof and reconstruct its true significance. Once again this purification presupposes his system, which in this case is his lengthy answer to the question, What is worthy of worship? If his version of the ontological argument articulates the Absolute as Spirit, it is because Spirit, not Anselm's transcendent creator or Spinoza's substance, is that than which a greater cannot be conceived by Hegel.

More troublesome to many than this question of whose version of the ontological proof is most adequate is the question whether any

[62] This has been made particularly clear by J. N. Findlay in the second part of his essay "Can God's Existence Be Disproved?," *Mind*, April 1948, reprinted in *Language, Truth and Value*, and in *The Ontological Argument: From St. Anselm to Contemporary Philosophers*, ed. Alvin Plantinga; and by John Smith in his emphasis on the importance for Anselm of discovering the appropriate philosophical formula for expressing the content of his religious faith. See *Experience and God*, Ch. 5. Another striking example indicates that such a preliminary reflection determines the neo-classical direction of Charles Hartshorne's version of the proof. He writes, "For reasons that I have given in various writings, I take "true religion" to mean serving God, by which I do not mean simply admiring or "obeying" him, or enabling him to give benefits to me and other nondivine creatures, but also, and most essentially, contributing value to God which he would otherwise lack. Even in this religions case, to "serve" is to confer a benefit, in precisely the sense that the served will to some extent depend upon the server for that benefit. This is genuine dependence ... In short, God with contingency but lacking dependence is not the God we can serve or, in what I think is the proper meaning, worship." "The Dipolar Conception of Deity," *The Review of Metaphysics*, XXI (December, 1967), p. 274.

version expresses a valid inference. To infer the reality of anything from its concept is, to say the least, highly unusual.

As it turns out, this way of putting the objection is one way of answering it. Just as Anselm had to remind Gaunilo that he was talking about God and not an island, Hegel reminds Kant that it is not a hundred thalers which is at stake. "But if it is correct that concept is not the same as being, it is truer still that God is not the same as one hundred thalers or other finite things. It is the definition of finite things that with them concept and being, concept and reality, soul and body, are different and separable, and that therefore they are perishable and mortal. While it is just the abstract definition of God that with Him concept and being are unseparated and inseparable."[63] This appeal to another kind of being and knowledge simply indicates that Kant's refutation of the argument begs precisely what is at question, namely whether there is anything other than the finite things for which ontological arguments are invalid.

But can Hegel go beyond this negative rejoinder to provide some intelligibility for the strange inference from concept to reality, from the rational to the real? He uses language which seems at first only further to mystify the doubtful. The concept "particularizes itself," "posits finitude," "generates reality from within itself," etc. This language, and the whole thrust of the ontological argument for Hegel, lose at least some of their strangeness when we remember that idea or concept for Hegel does not mean what it means for Locke or Hume, but rather what substantial form or entelechy means for the Aristotelian tradition. Relative to Aristotelian language, Hegel's references to the concept of a thing as its soul are not metaphors. The concept of a thing is the dynamic inner principle which guides the process of its development. It is "the shoot, out of which the whole tree develops itself. All the specifications are contained in this, the whole nature of

---

[63] SL, I, 102, gI, 75. Cf. II, 345, gII, 355. Hegel's invoking of the distinction between abstract and concrete in God raises the question of his relation to Hartshorne's neo-classical version of the ontological argument. He sees in Hegel "a man who is and wants to be in a perpetual systematic muddle between classical theism, classical pantheism, and something like neoclassical theism, with a dose of humanistic atheism, or the self-deification of man, thrown in for good measure." *Anselm's Discovery*, LaSalle, 1965, p. 235. As LP is understood in the present essay Hegel's position is considerably less muddled. He clearly wants nothing to do with either the kind of transcendence affirmed in classical theism or the finitude affirmed by neo-classical theism. His position is and wants to be a systematic mediation between classical pantheism and humanistic atheism. Hartshorne is misled, probably by Hegel's use of the abstract-concrete distinction, into sensing an affinity for neo-classical theism. But that distinction is present in Aquinas, and is no sure sign of the neo-classical. See "Temporality and Finitism in Hartshorne's Theism," *The Review of Metaphysics*, XIX (March 1966), pp. 561 ff.

the tree, the kind of sap it has, and the way in which the branches grow; but in a spiritual manner, and not preformed so that a microscope could reveal its boughs, its leaves in miniature. It is thus that the concept contains the whole nature of the object, and knowledge itself is nothing else than the development of the concept." [64]

It is clear that this last definition of knowledge is radically empirical rather than a priori and is akin to Aristotle's doctrine of knowledge as the immaterial reception of the forms. No speculative microscope can beat history to the draw. Only as the object develops and reveals what its concept already contains (in the sense that an acorn is already an oak and not a milk-pail) can the development of the concept come to consciousness for a subject and thus be knowledge.

It is also clear that the movement of thought or inference involved here is not from a present and known reality to the existence of an absent and previously unknown reality. It is rather a process of coming to a fuller understanding of the nature of a reality already encountered and only partially comprehended.

But Hegel intends to do more than suggest a bio-teleological model for describing the processes of nature and history when he says that the concept "particularizes itself," etc. He also means to assert with Anaxagoras that *nous* rules the world. Like Socrates, Hegel understands this to mean that the ultimate cause of the world arranges things for the best and that comprehension and justification go hand in hand. In order to make the point perfectly clear he assimilates the Anaxagorean doctrine to the religious doctrine of Providence. [65] The language Hegel invokes in defending the ontological argument is his philosophical translation of the Christian belief that the historical process is controlled and directed by an Absolute Goodness.

The clearest statement on this theme is in the *Philosophy of History*. "The only thought which philosophy brings with it to the contemplation of history is the simple conception of Reason; that Reason rules the world; and that the history of the world is thus a rational process. This conviction and insight is a hypothesis in the domain of history as such. In that of philosophy it is no hypothesis ... On the one hand, Reason is the substance of the universe, that by which and in which all reality has its being and subsistence. On the other hand, it is the infinite power of the universe, since Reason is not so powerless as to

---

[64] PR, I, 61, g15:77.
[65] *The Philosophy of History*, trans. Sibree, New York, 1956, pp. 11–13. *Die Vernunft in der Geschichte*, hrsg. Hoffmeister, Hamburg, 1955, S. 36–39.

be incapable of producing anything but a mere ideal, a mere ought having its place outside reality, who knows where ... That this Idea [Reason] is the True, the Eternal, the Absolutely Powerful; that it reveals itself in the world, and that in the world nothing else is revealed but this and its honor and glory – this is the thesis which, as we have said, has been proved in Philosophy, and is here regarded as demonstrated." [66]

These two features of Hegel's talk about the Idea particularizing itself invite the appellation historical Aristotelianism. They also invite certain questions or criticisms which can be mentioned briefly for the sake of further clarifying the issues at stake. The Aristotelian aspect, put in the context of historical processes, raises the question whether the spectre of historicism (see notes 10 and 40 above) does not hang over even the ontological argument in Hegel. Knowledge of the divine as a developing process is relative to the state of development at which it occurs and which it expresses. This makes it possible to explain why Anselm gave a theistic and Spinoza an abstractly pantheistic interpretation to the ontological proof. But it also makes us wonder whether Hegel's own version has a kind of obsolescence systematically built in.

A different sort of problem arises from the use of the ontological argument as theodicy. Nietzsche puts it bluntly: "The belief that one is a latecomer in the world is, anyhow, harmful and degrading; but it must appear frightful and devastating when it raises our latecomer to godhead, by a neat turn of the wheel, as the true meaning and object of all past creation, and his conscious misery is set up as the perfection of the world's history. Such a point of view ... has put history in the place of other spiritual powers, art and religion, as the one sovereign, inasmuch as it is the 'Idea realizing itself' .... [Hegel] has implanted in a generation leavened throughout by him the worship of the 'power of history' that turns practically every moment into a sheer gaping at success, into an idolatry of the actual for which we have now discovered the characteristic phrase, 'to adapt ourselves to circumstances.' ... If each success has come by a 'rational necessity,' and every event shows the victory of logic of the 'idea,' then – down on yours knees quickly, and let every step in the ladder of success have its reverence! There are no more living mythologies, you say? Religions are at their last gasp? Look at the religion of the power of

---

[66] *Ibid.*, pp. 9–10, g28–29. This passage and that referred to in the previous note are both from Hegel's own text, not from student notes.

history, and the priests of the mythology of Ideas, with their scarred knees."[67]

Marx makes the same criticism in his 1843 critique of paragraphs 261–69 of Hegel's *Philosophy of Right*. With reference to Hegel's description of the relation of family, civil society, and state, Marx writes, "They are not *as such* presented as rational. But they become rational again only in that they are presented as an *apparent* mediation, in that they are left just as they are, but at the same time acquire the meaning of a determination of the Idea, a result, a product of the Idea. ... Empirical actuality is thus understood as it is. It is also pronounced rational, but it is not rational through its own rationality but rather because the empirical fact in its empirical existence has another meaning than its own. The initial fact is not taken as such but rather as a mystical result." In short, Hegel "uncritically takes limited existences for the expression of the Idea."[68]

These criticisms are surely not the last word on the subject, and there are a number of ways in which Hegel can be defended against them. I have introduced them neither to defend them, nor to arbitrate the dispute to which they give rise. I have simply wanted to suggest that it is when Hegel approaches historical and political issues under the impact of his own thinking on the ontological argument that he gives ammunition to his critics along these lines. Recognizing this is of considerable help when one is trying to comprehend Hegel's perplexing comments on the ontological proof.

It may seem that only half of Hegel's theory of religious knowledge has been presented, since only the question of the knowledge of God has been discussed, while the question of the positive element in religion has been ignored. This would leave us with a theory of natural theology, but no theory of revealed theology. This incompleteness, however, is only apparent. It is true that we do not know precisely what Hegel will do with this or that particular doctrine of revealed theology. But we do know how he will handle every positivity, for we have seen his theory on this question at work. The three classical proofs are, before Hegel purifies them, just as positive, just as histori-

---

[67] *The Use and Abuse of History*, trans. Collins, New York, 1957, pp. 51–52. *Vom Nutzen und Nachteil der Historie*, in *Werke in Drei Bänden*, hrsg. Schlechta, München, 1954, I, 262–63.
[68] *Writings of the Young Marx on Philosophy and Society*, trans. and ed. by Easton and Guddat, New York, 1967, pp. 156–57, 179.

cally particular, as revealed doctrine. The ontological proof belongs to Anselm and Spinoza as much as justification by faith alone belongs to Paul and Luther. And just as Hegel purifies natural theology by reinterpreting it in the light of his own ontological logic, so he will free the essential truth of revealed theology from distortions due to the understanding. In the light of the discovery that for Hegel the cosmological argument ends in Spinozism, while the ontological argument, which Spinoza stressed, is just what leads beyond him, we should be prepared for some surprises in Hegel's purification of the various Christian doctrines. But for his general theory of religious knowledge we need go no farther. [69]

[69] Since Hegel regularly describes this purification as the raising of the content from its defective religious form (*Vorstellung*) to the adequacy of philosophical form (*Begriff*), Mure's treatment in this volume of the relation of *Vorstellungen* to philosophical thought is relevant here. One of Hegel's most important claims is to have provided a mode of thinking free of dependence on the imagination. It is also one of the most difficult of his claims to understand and evaluate.

ON ARTISTIC KNOWLEDGE
A STUDY IN HEGEL'S PHILOSOPHY OF ART

ALBERT HOFSTADTER

University of California, Santa Cruz

Is art knowledge?

On Hegel's view, it must be; for he maintains that art is called upon to disclose truth in the form of the sensible artistic construction,[1] and the disclosure of truth is certainly a cognitive process.

What is more, Hegel makes what must surely seem at first to be an extravagant claim for the power of art to disclose truth. For he locates art, along with religion and philosophy, in the sphere of absolute spirit. That means, art for him stands closer to ultimate truth than does empirical natural science, like physics, chemistry, and biology, as well as empirical psychological or social science, like individual psychology or economics or history. According to him the disclosure of truth we get from art gives us knowledge that is absolute and infinite, whereas the knowledge we have in empirical science is only relative and finite. The knowledge art gives us, although still intrinsically imperfect, lies on a plane that transcends empirical scientific knowledge.

Can there be any sense to such a grand claim?

Is the knowledge we receive in a Bach fugue – assuming there to be knowledge here at all – superior as knowledge to the knowledge that Newton gave us in his equations or that more recent physics provides about the external world? Is music closer to the truth of reality than physics? Can anyone in his right mind believe such an absurd declaration?

But we should be careful not to overstate the Hegelian claim. Hegel does not say that the musical composer knows more about nature in

---

[1] 12.89. (References to the *Sämtliche Werke* in the Jubilee edition edited by Hermann Glockner, Frommann, Stuttgart-Bad Cannstatt, are indicated by giving the volume number followed by the page number: e.g., page 237 of Volume 7 is denoted by 7.237. All such merely numerical references are to this edition. The translations are my own.)

its physical character than does the natural scientist. Quite the contrary; it is the empirical scientist, and he alone, who develops empirical scientific knowledge. It would be a fallacy to infer that because music is closer to the truth of reality than physics, the musician therefore knows more physics than the physicist. The musician is generally, *qua* musician, ignorant of physics as such; he does not even have to know the physics of sound and silence; what he knows, rather, transcends the physical altogether, even as it makes use of the physical – of physical sound and silence – in order to reach beyond the physical; and this knowledge of his, according to Hegel, is closer to the real truth of things, closer to true truth, than all the knowledge that could be furnished by the sum-total of all empirical sciences. The ignorant musician discloses truth more perfectly in his music than the most knowing physicist in his science. And the same holds of the comparison between artistic knowledge and knowledge in the psychological and social sciences.

Artistic knowledge does not stand in competition with scientific knowledge regarding the particular subject-matters of the sciences. It stands in competition, rather, with empirical scientific knowledge as such. Empirical scientific knowledge is knowledge at a lower level than that of art, a level that never reaches truth and reality in their ultimate shape. The prehistoric artist who painted in the caves of the palaeolithic age already knew truth and reality more truly than the most advanced of twentieth-century scientists. No matter how rudimentary his mental grasp, it was already in this respect more advanced than that of the sciences of the twentieth century with all their sophistication in mathematical theory and ingenious experiment.

But now, even if we do not overstate the claim, does it not remain simply bombast?

What validity can there be in such pomposities about the superiority of the knowledge of the ignorant musician to that of the knowledgeable physicist, of artistic imagination to scientific understanding, of the poem to the mathematical theory? Are we not confronted here by a paranoia of the sort that characteristically inhabits the metaphysical mentality?

Such a question eventually answers itself. Moreover one cannot supply an answer for someone else. Anyone who desires to know must live through and think through what happens in empirical science and in art, experience the disclosure of truth as it happens in both, and make the comparison on his own account. It is a matter, not of so-called empirical observation, but of genuine experience, going through a spiritual process and becoming aware of what has been gone through, in which this conscious realization is itself a spiritual process that fulfills more completely the life impulse dwelling within the whole experience.

At the end of the lectures on aesthetics Hegel said:

In art we have to do with no merely agreeable or useful pastime, but with the liberation of the spirit from the content and forms of finitude, with the presence and reconciliation of the absolute in the sensible and apparent, with an unfolding of truth which is not exhausted as natural history but manifests itself in world history, of which it itself constitutes the finest aspect and the best reward for the hard work in the real and the painful efforts of knowledge.[2]

If art is knowledge, then, it is not knowledge as over against a practice which would be its opposite; and it is not knowledge as an abstraction in comparison with the reconciliation of which he speaks – a reconciliation that unites within it at once the realization of the aims of both "the hard work in the real" and "the painful efforts of knowledge."

The knowledge that art is, is a knowledge which belongs to and is identical with ultimate human freedom, that freedom in which the spirit is liberated from the bonds of finitude, both in form and in content, and in which the absolute, with its infinite power of reconciliation, exists in presence. It is the same as the freedom that constitutes the whole sense of world history, and the unfolding of which is made in time in the unfolding of art, as well as of religion and philosophy.

The final purpose of the world, Hegel declared, is spirit's consciousness of its freedom and, precisely with that, the actual reality of its freedom.[3] In this statement, which sums up as well as any the general purport of Hegel's thinking, there is the clear identification of spirit's consciousness of its freedom (which consciousness can be understood as a form of knowledge) with the actual reality of its freedom, that is, with the liberation of the spirit in its own fulfilled being, not in some abstract side of its being that might be labelled "knowledge." The knowledge of freedom and the being and existence of freedom are, at the absolute level and standpoint, identical.

This entails that, since art exists as art exactly at the absolute level and standpoint, the identity also holds good in art. Art is, at once, the

---

[2] 14.580 f.
[3] 11.47–48.

consciousness and the actuality of spiritual freedom. And this means that in art the final purpose of the world comes into presence. To be sure, this presence is only a first one, the least of all the presences of authentic spiritual freedom; but it is the first, and its being so represents an infinite leap beyond every reality of freedom in the sphere either of abstract theoretical knowledge on the one side or of abstract practical action on the other. In art, the thinking and the being that exist as opposites in finite knowledge and action are for the first time brought into their true unity, in which thinking equals being and being equals thinking.

Once more: to be sure, this thinking is inchoate and immediate as thinking; it is only the real potentiality of genuine thinking; namely, it is only immediate beholding, intuiting. But even at this immediate level it has already succeeded in reaching the sought-for identification with being. In art, consciousness and actuality are one. In it, the fundamental opposites that are at odds with one another elsewhere first begin to join together, not disappearing into one another, but meeting and marrying, affording the spirit its first taste of the homeward return.

How can we make clear to ourselves this identity of thinking and being in art?

We must come to participate in it ourselves. Only by being this identity are we able to know it, that is, to think it truly. The knowledge of artistic truth is not a cool, abstract knowing about something from a distance. We can indeed obtain a certain distance from art while truly knowing it; but we can do this only by going through and beyond art, to religion, and eventually to philosophy.

There is no way of knowing the true, essential character of art by naturalistic observation, hypothesis formation, and theory construction, just as there is no similar way of knowing the truth of love. Much can, of course, be known in empirical abstractness about art, in the sense that we can know in that manner the things that cluster about the inner heart of art: schemes of composition, external forms, subject-matters, themes, historical data, biographies, etc. But the one thing that cannot be known in this way is the pure actuality of art as such, its essential reason for being, namely, the absolute truth and freedom that our spirit reaches when it attains the being of art. This is not empirical knowledge; it is experiential knowledge, knowledge that comes about in and through the actual living artistic experience and, in its immediate form, is identical with that experience.

This means at the same time that as subjective individuals we must arrive at enough spiritual freedom to be able to participate in the absolute freedom of art. To know truth, as truth opens up in art, the basic precondition is to realize the freedom that unlocks the truth and is the truth itself. You cannot learn this truth by reading it in a book – not even by reading it in this book, in these pages. Truth is freedom, and freedom is the return of spirit to itself. Only as you return, as spirit, to self, is it possible for you to be the free being that is artistic knowing.

How is it that art can be knowledge?

Art is supposed to be absolute knowledge. It is supposed to be not mere knowledge as over against something else that is not knowledge. Rather, it is supposed to be spiritual totality, freedom: both the consciousness (that is, the knowledge) of freedom and the actuality (that is, the realized being) of freedom, all in one.

In such absolute knowledge the fundamental oppositions that permeate man's finite life are overcome. The body in Nature, from having been a hindrance to the spirit and a weight upon it, has become spirit's willing and selfless organ. You can see it in all art, but it comes out beautifully in the dancer. The ordinary opposition between subject and object in consciousness, on one side the ego and on the other the ego's opposite, its object as other – this opposition has been overcome, and instead the object has become the ego's very own, its own self, and the ego has become an I that has grown up to the capacity for owning the other, an entirely non-selfish I.

In true artistic experience, in the experience of great and veritable art, you find your own self growing to this capacity and the object coming close to you, joining in the union of genuine affinity, so that your own life itself, during that interval, becomes seamlessly whole and self-sufficient, and you know it in its being so.

In a parallel way, the ordinary opposition between agent and patient that infects all finite practice is raised up into a condition of harmony and happiness, of blessedness and well-being, in which the two, beyond all mere acting upon and being acted upon, exist together in simple unity and perfect correspondence. You can experience some of this transcendent life by a kind of participation from without when you are the onlooker merely. But the truest and purest experience of it comes from the actual practice of art itself, creative and re-creative.

Who shall know the dancer from the dance?

The poet who has wrestled with words and world and has finally come to say his poem – in his saying he does not any longer act upon words and world, but rather, words and world are his acting, his saying, into which his being has entered and found itself in the being of these others, these words, this world.

Nor is the self which experiences in art the surmounting of the oppositions between spirit and body, subjectivity and objectivity, activity and passivity, a merely finite self that stands over against the social and historical world. Genuine artistic experience is never merely the isolated experience of a particular subject within itself. It is, on the contrary, a participation in the experience of a living culture – a people, a nation: Hegel uses the German word that combines both these senses – *ein Volk*. The musician composes in the musical medium and idiom of his folk, and all the more when he is the vehicle through which the medium and idiom are transformed in reaching new expressions. The poet composes in the folk language, the dancer dances in its bodily gestures, the architect builds in its architectural figures and sites. The artist's mind is impregnated with the mind of his people, all the more when his mind is the vehicle by which new thoughts, feelings, and aspirations are reached, and especially when, as with the Greeks, through his free creativity the people's gods receive their name and form, *von der Muse selber dem Dichter eingegeben* – given in inspiration to the poet by the Muse herself.[4]

How is it, then, that art can be such absolute knowledge?

The explanation is to be found only by following spirit in its own evolution into art. The nature of art as knowledge cannot be deduced from premises by an abstract logic of the understanding; for then the premises would have to contain already what the conclusion would assert, and there would be no life in this movement from premises to conclusion, only the death that belongs to the abstract logical intellect. For the same reason, there can be no valid argument from data to conclusion by means of statistical or probability measurements. The explanation has to consist in a growing insight that comes about by following and participating spiritually in the process of spirit's own living development.

Spirit cannot be explained by anything other than itself. It explains itself by explicating itself – unfolding in its own spiritual evolution. No one who is a stranger to speculative thinking, and to religion, could possibly comprehend what is happening when spirit gets to

4 13.69.

art; for spirit arrives at art in order to go through it to reach religion and speculation. It would be like trying to comprehend a hand reaching out to grasp a tool without knowing what it is to reach out for something or what a tool is and why anyone should want to get hold of it. This is not a denial of the existence of exteriority that can be known without spiritual insight. Modern science – especially the hardest-headed version of it, namely, the imitation of physics by behavioral science – can learn an immeasurable quantity of things external, but it remains blind to spirit because it remains blind to inwardness and intimacy. Only through sharing the inwardness and intimacy of spirit, however, can the way and life of spirit be grasped.

The first and last question which must be asked and answered if we are to comprehend not only the cognitive character of art but anything at all, is: What is spirit, mind, *Geist?* And the answer to this question, like the question itself, is not just a configuration of words. Mere words, as having externality attached to them, as participating in sound, which is their form in Nature, can never be either a question or an answer of spirit's. They are at most an expression, and the spirit must be there to give its life to them, to be their soul. That means: the question "What is spirit?" must be one that is truly inward. It must come out of its own spiritual need, even out of a certain despair, out of the spirit's experience of the negation of itself within itself – as for instance, out of the unhappy consciousness of the death of God, or out of skeptical doubt as to the being of truth, or out of the hell of the evil of subjective particularity that holds to itself, against all others, as the sole source of truth. Without the experience of spiritual life, living it oneself and, as far as possible, sharing in the life of others, one will never understand this question, much less grasp the significance of an answer to it.

Hegel's answer is:

Spirit is essentially this: to come to itself by the negation of negation, out of its otherness and through the overcoming of this otherness; spirit brings itself forth; it goes through the alienation of its own self.[5]

How is it that this essential nature of spirit, to be the return to self out of its own otherness, is to be understood as truth and, in one particular form, as art?

_____

[5] 15.435. See Georg Lasson, ed., *Vorlesungen über die Philosophie der Religion*, Hamburg: Meiner, Philosophische Bibliothek Band 60, *Die Naturreligion*, 1927, 1966, pp. 213–214; *Lectures on the Philosophy of Religion*, translated by E. B. Speirs and J. Burdon Sanderson, London: Routlege & Kegan Paul, 1895, 1962, 1968, Vol. 2, p. 82.

The concept of truth is fundamental in Hegel's thinking, not only about art but about all things in all their forms. In it Hegel found that identity of thinking and being, of the subjective and the objective, which, in its ultimate form, constitutes the absolute itself and which, when once found, provides the key that unlocks all gates leading to the sanctuary. As he said of himself, he aims everywhere in his philosophical efforts at the scientific cognition of truth, trying always to preserve the will to truth and the courage for it, a courage which is identical with faith in the power of spirit and which is the first condition of philosophical study. [6]

To ask the question of truth in Hegel's manner is to ask a question that is existential, not in the limited sense of Sartrian existentialism, which starts with disbelief in the essential, but in the profound sense that belongs to the striving for ultimate truth which gets expressed in the great art forms, religions, and thoughts of mankind.

When Christ spoke before Pilate saying: For this I was born and for this I have come into the world, to bear witness to the truth, Pilate asked: What is truth? Pilate's question is very different from Hegel's. Hegel, in asking what truth is, is asking – for instance, and in an ultimate way – what Christ is, who also said: I am the way, and the truth, and the life. The way, the truth, the life – these, all identical, are the central concern of great art, great religion, great thinking, everywhere. Thinking that devotes itself to them is existential in the profoundest sense, namely, in the sense that it itself has the courage and the will to seek to be what it knows and to know what it is, seeking the way, the truth, and the life that is its very own, truly own. It is existential not in being merely subjective, a matter of merely personal conviction, but in being grounded in faith and participation in existent truth itself, in truth's genuine striving to reach the existence of itself.

Hegel points out that the opposition between *Meinung* and *Wahrheit* – between opinion, subjectively appropriated mean-ing which is, as it were, mine-ing, and truth, or between the subjective that is onesidedly particular and the subjective that has matured through its encounter and eventual reconciliation with universality and objectivity – is already visible in the culture of the period of Socrates and Plato, a period, as he notes, of corruption in Greek life, and, we may add, not altogether unlike our own period. It is, he says, the same opposition which we observe at the time of the decadence of Roman public and

[6] 8.36.

political life under Augustus and subsequently. In this period Epicureanism, indifference to philosophy, as again in our own period, was widespread. It was in this sense of indifference toward philosophy, toward any seriously existential concern with truth, that Pilate answered Christ with the question: What is truth?

That, says Hegel, was spoken in a superior way, and amounts to saying: "This designation, truth, is a convention that we are finished and done with. We've gone further; we know that there is no longer any question of knowing truth. We have got beyond it.

And Hegel adds:

He who takes this stand has indeed gone past it.[7]

Truth in the philosophical sense must be differentiated from truth in its more customary sense. Customarily truth is understood as being an agreement or correspondence between an object and our representation of it. The object is one thing and the representation is another, and truth occurs when they are in accord. This hand has five fingers. I think: "This hand has five fingers." My thought – my representation of the number of fingers belonging to the hand – is in agreement with the object, the number of fingers of the hand. My thought, then, is true: thought and thing are in agreement; what the thought thinks the thing is.

This truth Hegel speaks of as correctness, *Richtigkeit*.[8] He does not deny its existence or its indispensability for life. And we too must acknowledge its worth. When extended, this correctness represents the truth that belongs to all finite knowledge – hence, to empirical science as well as to the knowledge of the commonsense world. Knowledge is finite when it is a knowing by a mind, on this side, of an object on the other side, different from this mind and its knowing. The knowledge is then finite, because it itself, as knowing, is one thing as over against the object known, as another thing. This difference

---

[7] See the discussion in the section on the history of philosophy as a stockpile of opinions, in his account of customary ideas about the history of philosophy, 17.38–42; in the English translation by E. S. Haldane, *Lectures on the History of Philosophy*, London: 1892, Vol. 1, pp. 11–15. See also Hegel's reference to this matter in the address to his audience at the opening of his lectures on the Encyclopedia Logic (not translated by Wallace), 8.34–35.

[8] See, for example, his statement about qualitative judgments like "the rose is red," "the rose is not red." Such judgments, he says, can be correct, but only in the sense in which so-called truth belongs to the limited sphere of perception, finite representation, thinking about objects. Philosophically speaking, no such judgment contains or expresses genuine truth, "true truth." 8.372. See also, 8.89–90; in Wallace's translation, pp. 304–305.

between the one and the other, the knowing (or knower) and the known, constitutes a limit and barrier that separates the two even in their close connection of accordance.

Moreover, because in this situation the knower and the known are not identical, there is always something in the known that must escape the knower. My hand has five fingers, yes; but the life of my hand, of my body, that courses through it and articulates it into a hand with five fingers – this escapes that judgment of mine; and, once I begin to know this life, that judgment becomes, not incorrect, but simply irrelevant, by-passed, superficial, lacking in true significance, hence lacking in truth.

The gap between knower and known, when the two are different and remain different, leads to the loss of insight and certainty that is so familiar to us in the ever-advancing success of modern empirical science. The empirical scientist never tires of pointing out that he does not deal in truth, does not know truth, does not even know what truth is supposed to be; all he does is to make hypotheses, theories, models, by means of which he hopes to be able to predict the consequences of given conditions.

This is as it must be. In empirical science man exists in his otherness toward existence, which then stands outside and over against him. He wishes to bring about a certain accord, however, between his thinking and this outward existence, Nature, in the broadest sense of the term, including human reality taken externally as empirical object. Ultimately, he wishes to control this reality, to dominate it and impress his own will upon it, as he does more and more with his technology. He seeks eventually a technology not only of the inorganic and organic, but of the human as well, so that he may engineer the structures and processes of human existence. In order to achieve this goal, he needs knowledge in the form of externality: the knowledge of causalities and reciprocities, laws that relate externals to one another. Therefore he must treat Nature in its externality, dealing with it in terms of concepts of the relationships of externals to externals, specifically, functions and laws that correlate phenomena as conditions and consequences, causal and reciprocal.

But on this very account he is forced to stay outside his object. As I lose hold of the life of my hand when I merely count its fingers, so does the empirical scientist lose hold of the life of the world when he counts the conditions and consequences within it, for in the end he loses hold of the spirit that rises up into world, ramifying into conditions and consequences, so that it may ascend into consciousness, self-consciousness, art, religion, thinking.

And the irony of it is that all the time he is himself an appearance of that spirit, in particular, a form of its consciousness. Consciousness, which provides the basic framework of all finite knowing, is that level of spirit in which spirit appears and exists as *ego*, as certainty of self. In consciousness I am aware of something other than myself – an object – and, precisely in being aware of it as other than myself, I am aware of myself as myself. I see the horse. The horse is an object to me, standing over against me, other than me; but just in that relationship of being other to myself, I myself am present to myself. I do not yet know the true reality that shows itself in horse and me and in the consciousness that embraces both of us. I have not yet reached an intuition, much less a representation or a thought, of the spirit that hides itself by showing itself to me in the horse and shows itself to me by hiding in the horse. I am as yet in the sphere of appearance, of correlation between things that are different, but a correlation in which one shows itself to the other and the other is conscious of it. It is a sphere of light, where the light lights up out of the darkness, assuming the form of the ego, which lights itself and lights its other, manifesting itself in the other while yet, because it stays with the other simply as other, ignorant of its true identity with the other. The empirical scientist has reached, according to Hegel, the third stage of consciousness, having passed through and preserved the values of the stages of sensuous consciousness and perceptual consciousness. He has reached the level of understanding, of abstractly intellectual consciousness, which knows its other not merely in the immediacy of being, by sensuous feeling; and not merely as something existing in the interconnection of things, as an instance of a universal, by representational perception; but by means of a certain kind of thinking – abstract intellectual thinking, which keeps things separate and relates them by means of the laws of their appearance.

The next step in the long march towards reason, freedom, and infinite truth would be to rise above the mere understanding, to move from this last outpost of consciousness to the beginning of self-consciousness, in which, as in the encounter with life, what is other for consciousness commences to reveal its identity with the self, so that the self's egoness begins to be transfigured into a foreshadowing of genuine community.

But to reach this self-consciousness the empirical scientist would have to die to his previous life. He would have to abandon egohood in moving toward a more concrete and living selfhood, joining with the other in a mutual participation, surrendering his will to intellectual power over the other. And this attainment itself would be one that had to be realized in a painful, difficult process of becoming and being self-conscious, beginning with appetite, going through the struggle for recognition in and through the other self (the master-slave relationship), and finally winning through to the true freedom of universal self-consciousness, the affirmative knowledge of self in the free acknowledgement of the other as free, where the other reciprocally has this same knowledge of himself in my self – the form of consciousness, Hegel says, of the substance of every essential spirituality as of every virtue: love, friendship, courage, honor, fame.[9]

And that would be only the beginning, since it represents a stage of spiritual being that is still merely subjective, still belonging to the particular individual as particular, having only begun to move into the objective existence of freedom as it occurs in social, political, historical reality, much less, then, having got to the point of entering into the absoluteness of spiritual existence as it takes the shape of art, religion, and speculation.

Truth in the philosophical sense is also an agreement; but instead of being an agreement between two things external to one another, it is the agreement of a content with itself.[10] Specifically, it is the agreement of a thing's concept with its existence, its existence with its concept. Hegel observes that this deeper philosophical sense of truth already appears partly in ordinary language, as when it speaks of a true friend, understanding by this one whose behavior accords with the concept of friendship, or when it speaks of a true work of art or a true state. It is this philosophical sense of truth that must concern us in seeking to understand the nature of artistic knowledge. Artistic knowledge is itself a certain kind of truth; it is artistic truth, the truth in and of art. It occurs in art works that are true – true art works which, being such, are true.

There is, according to Hegel, but one true truth. I put his statement down here so that it may stand before us, simply for itself, reminding us of the single point that must be held in mind all the way through.

God alone is the true agreement of concept and reality; all finite things, however, have some untruth in themselves; they have a concept and an existence, but

[9] *Encyclopedia*, 1830 edition, section 436.
[10] 8.90.

an existence which does not conform to their concept. For that reason they must perish, whereby the incongruity between their concept and their existence becomes manifest.[11]

Hegel gives the illustration of the animal as an individual thing. Its concept, he says, lies in its kind, the species, and the kind frees itself from the individuality of this single animal by death. Or as one might say, the message in the genes is self-replicative, and its meaning is not exhausted in this or that chromosome, cell, or organism; its manner of being is to get itself replicated over and over again in and through the genes, chromosomes, cells, organisms. The mode of existence the message has – the type of its tokens – lies in the process of renewed self-replication. To one familiar with Hegel's logic this immediately brings to mind the concept of the false infinite. A way, truth, and life that brings individuals into existence only so as to continue sacrificing them, over and over again, is one that, however real it is, nevertheless has also an untruth in itself, a concept and an existence which retain a certain incongruity. Therefore, in the order of the evolution of spirit, animal life itself must perish; it must "go to ground" into something higher than mere life.

What is higher than mere life is ... knowledge: knowledge both theoretical and practical but also, eventually, knowledge that is free, infinite, absolute, such as is had in art, religion, and philosophical speculation.

It is the knowledge which absolute spirit is.

The essential difference between this free, infinite, absolute knowledge that belongs to spirit and is spirit and is of spirit, and the knowledge that belongs to consciousness taken abstractly and is exemplified in the sciences and technologies of the modern world, is this: the truth of free knowledge is the agreement of its content with itself, its own concept with its own existence, whereas the truth of finite science, technology, and its associated practice is an agreement between their concept and an existence that is still different from and alien to that concept.

What is the concept of modern, finite, unfree science? It is not the concept of the electron, parity, relativity, the quantum, or whatever may be the shape of the particular theoretical-experimental concepts that appear within this science. It is the concept of the science itself, what it itself means to be and is, the indwelling universal of the science,

[11] 8.90.

its soul and character. This concept, at its very highest, is what Hegel calls in his logic "das Erkennen," the concept of cognition, whose essential counterpart and successor in the logical sequence is "das Wollen," the concept of volition.[12] Modern science is the living development of the concept of cognition in this sense of its particularity as compared with volition. This concept is like a dance that whirls from dancer to dancer as this and that man or woman takes up the scientific task and pursues it. It is at work in meetings of scientific associations, in deliberations of governmental committees awarding contracts for research, and in the structuring of universities, research institutes, publishing houses, museums, and similar agencies devoted to the development, manifestation, and spread of scientific knowledge.

Hegel employs the word "Erkennen" in two senses, one comprehensive and the other more circumscribed. In the comprehensive sense, both cognition and volition, the theoretical and the practical concept or idea, are called "cognition." In the restricted sense, the theoretical idea alone is called "cognition," and the practical idea is called "volition." Thus cognition as genus divides into the two species, cognition proper and volition. In fact, volition is just the more advanced form of cognition proper, and the whole movement is simply the movement of cognition in general. Cognition begins as theoretical; it advances to become practical; and it ends by proceeding beyond volition to the absoluteness of the idea as such – cognition fully developed, the truth of cognition. What we are at present concerned with is the idea of cognition in the circumscribed or stricter sense, the first stage of this total movement: theoretical cognition.

In theoretical cognition there is a subject and an object. It is a form of consciousness. Cognition exists first as a split between subjectivity and objectivity. The scientist experiences this split as one between himself, his mental activity, his thinking, on the one hand, and the world – specifically that aspect of the world, inorganic, biological, psychological, or social, which takes the shape of objectivity for him – on the other hand. The world exists as being, not simply as being himself, but as being other than himself. He takes this objective world to be something in and for itself, since his aim is to reach a knowledge of it. Even if philosophically he happens to be an idealist or a conventionalist or a relativist or some other such doctrinaire, so long as he is an empirical scientist and practices the process of theoretical

---

[12] 8.434–435, 435ff., 443ff.

cognition, there is something about the world which is, for him, other and, as other, having a being belonging to itself. Thus even if he knows how to treat the events and things of the objective world as mere phenomena, appearances, semblances, he nevertheless – in the words of Leibniz – has to treat them as phenomena that are well-founded, namely, that relate to a ground which affords them a certain being of their own, an orderliness in their mere phenomenality.

This split exists in theoretical cognition and it is there for a purpose. This purpose stems from the essential nature of spirit: to return to itself out of, in, and through, its other. The human spirit, as it takes the shape of scientist, distinguishes objectivity – the world, which is other as other – from itself as subjectivity, in order, precisely as subjectivity, to be able to reach out and find itself once more in and through the objectivity. This is what Hegel calls knowing's impulse or drive towards truth: cognition as such, theoretical cognition.[13] The scientist is for the most part unconscious of what he is and is doing here, since he has not yet been able to turn around upon himself but is still engrossed in the split and tension of subjective with objective. He is, however, the vehicle of an impulse, an instinctual drive, that urges him ever onward. All the while that he is conscious of his object, he remains unconscious of his underlying drive; he is locked in the structure and process of consciousness. The drive toward truth is not the mere sexual drive of Freudianism – although the drive of sexuality is itself a form, rooted in life, of the drive that in more advanced form occurs in science. The Old Testament knowingly speaks of knowing in sexual terms. The cognitive drive, in Hegel's sense, shows as clearly in Freud and the Freudians as in any other scientists. It is the more concrete, deeper-grounded, infinite drive of spirit toward its own fullness of being, for the accomplishment of which spirit uses everything: thinking, the belly, sex, the law, the police, property, the State, science, art, religion, speculation. It uses the scientist as cunningly as it uses the hero of the practical world and its history.

Thus we find the modern scientist inventing ever more ingenious experimental apparatus and theoretical models in order to push forward ever more, penetrating ever more deeply and extensively into

---

[13] 8.345. See also the following in my books: Chapter 2, "The Vocation of Consciousness," in *Agony and Epitaph: Man, his Art, and his Poetry*, New York: Braziller, 1970, and Chapter 5, "Truth of Statement," in *Truth and Art*, New York and London: Columbia, 1965, paperback edition Minerva Press. Both books develop, in a language contemporary with us, ideas essentially related to the Hegelian position outlined in the present essay.

the world, determining the objectivity of the world by his own theoretical subjectivity, the subjectivity of the conscious understanding. In this way he endeavors to overcome the onesidedness of his own subjectivity.

This subjectivity of the scientist, furthermore, must of necessity be a universal one. Only the universal is capable of overcoming the opposition of the world. The scientist's knowledge of the world cannot be limited to his personal individual experiences. His experiments have to be confirmable by other investigators, eventually and ideally by all competent investigators. His language, scheme of reference, mathematics, concepts, all these have to be able to be shared in common. His thoughts have to be able to be translated into a form intelligible to all. The ego which is the subject of the consciousness of science is never the mere particular ego of this scientist or that. It is, rather, a universal role, which anyone who wishes to be a scientist must learn to play, fit into, and take over as his own. Already in science – and this is no mean step of the spirit – the individual learns how to enter into the community in a universality of the spirit. This universality is still abstract and onesided, and therefore is not yet truly free; it is not a genuine communion; but it shows analogies to communion, which have hardly even been noticed in traditional and contemporary "epistemology."

The transcendental ego, first of Kant and later of the phenomenologists following Husserl, is primarily inspired by modern philosophy's subjection to the finite scientific concept of knowledge and philosophy's obedient service in working mainly to develop the theory of knowledge that mirrors the scientific process. The transcendental ego is a posited subjective unity which is supposed to be the source of constitution of the objectivity of the world. It is an abstraction from the true spirit and it shows itself to be such in the poverty with which it is afflicted when it tries to deal with the whole realm of right, morality, and ethicality, and even more with art, religion, and thinking.

Thus the picture we get of the concept of finite science is this: it is to be subjectivity which, in its onesidedness as abstract and universalized egohood in opposition to equally onesided, abstract, universalized objectivity, and under the influence of its own indwelling instinctual drive toward the free being of spirit, seeks to penetrate the objectivity so as to find itself. It is the conscious understanding seeking to push to the limit its intellectual seizure of the world.

How can it succeed? It starts as being empty, itself. It is the merely abstract universal ego, and all the concreteness that it needs exists as the world. It has to fill itself with the world, with being. In penetrating and permeating the world by its abstract intellectual forms, it can only open itself to the world's penetration and permeation of itself, the ego, for its content. This is the nature of the reciprocal relationship, *das Verhältnis*, of self and world in theoretical cognition. The process of filling the emptiness of the merely abstract form of intellect, filling the void that constitutes the spirit's hunger for being in knowledge, is exactly the process of what we have for centuries, and now in ever-heightening acceleration, been experiencing as "the progress of science."

But it is itself only a onesided process, and it can come only to onesided results. It is necessary. The human spirit will never escape it. It is our destiny, our fate. We must go through it. But we can know that while we are, as the Germans say, "making this experience," what is happening to us is that an irresistible drive is leading, in its onesidedness, to its own onesided issue. Our hope and our safety lie in balancing this onesidedness with another and, ultimately, in reaching and preserving the one truth that puts to death the two onesidednesses.

This process of theoretical cognition, says Hegel, is the first phase of the process of cognition in general. Cognition, in general, by its single activity as cognition, overcomes and transcends the split of the two opposed onesidednesses, subjectivity and objectivity. But to do this it has first to develop itself in two onesided ways, that of cognition proper (theoretical cognition) and that of volition (practical cognition). As he says, the process of cognition in general is itself, as such, immediately afflicted with the finiteness of this sphere and falls apart into the twofold movement of the instinctual impulse toward truth, put forth as two distinct movements.

One of these has just been outlined: the movement of the impulse in its theoretical form, which is that of superseding the *subjectivity* of the Idea by assimilating or absorbing the existing world (the world as being) into itself, into subjective representing and thinking, and thus filling its abstract certainty of itself with this objectivity, which counts thus as truly valid, as a content.

Why is this one side of the process of cognition, the theoretical side, to be understood as onesided and finite? The answer is basically the same as the answer to the question why consciousness itself is onesided and finite. It is because in theoretical cognition, as in consciousness generally, there occurs the split between the subjective and objective in such a way that the subjective presupposes the objective as being other than itself and as being an external world that has its own independent self-subsistence, complete in its being before, as it were, the conscious self discovers it. At the same time consciousness presupposes that it itself differs from that world, as subject from object, so that it exists in a relationship of externality with the world. This relationship is supposed to be one of reflection: the one side, the subject, presupposes the other side, while yet it does not apprehend itself as constituting it. Consequently the subject experiences the world as immediate, given, as found ready to hand.

Instead of the truth of the Idea being present, in which the unity of self and world is realized, there remains a difference and a distinction. The self's concept of the world is one thing, the world itself another. The self's concept is unified, universal, but empty. The world is manifold, various, and full, but it does not yet show the form of the self's concept. The presupposition is that as the self moves out toward the world, employing its powers of sense and intuition, representation and comparison, understanding and generalization, it will be able to weave the web of the world's form in the image of its own subjective concept. The Idea, as subject, is, as Hegel says, the certainty of the potential identity of the objective world with its own self:

Reason comes to the world with absolute faith in its ability to posit the identity and raise its certainty to truth, and with the instinctual impulse to posit the nullity of the opposition which, for it, is in itself or potentially a nullity.[14]

One way in which reason posits the nullity of the distinction between self and world, subjectivity and objectivity, is – as was noted above – the theoretical process, in which the subject absorbs the world, as being, into itself as thinking. The difference between being and thinking is then overcome by assimilating the being to the thinking. This is the path of the abstract understanding, the intellect of the empirical scientist.

It would not be too misleading a comparison to think of the instinctual impulse of this abstract intellect as being a hunger to eat up the world, to fill its gaping maw and destitute belly with the stuff of being. In a parody of the true religious movement, the Idea empties itself – a movement of self-humbling *kenosis* – so as to put all the

----

[14] 8.434.

worth of being on the other side, the side of the world, which then it will thereupon receive again into itself as a gift, being granted to it from being beyond itself.

This is the spiritual disposition which man is compelled to assume in taking on the role of understanding, or the empirical scientist. And one recognizes it existentially in the real, living scientist: the combination of the lordliness of reason as it lays claim to grasp the world by its understanding, and the humility of the emptied servant, laying down all his personal uniqueness – his feelings, his heart, what Hegel calls *das Gemüt*, his whole personal and emotional disposition, as well as his merely personal, particular opinion – in serving the universal cause of reason as the vehicle of understanding. I use the term "existential" here with full intention to emphasize the existential quality of the enterprise of empirical science.

It is a peculiar paradox, in which the self, by separating itself from the world as other and alien, does so precisely in order to overcome and deny that separation and alienation. It makes itself finite, limited by an essential other, in order to overcome this finiteness. But even when it succeeds in the overcoming it remains finite. For the unity it has achieved with the world, though stuffed full of the world's being, is wholly poverty-stricken from a spiritual viewpoint. There is nothing recognizable in the absorbed being of the world that belongs truly to the self, that shows the self's own true being. What of the self is there is merely the form of the abstract intellect, the understanding, a mold from which the substance of the self has been removed in the kenotic process, just in order to become the emptied vehicle of theoretical cognition.

The self that has succeeded in its theoretical aim must come to recognize that in realizing its concept the reality turns out not to be adequate to the concept. Or equally, the concept turns out to be insufficient to be a true concept of the self. Empirical science starves me. It gives me the world, but it is a world without soul, a spiritual vacuum. The knowledge it gives me of the world, being a knowledge of conditions and consequences, or relationships of causality and reciprocity, gives me at the same time the basis for exercising power over the world. Modern man, by his empirical science, has begun to realize the dreams of the ancient magicians; like a sorcerer, he waves his wand and recites his charm and lo! the world obeys him. But this same powerful knowledge shows me nothing at all that could offer me the slightest motive for using that power. Therefore, as I participate in that knowledge and that magic, I feel within myself a deep split and begin to realize that my truth lies beyond.

Man's empirical-scientific self is a false self, in the philosophical sense of falsehood. Its concept and its reality are not in thorough agreement. The basic concept of the self, the Idea, is only half-represented by the concept of empirical science itself, the concept of absorbing the world's being by means of understanding. In trying to actualize itself as empirical science, the self, whose truth lies only in the Idea, falsifies itself, has, as it were, a "false consciousness" of itself, and this falsehood catches up with it in the end. The truth it achieves turns out to be finite. In achieving this truth it comes to its own limit, and ultimately it is compelled to recognize that limitation.[15]

The second way in which the split between subjective and objective, thinking and being, self and world, is overcome is that of volition, or the practical activity of the Idea, which aims at superseding the onesided *objectivity* of the Idea. It recognizes the spiritual emptiness of the world and it seeks to fill that emptiness with the subjective content it lacks. The world that cognition proper presents to us is itself onesided. It is a semblance, a mere collection of contingencies and intrinsically null, void, invalid forms. This world, onesidedly separated from the subjective, appears to the subject of necessity as being without any rights. All right stands on the side of the subject. The merely objective world only *is*; the *ought* stems from the subject and his rights and duties. When the subject separates the world from himself in such a way, having in this division the certainty of the nullity, the nothingness – the invalidity, worthlessness, and utter triviality – of the world and all its contents, then his standpoint is that of volition, and as subjective Idea he himself assumes the shape of the

---

[15] Hegel's account of the finiteness of "cognition proper" in the Encyclopedia Logic is no doubt too simple. It supposes that cognition proper presupposes the view of the knowing subject as a *tabula rasa*. But more modern studies of empirical science show how large a role is played in the constitution of empirical knowledge by the activity of the subjective intellect, and science itself acts with much know-how in fashioning its own shape. In this respect empirical science is more rational in Hegel's sense than he himself allows. But the finiteness of empirical science, the emptiness from which it never recovers, no matter how much it fills itself by assimilating the world to its intellectual forms (thus satisfying its own power impulse), is an emptiness of spirit. Science can offer nothing to touch the will, except what the will gives to it by willing to be science. The will has to call upon itself to initiate the process of its own freedom. Science reaches its limit when the limitation of its *concept* appears. Science has limited itself, in its concept of itself, by restricting itself to the abstract intellectual understanding of the world.

good, which Hegel defines as the subjective Idea as determined in and for itself and as simple self-identical content.[16]

As the concept of finite science is the concept of overcoming the onesidedness of subjectivity by absorbing and assimilating the world's being, so the concept of volition is the concept of overcoming the onesidedness of objectivity by impressing upon the objective the essential character of the subjective, namely, its inwardness.

Onesided objectivity, the objectivity we know from empirical experience and science, is the sphere of externality – of space and time with their relationships of sequence, juxtaposition, separation, and isolation, and of connections like causality and reciprocity which, with all their supposed necessity, nevertheless keep apart, exactly by that necessity, the things they connect. No inwardness, interiority, shows anywhere in the onesidedly objective world. That also is why the empirical scientist as such does not know what to make of inwardness and easily succumbs to the temptation to call it nothing and dismiss the language of inwardness as meaningless. And, to be sure, it is indeed meaningless for the realizing of his immediate concept, which nowadays takes the title of "behavioral science." Modern positivism, in all its varieties, represents this – what can only be called – falsehood of the spirit to itself. It is a falsehood that comes about as a necessary stage in the search for truth, and has its own justification; but it has to be transcended, and the transcending of it is at the same time the rightful judgment upon it.

Corresponding to the instinctual drive of reason as theoretical towards the truth of understanding, there is the instinctual drive of reason as practical towards the accomplishment of the good. This too is a way of knowing, in a genuine and important sense of knowing. Although ordinarily practical action is opposed to cognition in such a way as to refuse the name of knowledge to it, that opposition is only relative and finite, and a deeper comprehension of practical action reveals it to be knowledge in a sense even truer than that of onesided cognition. Knowing is not an action that takes place merely "in the head," so to speak. In knowing something I am involved in a relationship with it. The dominant form of this relationship – at least initially, and in a lasting fashion as the process of *Aufhebung* continues, with its cancelling, preserving, and lifting to a new level – is *consciousness*, the relationship of subject to object. Insofar as the object is differentiated

16 8.443.

from the subject, and the subject does not yet comprehend its own self in and through the object, but sees the object exclusively as its other, then knowledge of the object and self-knowledge are separate from one another, even though they are intimately intertwined. As I see and know the things of the external world I am at the same time and through that very knowing "certain" of myself. This "self-certainty" is located in my feeling as this feeling exists in my perception of things. Through the influence of the perception of things I am enabled to feel my own self in an immediate certainty of my own being. The two, external perception of thing and self-feeling, are different but connected. This is still a very primitive stage of self-knowledge. This self-feeling of mine includes feelings of the agreeable and disagreeable, the first stirrings – as yet unshaped and inchoate – of soul life towards appetite and desire, ultimately towards the articulated will and character of genuine human freedom. But as yet it is all feeling and nothing but feeling: spirit and its self-knowledge in the purest immediateness. That is, at the level of mere consciousness, the only self-consciousness I have is, as it were, still unconscious. It is immediate unarticulated feeling. This primitive, rudimentary self-consciousness is present, in its undeveloped form, in the most advanced empirical scientist as it is in the least educated peasant or worker, so far as these men and women are merely conscious.

But consciousness itself exists only as a stage in the development of self-consciousness. The whole reason for consciousness lies in the self's need, in order to become self-conscious, to articulate for itself a world which at first appears as external and other, but which will later be penetrated and permeated by the quality of selfhood, subjectivity, and spirit, namely, interiority, so as to reflect back to the beholding subject its own mode of being, eventually its own self. [17]

It is here that the truth of the Fichtean philosophy becomes evident. The self builds a world for itself because it needs the world as the sphere in which it can engage in its destined task of liberating itself. As Hegel never tires of saying, freedom is being with what is other as with own, with self. To be free, the self needs to have a world which is its own world, its homeland, the place where it finds its own, its own being, its own selfhood. And this is the meaning of practice.

Practice, action, activity: these are words for the process by which the subject arrives at the apprehension of his self in the other. Prac-

---

[17] Cf. "The Vocation of Consciousness" in *Agony and Epitaph.*

tice is the process of self-consciousness, of becoming and being conscious of self. The child who throws stones into the pond, beholding with satisfaction the expanding ripples, has – to be sure, in a still rudimentary way – imposed himself upon the watery stuff, giving it a shape and movement that follow his originally interior purpose. He has "realized" – made real – something that was at first merely interior, ideal. All practice is the realizing of the ideal, the externalizing – *die Äusserung* is Hegel's word, which carries the senses of utterance, statement, and manifestation, expression, as well – of the internal. Its meaning lies in the fact that only in and through such "outering" can the internal be recovered. This is the nature of spirit: to externalize itself so as to be able to recover itself in the external. Practice is the activity of the spirit, the activity of exercising its freedom.

The essential characteristic of practice is the self's recognition of itself in the other upon which it practices.

The consumption of matter as food is a process by which the animal not only ingests the material but the soul knows the other as potentially itself, as having no right other than the right to serve the self, as having its essential being in the self. That is why man, as living soul, feels he has the right to eat other living things.

The practice of the master-slave relationship is the carrying out of the struggle for recognition, namely, for acknowledgment of the essentiality of the master's self in and through the existence of the other as slave.

And so on, through all forms of practical activity. Any action of mine, whether legal or illegal, moral or immoral, ethical or unethical, is a way of imparting the predicate "mine" to a behavioral sequence in the world. In my action I have placed myself into the external world; and so far as I have had the consequences in my design (purpose, *Vorsatz*) they are the embodiment of my self, as far as mere external action is able to embody selfhood. That is why the act is, to that extent, recognized by others as by myself as being mine, and is imputed to me as my responsibility, even my guilt.

My practice in art, as creator of poetry, music, sculpture, is an even more advanced form of giving the predicate "mine" to things. The "mine" is now highly advanced, being no longer merely privately personal, but also reflecting and reverberating with the spirit of my culture and people.

The practice of the cult in religion represents the penultimate stage of such self-consciousness, since in it there occurs the reconciliation of God and man in its realized form of the communal congregation's being. God himself comes to self-consciousness in and through the practitioners of the cult as the holy spirit in its communal congregation. The German word for this congregation is: *die Gemeinde;* at its center is the truth of the *"mein"*; and it is the same with "gemein" and "allgemein," the words for what is common and universal.

Philosophy is as much practice as it is cognition proper. It is neither and both, since it is the suspension and elevation of the two into an ultimate form of contemplation which is the being of man as spirit when he reaches the ultimate goal of being truly free. This goal is the knowing of self in other in its truest form. And here, being is nothing but knowing and knowing is nothing but being; being is all knowing and knowing is all being; not being as merely immediate, in the way in which it begins so abstractly in logic, but being as the final mediated immediateness as it ends the entire life-process of the spirit.

To understand Hegel's thinking about volition and its realization in practice one must look to the field in which self-consciousness is carried out as such. This is not merely the subjective domain of self-consciousness, which he treats as one stage of subjective spirit in the philosophy of mind or spirit; for that subjective domain is itself merely abstract and unrealized when it remains only subjective. It needs to be realized. The concept of self-consciousness needs to develop its own *Dasein*, its own specific existence and reality, as outside the subjective sphere, at first alienated and estranged, in order to recover itself there. This realization occupies the whole of what Hegel calls "objective spirit." The treatment of it occupies a large part of the *Phenomenology of Spirit*, the *Encyclopedia of the Philosophical Sciences*, and other works, but his fullest and clearest treatment of it is in the *Philosophy of Right*. For right, *Recht*, is indeed one of the exact names for the objectivity of self-consciousness. Other names are: will, freedom. The Idea of will or of freedom is: consciousness of the identity of the self in its other, that is, self-consciousness. Therefore all phenomena in which spirit orders and disposes existence so as to realize this identical self-consciousness are phenomena belonging to will, freedom, right.

The abstract universal right that constitutes the sphere of legal phenomena, the abstract particular subjective right that constitutes the sphere of morality, and the concrete right, uniting particular subject and universal community, that constitutes the sphere of ethicality and that finally issues in the state and world history – all these are the shapes assumed by self-consciousness proper. Only a comprehension of them as stages and standpoints in the development of true self-consciousness can provide a true, that is a philosophical, understanding of what in fact is happening in the world of culture. Studies of law, morals, politics, history which remain empirical and assiduously eschew philosophical contemplation determine themselves to their own finiteness. They are necessary and justifiable, just as empirical natural science is; but no summing of them, no integrating of them enables man to advance to the next stage. Only the treatment of them as history of consciousness, and indeed in these stages as history of self-consciousness, has in its hands the concepts by which they become intelligible, since these are their very own concepts, the concepts whose endeavor at self-realization they are.

But consciousness and self-consciousness, both of them, when realized as genuine knowledge, the first in the theoretical knowledge that gives us the understanding's science, and the second in the practical knowledge that gives us the objective world of law, morality, and ethicality, still fall short of fulfillment of the basic instinctual drive of spirit. Both of them are finite. We have already seen above what constitutes the finiteness of theoretical cognition. And, just as this finiteness consists in the split between self and world, subject and object, which is never finally overcome in theoretical cognition, so the finiteness of practical cognition also lies in the split between the world as it exists on its own account and the ideal, the ought, which the self holds up to it, and whose realization the self comprehends as the good. The world as such, as the genuinely objective over against the subject's selfhood, is not good essentially. Unless the world existed as alien and foreign to the self, there would be no world at all; for the self needs the world as the stuff on which it has to impose its will, the arena in which it has to achieve its freedom. Hegel therefore describes the finitude of volitional action as "the contradiction that, in the self-contradictory determinations of the objective world, the purpose of the good is just as much executed as it is not executed; the purpose of the good is posited as actually real and at the same time as merely possible." And he observes that this contradiction puts itself forth as "the infinite progress of realization of the good, which is fixed in it merely as an ought."[18]

As intelligence first empties itself of reality in order thereupon to stuff its emptiness with the world's reality, so will empties the world

---

[18] *Encyclopedia* of 1830, section 234; 8.444.

of ideality in order thereupon to impose upon it the self's own ideality. Neither intelligence (theoretical reason) nor will (practical reason) is ultimately reasonable. Neither of them sees or is the truth in the truth's own fullness. And spirit's own indwelling instinctual drive toward truth leads it onward to a final shape of reason which is the truth of knowledge and, at the same time and in that very respect, the ultimate truth of being.

The concept of this truth is more concrete than the concept of the understanding's theoretical-empirical science, and it is more concrete than the concept of the will's practice. As a subjective form, such as is dealt with in philosophical psychology, Hegel calls it simply: *reason, Vernunft.* One of his simplest definitions of it reads:

Reason is the highest union of consciousness and self-consciousness or of knowing an object and knowing oneself. It is the certainty that its determinations are just as objective, just as much determinations of the essence of things, as they are our own thoughts. It is just as much the certainty of itself, subjectivity, as being or objectivity, in one and the same thought.[19]

In this form of subjective existence, in which my knowledge of an object is such that in it I am knowing myself, and in which my self-knowledge is such that, in knowing myself, I am knowing the objective essence of things – in this form of existence, the concept that makes reason what it is has already begun to take shape in reality, in the reality of subjective spiritual being. That concept, taken by itself in abstraction from its realization in the element of subjectivity, is what Hegel calls the *Idea*. The Idea is precisely the concept of the unity of theoretical and practical cognition; it is the unity of the theoretical Idea and the practical Idea: "will knows the end as its own and intelligence apprehends the world as the concept become actual."[20] The idea is the concept of ... itself. The earlier concepts involved a split between their subjective and their objective components – as we have seen in the concepts of theoretical knowledge and practical knowledge; and, in attempting to overcome the split, they emphasized onesidedly either the subjective or the objective. The Idea is the concept of the fully reconciled identity of subjective and objective. The element in which the subject discovers objectivity is the element of his own subjectivity; the element in which he produces ideality is, again, the element of his own subjectivity; and both the expressions just used are wrong: at the level of thinking represented by the Idea,

[19] 3.111–112 (a passage in the Nürnberg *Propädeutik*)
[20] 8.445.

the subject no longer discovers something given as existing beforehand, but rather exists as luminous insight into self, and the subject no longer produces something other than himself as containing his ideality, but rather is self-conscious in his very being, because his being is nothing but self-consciousness, manifestation, revelation. The Idea, taken abstractly as a mere logical concept, may be viewed as the essentially self-fulfilling project of this ultimate unity.

Every creative artist and every religious person is and knows the Idea, not as the philosopher does, by thought such as is being expressed in these words, but in the former case by artistic intuition and in the latter by religious representation.

The artist knows the Idea just insofar as the art work takes shape under his hands. For what takes shape there is something given to intuition as an image, a *Bild*, which embodies a meaning; and the meaning it embodies is precisely: the Idea. What gives essential aesthetic character to an art work is its embodiment of the ownness, that is, the ultimate belongingness of objective to subjective and subjective to objective, that constitutes the essence of spirit, an essence which we think abstractly as Idea, Truth, Freedom.

When we experience an art work as art, we experience this meaning intuitively in the work as a given object. As we dwell in that intuition, beholding during that moment, we are existing in the absoluteness of absolute spirit. We are then knowing in the absolute sense of knowledge, for which Hegel reserves the verb *erkennen*, as contrasted with *wissen*. The self that is doing the knowing, while it is your or my particular self, is that particular self purified and transfigured by being reconciled with universality: it has lost its selfishness, its mere egoity, in the intuition, and for this brief period it has been healed of its finiteness. The object that is being known is just the self doing the knowing. But it no longer stands over against the self as being another. To be sure, there is still a certain externality, since it is apprehended only in an image, therefore only in a construction of sense and/or imagination. There is here still a certain split, between the sensuous and the spiritual, within the mind itself. But despite that split a miraculous passage has taken place; the sensuous has really been transfigured, and it lives wholly in the realm of the spirit as it exists as aesthetic image or semblance.

The trouble is, however, that, miraculous as the transfiguration of the sensuous may be in art, it must ultimately fail, just because the sensuous is not the true *Dasein*, not the true mode of specific existence and realization of the spirit. What is more, art itself, in its being and its history, is nothing but the development of this very insight, namely, that art is not the finally (and therefore truly) true mode of existence and realization of the spirit. The knowledge achieved by the human spirit in art is exactly this knowledge, that the spirit must go through and look beyond art to its ultimate truth and freedom. Art achieves this knowledge, not in the rarefied ether of philosophical thought but in the very intuition itself, sensuous and sensibly immediate, that makes it art. It is an artistic knowledge of the spirit's ultimate destiny. Therefore when we speak in Hegel's language of art as being immediate knowledge of absolute spirit, the qualification of immediateness must be emphasized and constantly born in mind. The artist cannot say his truth and knowledge in the way of the philosopher; he has to show it; even the poet's saying is, essentially, a showing.

It is sometimes erroneously thought that for Hegel art is the sensible realization, for intuition, of the beautiful. In this interpretation Hegel is supposed to have thought that the purpose of art is to express in sensible form the content of the Idea, the essential content that defines the spirit and its absolute freedom. And since the Idea, when it is adapted to sensible presentation, is the Ideal, and the presentation in sense of the Ideal is, by Hegel's definition, beauty, the conclusion is drawn that for Hegel the task of art is the presentation or expression of the beautiful. Aesthetics would then be the science, not of all art, but only of "fine art," or, as the German phrase goes, of "beautiful art" – *der schönen Kunst* – the art of beauty.

There is no doubt that such an interpretation of the Hegelian aesthetics is tempting, since Hegel does limit aesthetics to artistic beauty, as against beauty in nature, although he has an extensive discussion of the latter. The lectures on aesthetics even begin with the bald statement:

These lectures are devoted to *aesthetics;* their object is the broad *realm of the beautiful,* and more specifically their field is *art* and, indeed, *fine or beautiful art.*[21]

And following some critical remarks about the unsuitability of the name "aesthetics," as well as "callistics" (the science of beauty, which is too broad, covering the beautiful in general, in nature as well as art) Hegel says that the proper expression for the science is "philosophy of art" and more specifically "philosophy of fine or beautiful art," "Philosophie der schönen Kunst."

[21] 12.19.

There is a certain truth to this interpretation. Nevertheless it must be realized that art – and art precisely in the sense in which this philosophy of art thinks of it – is not only art of the beautiful. Art of the beautiful, art that devotes itself specifically to the unfolding of beauty and its full presentation, is just one form of art. It occurs in a certain place in the history of art, preceded and followed by art that does not devote itself specifically to the full presentation of the beautiful. The art of beauty is classical art; this is one of the three great art forms, the other two being symbolical and romantic art. The history of art is the evolutionary process in which art is born as symbolical, grows to classical florescence, and dies away in the romantic. Art is as much, and no more, essentially the presentation of beauty as a plant is the blossoming of its flowers.

We could if we wished introduce a sharp distinction – one, however, which Hegel does not himself literally employ – that would say: it is the task of art to reveal the beautiful, but it is the destiny of art to transcend that revelation – in essence, to transcend itself. This self-transcendence would be the process in which art, as art, becomes non-art, as it develops into religion. To understand the nature of this self-transcendence would allow us, at the same time, to understand the inner contradiction of art, or why art has to make itself non-art, why the ultimate calling of art is not just the revelation of the beautiful but also the annihilation of the beautiful. It would help us to comprehend how and why the knowledge that art is, is the knowledge of the ultimate falsehood of beauty. While it would remain true that art's central concern – central even in the literal sense of being its middle stage – is with beauty, we would see that its final concern is not only to show beauty but further and beyond that to show the dissolution of beauty as being ultimately inadequate to express truth.

The basic task set to art by the spirit as it develops toward true freedom is to know absolute truth in the immediate mode of sensible intuition. Absolute truth is the self-accordance of spirit's concept, the Idea, with its reality, subjectivity. Absolute truth and freedom are the same thing. They differ only in the emphasis we put on their expression. Both consist in the self being with the other as with its own, or the spirit returning to itself in and through its other. Freedom emphasizes more the other and its overcoming or the passage through it; truth emphasizes more the being with it in ownness and identity. But to be with other as with own, to be self-identical in otherness, this is the ultimate form, nature, and content of truth, freedom, and spirit itself. And the basic task set to art by its very own self as spirit seeking its true freedom is to show this content in a sensible image. If this content is shown to spirit by itself in a sensible image, then spirit there possesses itself for its own precisely in this immediate way of sensible intuition, and consequently is itself, in knowing itself, in this immediate way.

This basic task however is an impossible one. It cannot be performed. The impossibility, when you know it, is enough to break your heart; and, indeed, your heart must be broken in this way if you are to take new heart to make the next step in the glorious but hard road of the spirit. The reason it is impossible is that the self-accordance of the Idea with its correspondent reality can occur only where that reality is the reality, the *Dasein* or form of definite existence, of subjectivity; and subjectivity, by its essential nature, is interiority, not exteriority, whereas the sensible is, equally essentially, exteriority as such. Only interiority is capable of being spirit, self-return in and through other. To ask to show spiritual truth and freedom in sensuous form is to ask to show interiority in exteriority. It is a contradictory demand.

Art can perform, as was said above, a miracle in this direction – the miracle called beauty. You could not have predicted it. Beauty has to be seen to be believed. In beauty, as much of spiritual totality as can be descried in sense is brought out and made explicit. The Idea, the realized and concrete concept of truth as accordance between concept and existence in the mode of self-accordance, has been fashioned forth into actual reality and has entered into immediately correspondent unity with this actuality. In this shape it has left its conceptual abstractness and become the individualized Idea, the Ideal. The task was to make perfectly adequate to one another the Idea and its configuration as concrete sensible actuality. This done, the Idea, as actual reality which has been fashioned in accordance with its concept, is the Ideal. [22]

This is the highest point that art can reach as art. It was reached by classical art, especially the art of Greece, and in particular the art of Greek sculpture in its high classical period. Only classical art, says Hegel, gives the production and intuition of the perfected Ideal, and sets forth this Ideal as realized. [23] The Ideal is artistic beauty; artistic beauty is the Ideal; it is the true Idea of beauty. Classical art, and

[22] 12.112.
[23] 12.117.

especially the classical art of the ancient Greeks, is the highest art. Of it Hegel says:

Only in the highest art do Idea and presentation truly correspond to one another in the sense that the shape of the Idea is intrinsically the shape that is true in and for itself, because the Idea it expresses is itself the veritable Idea.[24]

The beauty that classical art reached, being true beauty, was all that beauty could be, and of it Hegel says:

Nothing can be and become more beautiful.[25]

This means: if you wish to know what the truth and freedom of the spirit are, behold the sculpture of Phidias. Open your eyes to the truth there revealed: the intrinsic self-accord of Idea and actual form. In its infinite intrinsic rightness, in which everything is as it should be, and all that ought to be is there, it manifests in an image, for spiritual intuition, what you are in search of.

But one must add: as far as it is possible for a sensible image to show this, at all.

And one must then add: everything there is not as it should be, and not all that ought to be there is there.

For even in classical beauty, in its highest reaches, there is a disturbing note, a trouble that reverberates throughout the whole.

In art, spirit attempts to express itself in sensible form for direct intuition. Expression is successful, in general, when there is perfect correspondence between the inner meaning and the outer figure. The concept of beauty is the concept of such perfect correspondence between the spiritual Idea, as inner meaning, and the outer figure. Now as Hegel said, symbolical art *seeks* that perfect unity of inner meaning and outer figure, which classical art *finds* in the presentation of substantial individuality for sensible intuition, and which romantic art *transcends* in its ascending spirituality.[26]

Art's success in this enterprise of expression is at the same time its recognition of its own failure.

Classical art finds a perfect unity of meaning and figure, but in order to succeed in this way, it has to settle for an imperfect content. Its content is the substantial individuality of spirit rather than its absolute subjectivity The spirit in the form of substantial individuality is a spirit which, though freed from the contingency and particularity of

---

[24] 12.113.
[25] 13.121.
[26] 12.406.

inner and outer, is still filled only with a particularized individuality: it appears as one of many gods, as one specifically independent form of free and perfect spiritual subjectivity which can find an external body, a perfect anthropomorphic body, as its mode of existence and vehicle of expression.

In classical art spirit has gone outside itself into its own other, Nature, the sensible element. It has alienated itself in the naturalness of sensible expression. Classical art is the midpoint of the spirit's enduring of its alienation of its own self. In this classical mode of alienation, which is art's acme of perfection, spirit has succeeded in realizing the maximal possibility of actual expression of its content in sensible form. At the same time, spirit begins to realize that sensible form is inadequate to hold within itself anything more than that. The sensible form can contain within itself spirit's substantial individuality but it cannot contain spirit's absolute subjectivity, its uttermost truth – the intimacy that binds spirit to spirit in absolute self-knowledge, freedom, and love.

Art itself realizes this fact in its own way *as art*. The beginning already lies in classical art itself. In its heart classical art feels the pain of its own mortality. Already within classical art and at the very moment of its perfection, a shadow falls on the perfect artistic image. For the gods are gods. They possess a majesty that raises them above anything merely natural, since they bear within themselves, pregnantly, the unborn absolute subjectivity. This majesty is a spiritually interior being. It stands in conflict with the gods' beauty, which is external and bodily. The conflict is present even though it does not stand out as a difference and division between the inner spirituality and the exterior appearance. Consequently the negative character is immanent within the whole, expressed in the whole itself. "This," says Hegel, "is the breath and fragrance of sadness within the spiritual majesty, which keen-spirited men have felt in the divine images of the ancients, even along with beauty perfected into loveliness." [27]

The repose of a god is not that of self-satisfaction, a finite emotion. The god's individuality, both in spirit and in figure, coincides only with itself as at the same time free universality and spirituality that lies within itself. It is this universality which has sometimes been identified as the "coldness" of the classical gods. But such coldness exists only for the modern temperament that seeks intimacy in the finite. Considered for themselves, the gods

[27] 13.77.

have warmth and life; the blissful peace that is mirrored in their bodily shape is essentially an abstracting from the particular, an indifference towards the transient, a surrender of the external, a renunciation – not painful and full of care, yet a renunciation – of the earthly and fleeting, as spiritual serenity looks profoundly over death, the grave, loss, temporality, and just because it is profound, contains this negative within itself ... The blessed gods mourn, as it were, over their blessedness or bodilyness; we read in their forms the destiny that stands before them, and its unfolding, as an actual emergence of this contradiction between majesty and particularity, between spirituality and sensible existence, which leads classical art itself toward its downfall.[28]

This shade, this breath and fragrance of downfall – which is at the same time an ascension – which is only just able to be felt as a premonition in classical art, this element of negativity toward the particular, earthly, perishable externality of existence, becomes in romantic art a central feature.[29] For the essential knowledge which romantic art is and gives to us is the knowledge of the infinite nature of spirit, in and for itself, as over against and as recovered from every form of externality, and that means, from every form of the natural. Romantic art does not tell this to us. It does not speak in the language of grammar and logic. It shows it to us, directly, immediately, in its ever-varied images. But it does show it to us, and in doing so it gives us a profound insight into the ultimate shape of truth and reality, far beyond what any positive science of externality can represent in its formulae. For it shows us by its hints and suggestions what lies deep in the depths of potentiality – the *Ansich* – of Nature and of the Idea of which Nature is the outward shape: the infinite freedom of absolute spirit.

We do not actually see this freedom in romantic art. True freedom cannot be seen in a sensible presentation. It is spiritual, interior, in and for itself. The element in which it has its proper existence is the element of interiority, namely, subjectivity. And the truth and freedom of subjectivity consists in subjectivity finding in its other – not Nature, but other subjectivity – its own, itself. The infinite freedom of the subject lies in the most concrete, uttermost identity that can exist, the identity of absolutely free spirits. This identity is the one peculiar to inwardness and interiority. It is an identity that can subsist only between beings whose essential nature is interiority.

Hegel uses as a designation for it the term *die Innigkeit* – warm,

---

[28] 13.78.

[29] For a more detailed version of Hegel's notion of the romantic see my article (from which some parts of the above two paragraphs have been reproduced here) "Art: Death and Transfiguration. A Study in Hegel's Theory of Romanticism," in *Hegel in Comparative Literature*, special editor Frederick G. Weiss, *Review of National Literatures*, Volume I, Number 2, Fall 1970, pp. 149–164.

tender, sincere intimacy. Intimacy is not just inwardness. It is the truth of inwardness. Inwardness exists for the sake of the coming into being of intimacy; intimacy is the for-itself of what inwardness is in itself. To comprehend it, and that means to be it, the human spirit must go through romantic art and again through absolute religion, and eventually come to think it as these words are now trying to express the thought. The comprehension must come out of learning the direction towards which romantic art points, living within the intimacy of the spirit in its communal congregation, and, through this education of the spirit, reaching the point of thinking the philosophical thought that is intimacy's purest and last form of existence. This thought is not taught in the academies. It is not philosophy in the current academic sense. He who thinks it, and is it, knows it; he who thinks it, and knows it, is it.

The task of romantic art is: by means of art to do away with art. It is: by artistic means to show the falsehood of art's means. This negative function is however not abstractly negative. It is one side of a more concrete function which is, as in all art, to show truth in the mode of intuition. Now the truth is: intimacy, *die Innigkeit*. It is spirit which has reconciled itself with itself in its own element of subjective interiority. Art which is to show the truth must therefore show this inner purely spiritual reconciliation. It cannot show it as such. What, then, can it do?

Classical art tried to show truth. But its comprehension of truth was failing. Its Idea of truth was the Idea of the Ideal, of the inner harmony of the natural-spiritual being. Its faith was a faith in the possibility of existence of spiritual truth in natural form. The Greek gods were instances of such beings: natural forms ensouled by divine spirits, the spirit and the form being harmoniously one.

But the true nature of spirit is subjectivity and interiority, which can find its true other, with which it can be truly reconciled, only within its own element – subjectivity and interiority, as over against the merely living individuality and substantiality of the classical mode of existence. The natural, although it is the stage of the outward existence of the spiritual, is for that very reason also the opposite and deadly foe of the spiritual. It is the spirit estranged from itself. The spirit's estrangement consists in externality, Nature, because spirit's own proper being is internality; spirit can estrange itself from itself only by turning into its own opposite, the external, Nature.

Greek religion, which was the religion of beauty and which found its proper expression in the art of beauty, by trying to articulate truth as the harmony of spirit and Nature, was putting forth, in deepest irony, the absolute falsehood that the truth of being lies in the identity of spirit with Nature. The identity that spirit seeks to recover in and through Nature is not one in which spirit remains within Nature, but one in which spirit has returned to itself from having been outside itself in Nature. This is the truth as articulated by Christian religion, and its corresponding mode of intuitive expression is, not the art of beauty, but romantic art.

By "romantic art" Hegel means, not merely what we are accustomed to call by that name, a certain art tendency that began in the later eighteenth century and extended into and through much of the nineteenth. He means the art expressive of the spirit that belongs to the Christian West, taking its inception with Christianity and sharing the destiny of Christianity. Early Christian architecture, painting, and sculpture, the Gothic cathedral, the poetry of chivalry, yes even the "high classical" art of Leonardo, Raphael, Michelangelo, are just as much constituents in the historical existence of the romantic art form as, in his eyes, Goethe or Schiller. And for us who have seen art continue to multiply its shapes since Hegel's day, the newer modes – impressionism and expressionism, naturalism and symbolism, realism and abstraction, cubism, constructivism, dada, surrealism ... I forbear mentioning the art ripples of the day – bring out even more clearly the essential import of his concept of the romantic. The age in which we have been living, in which the Western world came to dominate world history, and which in its religious aspect can be understood as the Christian era, can be understood in its aesthetic-artistic aspect as the Romantic era. It is decisively important to bear in mind the broad scope of Hegel's concept of the Romantic, since for him romantic art is not just the pale dreaming of a Tieck or a Wackenroder, but the deeply living and suffering and courageous hoping and working of the greatest artists the West produced after the classical art of Greece and Rome had fulfilled its vocation: transcendent creators like Dante, Shakespeare, Milton, Goethe, and their compeers in the other arts. All of the great art of the Christian West has been romantic, in Hegel's sense of the word.

If romantic art, unlike classical art, is not an art of beauty, then what is it?

We need not deny that there are many beautiful expressions in romantic art. But they do not give its ultimate content; they are there only for ulterior purposes. Romantic art is not an art of harmony but of disharmony; it is an art, not of the realization in external shape of norms of balance, measure, and proportion, but of the exhibition of imbalance, unmeasure, disproportion. It is, in a pregnantly expressive description of it by Hegel, an art of *Zerrissenheit* – tornness, disruption, inner strife and confusion.

The basic feature of the classical ideal is a serene repose and bliss, a self-sufficiency in its own self-closure and satisfaction.

The ideal artistic figure stands there before us like a blessed god. Need, wrath, interest in finite circles and ends – these do not have an ultimate seriousness for the blessed gods; and this positive retraction into themselves in connection with the negativity of everything particular gives them the characteristic feature of a cheerful serenity and tranquillity. In this sense, Schiller's saying holds good:
"Ernst ist das Leben, *heiter* ist die Kunst." [30]

Hegel is quick to point out that the tranquillity and repose of classical art is not truly exemplified by a satisfaction without struggle, but rather when, as he says, a deep breach has torn apart (*zerrissen*) the subject within himself as well as in his whole existence; and he cites the case of the tragic heroes who are represented in such a way that although they are overcome by fate, and succumb, nevertheless their heart and soul snatches itself back from destruction into simple being-with-self, as it says: "It is so!"

The subject then remains ever true to himself; he yields up what has been plundered from him; but the ends he pursued are not just taken from him; rather, he lets them fall, and he does not lose his own self along with them. Man, subdued by Fate, can lose his life, but not his freedom. It is this self-dependence which makes it possible, even in suffering, still to keep a serene tranquillity and to let it show forth. [31]

Classical art shows this repose.

It is different with the romantic. It too has a positive feature to exhibit – its own kind of bliss, gaiety, serenity; but it no longer remains with the serene satisfaction and sufficiency of the classical. The romantic smile is one that shows only through tears. In romantic art

the tornness and dissonance of inner being goes further, as in this art, generally, the oppositions that are presented go deeper, and their disunion can be retained ... Nevertheless in romantic art too, although in it suffering and pain affect the heart and subjective inner being more deeply than among the ancients,

[30] 12.218.
[31] 12.219.

there can occur the presentation of a spiritually intimate tenderness, a joy-fulness in resignation, a bliss in pain and rapture in suffering, yes even a volup-tuousness in the agony of torture.[32]

Hegel had various stages of Christian art in mind – we could ourselves put forth, as one among a thousand exhibits, the art of Bernini. Hegel speaks also in this connection of serious religious Italian music, in which this joy and transfiguration of suffering permeates the ex-pression of complaint.

In the romantic everywhere, this expression is the smile through the tears. The tears belong to the pain, the smile to the serene gaiety, and thus the smiling in the weeping signifies this repose-within-self in torment and suffering.[33]

As Hegel says, this must not be a merely sentimental affection of a subject vain about his small "miserabilities," but has to appear as the composure and freedom of the beautiful in despite of all suffering and pain; and his instance is Ximenes, in the romances of the Cid, of whom it was said: How beautiful was she in tears!

But the smile through the tears is itself only one romantic form of appearance. Hegel himself points out the relationship of the principle of modern irony to the romantic principle.[34] He is critical of it as lacking in artistic holding power because of its lack of true seriousness and its tendency to end in mere emotional yearning. What connects it with the romantic is the feature of absolute negativity, in which the subject relates itself to itself in its annihilating of definitenesses and onesidednesses. The real principle of the romantic, which lies at the core of everything belonging to romantic existence, is this absolute negativity of subjective self-reference or, in other words, of infinite subjective freedom. Had he been able to observe him, Hegel would have found in Kierkegaard, for instance, an extremely instructive case of the romantic principle at work in all the dimensions of absolute being: artistic-aesthetic, religious, and philosophical!

The ground-principle of romantic art, says Hegel, is the rise of spirit to itself, by which it regains within itself the objectivity which otherwise it had to seek in the external and sensible mode of existence; now it can feel and know itself in this union with itself.[35] In romantic art the spirit comes to realize that its own truth does not and cannot lie in union with the external, that its own ultimate home is not the

[32] 12.219.
[33] 12.220.
[34] 12.221.
[35] 13.122.

natural world, that its truth does not consist in immersing itself in bodyhood. On the contrary, he says, spirit becomes certain of its truth only by leading itself out of the external and into its own self-intimacy, and by positing the external reality as an existence inadequate for spirit itself. It is especially this positing in the artistic mode of intuitional showing that gives to romantic art its characteristic modes of appearance. Romantic art, in showing truth, must show – and does show, everywhere, over and over again, and in ever new shape – the return of inwardness to itself out of all outwardness. It does this by distorting, tearing apart, dissolving the outward form.

The phenomenology of romantic art, and with it of the whole of cultural life as it falls within the era of the romantic, is a manifold and rich field. Unlike the phenomenology of the classical, which has the one central unity of the spiritual and natural as its focal point, the phenomenology of the romantic has to contend with a potentially infinite number of shapes. The reason is to be found in the infinitely negative character of romanticism itself. While the romantic spirit performs the single task of returning to spirit's own self-intimacy, it does this by moving out of self-estrangement in outwardness and naturalness; and the spirit can move out of the outward from any point at which it finds itself in the outward. Thus there can be a romanticism which negates the present by looking back to the past, or ahead to the future, or above to the eternal; there can be a romanticism which departs from existence in longing and yearning, in bitterness and anger, in hope or in revenge, evolutionary or revolutionary, sane or insane; there can be a romanticism of drugs and a romanticism of political revolution.

This is why some students of romanticism, following A. O. Lovejoy, came to think that there were many romanticisms but no single reality that could be called by the name. They had at least this point in their favor: the one thing that romanticism is, as a reality, is the principle of the negation of the unique unity of the classical, a negation which can be carried out in different directions; and insofar as romanticism shows its negation in the form of the image, it has many images to offer. Like the so-called infinite judgment, which says what the subject is by affirming the predicate in a merely negative form, so the romantic makes its affirmation by negating everywhere the specific naturalness and exterior articulation in showing that none of them is adequate to express essential spirituality.

This is why, also, the language of romanticism is the language of

negativity; for romantic art has to show everywhere the basic opposition between the spiritual and the natural, in order to raise the
spiritual back to itself out of the natural. And if romantic art still holds
on to the task of making itself beautiful – in Hegel's day the romantic
principle had still not fully emancipated itself from the death-grip of
the classical principle of the aesthetic, namely, the beautiful – nevertheless, Hegel points out, beauty in the hitherto existing sense remains
subordinate for it, and becomes the spiritual beauty of what is inner
and for itself, as spiritual subjectivity infinite within itself.[36]

We, however, who inherit the experience of a century and a half of
further historical development, are able to see how much less the
spirit is tied to the classical aesthetic as it searches in every way to
break through and break apart – *zerreissen* – the restraints of naturalness. Especially in this twentieth century, the century of expressionism,
cubism, surrealism, and dada, and all the minor tendencies that have
sprouted from this main stock, it has become more and more clearly
visible how infinite subjectivity, by the necessity of its own infinite
freedom, seeks to break the hold of exteriority and naturalness.

In his book *Concerning the Spiritual in Art* Kandinsky celebrated
Arnold Schönberg's breaking of the hold of tonality – that stronghold
of the classically natural and beautiful – in music as he strove to find,
in what outwardly appeared cacaphonic, the expression of an inner
spiritual beauty. But since those days of the first and second decades
of the century, even inner spiritual beauty has become irrelevant for
artists in the forefront of spiritual discovery. Every form of the
negation of the natural and immediate, every form of what has been
established spiritually in the articulation of expression and therefore
suffers from a certain finitude (since expression has to use the naturally
given media and consequently has to fall to some extent into externality
and finitude), every possibility of showing the degradation of the
spiritual in its natural existence – in horror, obscenity, shock, dullness,
ugliness, and boredom – has been progressively drawn into the picture.

Contemporary art – more vividly romantic than art has ever before
been – forcibly opens our eyes and thrusts before us the disfigured
corpse of the beautiful and makes us see, whether we like it or not,
the downfall of an illusion. You may not think that Andy Warhol is a
great artist, great man, or great spirit, but the spirit has pushed him
forward, too, to serve its purposes, just as it makes use of crime and

[36] 13.122.

the criminal to bring to birth the idea of morality and just as it makes use of death to transfigure life into its own eternal truth of being.

These are only some lines that tell fragmentarily of the knowledge that art is. The subject is deep and manifold, as befits its nature, which is the free being of the spirit in its first native form of truth, that of artistic beholding.

The artist and the experienced beholder of art know this truth in the manner of its own being. They are intuitive knowers, whose knowing takes the subjective form of intelligence in its pure immediateness, in which the content is given directly to mind as from without. The great artists of our century have known, in ever deeper and sharper ways, what Hegel spoke of in the early nineteenth century, and their struggle has been to bring this knowledge out, to show to us where it is that we ultimately belong – not, as classical art envisaged it, or as the would-be imitators of the classical in every age ironically repeated, absorbed and exhausted in our essence by our position in Nature, so that the whole meaning of human existence could be shown in the form and life of a Greek god, but returned to the essential inwardness of the spirit of which Nature is merely an outward manifestation, the essential inwardness for which we have to stammer the name "intimacy," "die Innigkeit."

The meaning of intimacy, however, is to be comprehended in its truth only as we move out of the immediateness of artistic intuition into the mediation of religion and through it make the return, in thinking, to that very intimacy itself.

TRUTH IN THE PHILOSOPHICAL SCIENCES OF SOCIETY, POLITICS, AND HISTORY

HENRY PAOLUCCI

St. John's University

To the question "what is truth?" Hegel replies (with Socrates and Aristotle and most other systematic thinkers of the West) that it is a ratio. He holds that it is not simple but composed, and that, in the pursuit of knowledge, it comes not among the first things, but among the last. More precisely: truth for Hegel is neither a subjective idea in itself nor an objective thing in itself, neither a universal abstractly conceived nor a particular empirically apprehended, but an adequate linking-together in reason (*ratio*) of thought and thing, universal and particular.

The entire Hegelian system as we have it in the *Encyclopedia of the Philosophical Sciences* is unmistakably an analytical exposition of truth as a ratio. Its three major parts develop the truth of idea as *idea in itself* (Science of Logic), the truth of thing as *idea in its otherness* (Philosophy of Nature), and the truth of the adequation of idea and thing as *idea come back to itself out of that otherness* (Philosophy of Mind).[1] Each of the parts, in turn, mirrors the structure of the whole; and so do the parts of the parts, down to the simplest constituent propositions, for every proposition or sentence capable of expressing even a modicum of truth is, according to Hegel, a linking together of subject and predicate, of particular and universal, of thought and thing.

The sciences that especially concern us here – the social, political, and historical sciences – are parts of a part of the Philosophy of Mind which, like the other two major divisions and the system as a whole, presents its contents first as idea (Subjective Mind), then as thing (Objective Mind), and finally as an adequate linking-together of idea

---

[1] *The Logic of Hegel* (Part I of *Enzyklopädie*), trans., William Wallace (Oxford, 1892), pp. 28–29 (§ 18). This work is hereafter cited as *HL*; translations adapted slightly in accordance with German text (Henning, 1840, 1955).

and thing (Absolute Mind). The conclusion is hardly to be avoided, therefore, that in the least parts as well as in the whole of his system, Hegel quite deliberately sustains the classical definition of truth which, in its Latin form, survived into modern times as a commonplace of medieval philosophy: *veritas est adaequatio intellectus et res*.

Immanuel Kant, it is important to recall, had rejected that traditional notion of truth. Or rather, in his celebrated *Critique of Pure Reason*, he had begun by granting it, but only to dismiss it at once as something trivial. And Hegel criticizes him for it, particularly in the *Science of Logic* (Johnston and Struthers, Vol. II, p. 227), where he defends the medieval commonplace as "a definition which is of great, and even of the highest value." Against Kant, he there argues that if the old notion of truth

is recalled in connection with the fundamental assertion of transcendental idealism, namely, that cognition by means of reason is not capable of apprehending the things-in-themselves, and that reality lies utterly outside the Notion [Begriff], then it is clear immediately that such a reason, which cannot establish a correspondence between itself and its object (the things-in-themselves), is an untrue idea; and equally untrue are things-in-themselves which do not correspond with the Notion of reason, a Notion which does not correspond with reality, and a reality which does not correspond with the Notion. If Kant had kept the idea of an intuitive understanding close to this definition of truth, then he would not have treated this idea, which expresses the required correspondence, as a figment of thought, but as truth.[2]

Because he adhered to an untrue idea of what truth is, Kant was foredoomed to fail in his attempt to assess the capacity of human reason to arrive at truth. Hegel characterized as a "mark of the diseased state of the age," the general adoption of the "despairing creed that our knowledge is only subjective." The natural belief of ordinary men in all ages gives the lie to such a view. Rightly understood, truth is objective; rightly understood, thought coincides with thing. Hegel cites Dante's insistence (*Paradiso* iv, 124–30) that the human intellect is certainly capable of attaining truth, and that, indeed, nothing short of truth can satisfy it. The business of philosophy, he concludes against Kant, is precisely to confirm the old belief that it is "the characteristic right of mind to know the truth" and thus "to bring into explicit consciousness what the world in all ages had believed."[3]

In his *Science of Logic*, Hegel refers us specifically to his *Phenome-*

[2] *Hegel's Science of Logic*, trans. W. H. Johnston and L. G. Struthers (London, 1951), Vol. II, p. 227.

[3] *Hegel's Philosophy of Mind* (Part III of Enzyklopädie), trans. W. Wallace and A. V. Miller (Oxford, 1971), p. 180 (§ 440). This work is hereafter cited as *PhM*; translations adapted slightly in accordance with German text (Boumann, 1958).

nology of Mind for a detailed analysis of the limitations of Kant's approach to the question of knowledge. Kant's basic defect, according to Hegel, was that he "neither considered nor investigated the truly speculative ideas of the older philosophers about the notion of Mind," taking his departure in this area exclusively from Hume's skeptical treatment of the rationalist metaphysical doctrine of the mind. In his *Phenomenology* of 1806, Hegel assumed that same vantage point, accepting the Humean and Kantian formulations of the problem of truth; but then he went on to rectify the Kantian errors, giving us a vivid account of the riot of thought through which the mind, driven by doubt, must pass in rising to the level of "insight into what knowing really is."[4]

Of the *Phenomenology of Mind* it has been correctly said that it is the germination of a living seed which absorbs and consumes its environment in preparation for its own systematic growth, which is yet to come. In the process of getting to know what knowing really is, the mind initially takes for granted "the existence of the concrete formations of consciousness, such as individual and social morality, art and religion." But to arrive at its goal, it must free itself of all that it has received or absorbed uncritically. Thus – Hegel explains in retrospect – the development of consciousness traced in the *Phenomenology* involves a sort of cultural unravelling "of the matter or of the objects properly discussed in the special branches of philosophy." What belongs in the ratio of truth of the complete system is "prematurely dragged into the introduction," and that makes the exposition intricate.[5]

Practically all the distinguishable sciences of the three parts of the *Encyclopedia* make an appearance of sorts in the *Phenomenology of Mind* – but not in the form of truth. Their vast cultural wealth is poured into the consciousness of the individual mind to nourish it the way food nourishes the individual body. Just as the body in its growth from the fertilized egg recapitulates the great chain of animal forms that are implicit in its nature, so the mind of the individual recapitulates the experience of the family, civil society, state, and period of history into which it is born. Through self-criticism, conscious Mind, which is initially a captive of its cultural environment, must emerge, finally, as Free Mind, ready for the logic of truth in its systematic form. There is no avoiding that preliminary illogical, almost riotous confrontation

---

[4] *The Phenomenology of Mind*, trans, J. B. Baillie (London, 1931), p. 90; adapted slightly (Hoffmeister, 1949).
[5] *HL*, p. 59 (§ 25).

with the fullness of human culture, however; for a large part of the task of preparing the mind for genuinely philosophic science is precisely to unravel the complexities of existential experience, and thus "to show how the questions men have usually raised about the nature of Knowledge, Faith, and the like – questions which they imagine to have no connection with abstract thoughts – are really reducible to the simple categories which first get cleared up in Logic."[6]

The *Phenomenology of Mind* is not to be confounded, therefore, with the system of the *Encyclopedia*. The former is an existential treatise in the modern sense. Whoever takes up the question of knowledge as posed by Hume and Kant and their disciples in our own time is certain to find himself at one turn or another of the path of the *Phenomenology* – which is a preparatory work of Conscious Mind. The *Encyclopedia*, on the other hand, is the consummate work of Free Mind. It presupposes that Conscious Mind has become Free through insight into what philosophic truth really is: an *adaequatio intellectus et res*, developed into a universal whole, each part of which consists of a ratio of ratios, analyzable downward in its rational necessity to the least meaningful linking-together of the basic parts of speech.

I. THE HEGELIAN-ARISTOTELIAN PERSPECTIVE

Because the truth of the Hegelian system is the whole in its organic articulation, there can be no specially favored beginning, no basic introductory science so completely true in itself that it must stand first. The notion of a beginning in philosophy has meaning, Hegel writes, "only in relation to a person who proposes to commence the study, and not in relation to science as science."[7] The system in its truth is a great "circle of education" without beginning and without end – a circle that freely turns upon itself, carrying its constituent sciences around with it, each in its distinctive place, fixed there by a rational necessity, each offering a distinctive approach (neither more nor less valid than any other) to the truth of the whole.

Only Free Mind can know the whole truth in its freedom; yet, paradoxically, it is only through knowledge of the truth that Mind is made free. As often as he discusses what true knowledge is and what results from reason's absorption in it, Hegel confronts this paradox. Repeatedly, he cites the Biblical admonition: "You shall know the truth and

---

[6] *HL, ibid.*
[7] *HL*, p. 28 (§ 17).

the truth shall make you free." And almost invariably, he couples with it Spinoza's paradoxical formulation of the ancient truth that freedom is "insight into necessity." Hegel thus sums it all up in the opening pages of his *Encyclopedia:*

> Truth is only possible as a universe or totality of thought; and the freedom of the whole, as well as the necessity of the several sub-divisions, which it implies, are only possible when these are discriminated and defined, ... Each of the parts of philosophy is a philosophical whole, a circle rounded and complete in itself. In each of these parts, however, the philosophical idea is found in a particular specificity or medium. The single circle, because it is a real totality, bursts through the limits imposed by its special medium, and gives rise to a wider circle. The whole of philosophy in this way resembles a circle of circles. The idea appears in each circle, but, at the same time, the whole idea is constituted by the system of these particular phases, and each is a necessary member of the organization.[8]

Like the satellite epicycles of the ancient and modern astronomies, each science of the system of sciences has a separate center of its own and a relatively independent progression of its own around that center. The ultimate moving principle is that of the whole; but that is by no means an exclusive or restrictive principle. On the contrary, as Hegel writes, "genuine philosophy makes it a principle to sustain every particular principle."[9] Indeed, because its organic connection with the whole leaves it relatively free in its self-centered progression, every one of the specialized disciplines of the *Encyclopedia* has a tendency to "burst through" the limits of its special medium and extend its sway at the expense of its neighbors. The science of history, for instance, has always had an insatiable appetite for devouring neighboring disciplines, claiming that its sweep ought to encompass all that is humanly known or knowable. Similar claims have been advanced more recently by political science, sociology, economics, psychology, anthropology, and even bio-chemistry. Obviously it is only the systematic discipline of the whole, however arrived at, that can by rational necessity keep the constituent disciplines in place.

The organic conception here is far removed from the Kantian critical perspective. The premises of transcendental idealism with respect to the nature of mind and truth are abandoned in favor of the dialectical realism of Aristotle. Of this there can be no serious doubt. The staggeringly humble tribute to Aristotelian thought in the concluding lines of the *Encyclopedia*, where Hegel expresses his own loftiest

8 *HL*, pp. 24–25 (§ 14, 15).
9 *HL, ibid.*

thought in Aristotle's Greek, is well known. What needs to be stressed here is that the Hegelian system in its entirety – as distinct from the introductory *Phenomenology of Mind* – is essentially Aristotelian from its immediate approach to the question of knowledge to its full exposition of truth as Absolute Mind.

In his *History of Philosophy*, Hegel credits Aristotle with the initial logical insight into what knowing really is, praising him especially for the clarity of his distinctions in remarking how, even in its most abstract expression, truth is not something simple but a ratio. Aristotle had emphasized in his *De Interpretatione* (which is essentially a grammar of logic), that subjects and predicates and linking verbs, "as isolated terms, are not yet either true or false," for "truth and falsity imply combination and separation." Of the process of combination in thought, Aristotle had said further (in a very "Hegelian" vein): "Neither are 'to be' and 'not to be' and the participle 'being' significant of any truth, unless something is added, but imply a copulation, of which we cannot form a conception apart from the things coupled." [10]

It is on the insight so abstractly expressed here that Hegel constructs his grand "cycle of education." Ultimately, the "things coupled" in his *Encyclopedia* are all the constituent truths of all traditional disciplines of scientific knowledge, ranging from the abstract sciences of logic and mathematics, through the mechanical, physical, and organic branches of natural science, to the cycle of man-centered studies that culminate in the sciences of artistic making, religious behavior, and God-centered metaphysical speculation. Just as in the mathematical sciences, the goal is a formulation of truth as a set of mathematical ratios, so in the all-comprehending system of sciences, the goal is an all-comprehending philosophical ratio of ratios. Though he did not attain it himself, Aristotle had projected just such a goal for philosophy; and to realize it has been, according to Hegel, the proper task of philosophy ever since. Hegel is thus characterizing his own philosophic labors of a lifetime, as well as the limits of Aristotle's achievement, when he remarks in the *History of Philosophy* that

the whole of Aristotle's philosophy really requires recasting, so that all his determinations can be brought into a necessary systematic whole – not a systematic whole which is correctly divided into its parts, and in which no part is forgotten, all being set forth in their proper order, but one in which there is one living organic whole, in which each part is held to be a part, and the whole

---

[10] *The Basic Works of Aristotle*, ed. Richard McKeon (New York, 1941). p. 41 (adapted in accordance with Bekker, *De Interpretatione*, 16ᵇ 19–25).

alone as such is true. Aristotle, in the *Politics*, for instance, often gives expression to this truth.[11]

That his *Encyclopedia* is offered as a recasting of the Aristotelian philosophy, Hegel himself assures us quite explicitly in many places, and perhaps most explicitly in his introduction to the Philosophy of Mind. There he says that "the books of Aristotle's *De Anima*, along with his discussions on the *psyche*'s special aspects and states [discussions pursued in the *Nichomachean Ethics*, *Politics*, *Rhetoric*, *Poetics*, *Metaphysics*, and related writings] are still by far the most admirable, perhaps even the sole work of philosophical value on this topic." And his conclusion is that "the main aim of a philosophy of mind can only be to re-introduce unity of idea and principle into the theory of mind, and so reinterpret the lesson of those Aristotelian books."[12]

Following Aristotle's lead, Hegel distinguishes three developmental phases, or functional aspects of Mind, to which the designations Subjective, Objective, and Absolute correspond. In its subjective development, Mind acts to rationalize, or assimilate to its own nature, an animal actuality which is only potentially human. The Aristotelian leads for this phase are clearly indicated in the *De Anima*. In its objective development (and here Hegel follows closely the leads of the *Ethics* and *Politics*), Mind shapes for itself the rational, or *mindful* realities of family-life, civil society, and states, whose coming into being and passing away constitutes the course of history. Finally, in its absolute development (corresponding to the sphere of Aristotle's *Metaphysics*, Book X of the *Ethics*, the *Poetics*, and related passages of the *De Anima*), Mind transcends objective history, arresting time in the aesthesis of inspired art, overcoming mortality in the ecstasis of revealed religion, and assimilating itself to God (*nóesis noéseos nóesis* – thought thinking thought) in the experience of *sophia*, where the highest intuitive and discursive reasoning – the *nous* and *epistēmē* of Aristotle – are one.

It is important to keep in mind the essentially Aristotelian perspective in all of this, so that we may guard ourselves against the error of students of Hegel who don't know Aristotle and who insist on approaching the Hegelian system through Marx or contemporary

---

[11] *Hegel's Lectures on the History of Philosophy*, trans. E. S. Haldane and Frances H. Simson (London, 1955), Vol. II, p. 223. This work is hereafter cited as *HPh*; translations adapted slightly in accordance with German text (Michelet, 1840).
[12] *PhM*, p. 3 (§ 378).

existentialism: the error of imagining that Hegel is straying off on some needlessly obscure, tortuous new path of epistemological speculation, spurred on by his apparent mania for triads, at precisely those turns of his exposition where he means to be most respectful of the Aristotelian tradition.

II. THE SCIENCES OF OBJECTIVE MIND

Within this broad Aristotelian design, Hegel distinguishes almost all the "disciplines" that have traditionally enjoyed academic status as sciences of human nature and conduct, and several that have acquired such status since his time. For most of the minor sciences, the definitions are necessarily brief in the *Encyclopedia*, in keeping with its character as a handbook; but many cursorily treated there are considered at length, with particularized discussions of methods of study and scientific validation, in the *Philosophy of Right, Philosophy of History, Philosophy of Fine Art, Philosophy of Religion*, and *History of Philosophy*, all of which are elaborations of the Philosophy of Mind.

From the standpoint of classification in the social or behavioral sciences, Hegel's broad distinctions of Subjective, Objective, and Absolute are very instructive. In his day they might have served, as he said, to re-introduce "unity of idea and principle" to a field where speculative chaos reigned. And one ventures to suggest that a general acceptance of them now might greatly facilitate the task of the many hard-pressed academicians who are today charged with regulating the seemingly endless, overlapping, proliferation of specialized disciplines in the field.

The sciences of society, politics, and history, strictly defined, make up the cycle of Objective Mind. But as they presuppose the "results" of the preceding sciences of Subjective Mind, it will be necessary, by way of introduction, to review cursorily the matter and form of those sciences.

Under Subjective Mind, Hegel distinguishes the sciences of anthropology, phenomenology, and psychology – all of which today qualify, on some one or another of the modern listings, as social or behavioral sciences. Anthropology is defined, in accordance with its etymological meaning, as the most general of the sciences of man. It focuses on the least common denominator of manhood: on the very *idea* – as Plato would say – of *anthropos*; or rather, in Aristotelian terms, on the characteristic act of manhood, through which the physical, self-nutritional, sentient, passionate, and emotional activities of an animal existence are "humanized."

The systematic science of phenomenology (not to be confounded with the "voyage of discovery" which prepares the mind for true science), presupposes the humanizing activities studied in anthropology. On its higher level, phenomenology traces the activities of Mind that transform animal awareness into thoroughly human consciousness, then into self-consciousness, and finally into that doubling, or "mirror-ing" of self-consciousness which Hegel calls Reason (*Vernunft*) in full potency, as distinguished from the mere Understanding (*Verstand*) of consciousness and self-consciousness.

Psychology takes up the activity of Subjective Mind where phenome-nology leaves off, tracing its development, through self-analysis, on the levels of theoretic and practical reason, to the level of potentially productive, or *willful* reason. As in the Freudian psychological self-analysis, so in the Hegelian, what emerges is the perfection of Subjective Mind as "Free Mind" – as mind become master in its own house (to use the renowned Freudian expression) and able, therefore, to over-come its subjectivity.

Anthropology, phenomenology, and psychology, thus defined, are introspective sciences of man. There are no objective "phenomena," no "evidences of things seen" to be "saved" by them. For validation of their measure of truth, scientists specializing in such fields must rely ultimately on subjective insight. In this respect, their relationship to the sciences of Objective Mind that immediately follow parallels the relationship of the Science of Logic to the Philosophy of Nature in the system as a whole.

Like the sciences of mechanics, physics, and organics that make up the Philosophy of Nature, the sciences of Objective Mind are objective in the strict sense. In both spheres the method of scientific study is therefore essentially the same. There are, on the one hand, external phenomena which must be taken for granted as empirically given, and, on the other, principles of thought, or organizing ideas, elaborated as hypotheses, that are not empirically given. The external phenomena are the "things," the hypotheses are the "thoughts" that must be adequately "linked-together," in reason, if the sciences of Objective Mind or those of the Philosophy of Nature are to have a valid ratio of truth in them.

It is, indeed, only the specific content or subject matter of the sciences of Objective Mind that distinguishes them from the natural sciences, in Hegel's scheme. Instead of testing the adequacy of their generalizing notions or hypotheses through direct observation of the characteristic motions of empirical phenomena on the level of mechanics, physics, and organics, they do so through direct observation of the phenomena of man, as he actually lives now, or has lived in the past, in family, civic, and political association with his fellows.

Again and again, in the *Philosophy of Right* and the *Philosophy of History* (which together cover the same ground as the section on Objective Mind in the *Encyclopedia*), Hegel reminds us of the obvious fact that the evidences of man's present and past existence as a social being have an objective authority for our consciousness at least as compelling as that of the "sun, moon, mountains, rivers, and the natural objects of all kinds by which we are surrounded." [13] Indeed, he insists that, since the aim of empirical science is to trace the operation of rational laws in the phenomena under study, the social sciences are specially favored in this respect. For it is the rational activity of man – the practical and productive reasoning of his Free Mind – that fashions the human institutions and institutional histories that are the proper objects of study in the theoretical sciences of Objective Mind. As Hegel explains in the Preface to the *Philosophy of Right*:

So far as nature is concerned, people grant that it is nature as it is which philosophy has to bring within its ken ... that nature is inherently rational, and that what knowledge has to investigate and grasp in concepts is this actual reason present in it; not the formations and accidents evident to the superficial observer, but nature's eternal harmony, in the sense of the law and essence immanent within it. The ethical world, on the other hand [the world of family, civil society, statehood, and history], is somehow not authorized (according to the bias of some) to enjoy the good fortune which springs from the fact that it is reason itself which has achieved power and mastery within that element and which maintains and has its home there. [While nature is assumed to be immanently rational] the universe of objective mind is thus supposed rather to be left to the mercy of chance and caprice, to be God-forsaken; and the result, from this standpoint, is that if the ethical world is Godless, truth lies outside it, and at the same time, since even so reason is supposed to be in it as well, truth becomes nothing but a problem.[14]

Hegel very emphatically denies the view that the natural sciences – and particularly the mathematical sciences of celestial and terrestrial mechanics (astronomy and physics) – ought to be regarded as the sciences *par excellence* upon which all other sciences, and particularly

---

[13] *Hegel's Philosophy of Right*, trans. T. M. Knox (Oxford, 1956), p. 106 (§ 146). This work is hereafter cited as *PhR*; translations adapted slightly in accordance with German text (Gans 1833, 1952), making use also of the translation by S. W. Dyde (London, 1896).

[14] *PhR*, p. 4 (Preface).

the social sciences, ought eventually to pattern themselves. His arguments against such an assumption illuminate the seeming paradox of
the fact that, when Sir Francis Bacon proclaimed a new beginning for
natural science in the 17th century, he took his cue (as he acknowledges)
from the founder of modern political science: Machiavelli. What
Machiavelli had so successfully done with the science of politics, Bacon
argued, ought to serve as a model for what obviously needed to be done
for the advancement of a long-stagnated natural science. With profound insight into the making of states, Machiavelli had undertaken
to trace the *laws of statecraft* as statecraft really *is*, rather than as,
according to the moralists, it *ought to be*.

How can natural scientists apply Machiavelli's example in their
field? How can the method of Machiavelli's political science be made
to stand as a model for chemists and physicists? Bacon's brilliant
suggestion is that chemists and physicists should hereafter apply
themselves to the study of empirical phenomena that are, like states,
man-made – phenomena to be produced by a *craft* which is of the same
order, though on a much more primitive level, as Machiavelli's *state
craft*. That Baconian *craft*, through which natural science might hope
to match Machiavelli's political science, is, of course, the craft of
experimentation. Needless to say, scientific experiments as Bacon
conceived them are man-made. And precisely because they are man-
made, with human reason built into their minutest detail, study of
them to ascertain their laws is much more rewarding than the study
of empirical phenomena that are not man-made.

Experimental science – the glory of the modern world – is thus,
from Hegel's point of view, a very specialized part of the social or
behavioral sciences: a specialized part that is accurate in its results,
from a logical mathematical point of view, to the measure of its relative
emptiness. An experiment with a lever in a laboratory, for instance,
is man-made in the same sense that the new state of Israel is man-made.
And it is no doubt true that a Ben Gurion, who has actually experi-
mented with the making of states, is probably much better able to
comprehend the truth of the science of politics as Hegel expounds it,
than the average experimenter with levers, who fails to recognize the
social nature of experimental science, is able to comprehend the truth
of the science of mechanics.

Giambattista Vico had of course made the same point in his *Scienza
Nuova*. What mankind has itself made men can know better than they
can know the natural things that God, or chance, has made. And this

is true, for Hegel as for Vico, ranging upward from the least artifacts of primitive peoples, through all the utilitarian products that serve human ends in civil society, to all the things of fine art, religious worship, and high philosophy that constitute the grandeur of history's great states, empires, and world civilizations.

The same Free Mind of man that "makes" a controlled experiment in a physics laboratory has, needless to say, also made the laboratory itself, as well as the "Advanced Institute" of higher learning that envelops it, and the surrounding college town, civil society, and political order apart from which the pursuit of science is an impossibility. Free Mind is, as we noted, the perfection of Subjective Mind, or Mind which, through psychological self-analysis, has overcome its subjectivity and is able, therefore, to objectify, or make actual, what it implicitly is.

Free Mind first manifests itself objectively, writes Hegel, through the assertion of a universal, willful claim on all it surveys; and the disciplined study of that characteristic act of Mind as Will is distinguished by Hegel as the science of Abstract Right, or theory of Law – first of the philosophical sciences of Objective Mind. In asserting its willful claim on everything, Free Mind acts as if it knew no bounds – as if it had actually heard the God of *Genesis* say to it: "Be fruitful, and multiply, and replenish the earth, and subdue it: and have dominion over the fish of the sea, and over the fowl of the air, and over every living thing that moveth upon the earth." But, as in *Genesis*, so in the Hegelian system, Free Mind, in solitary possession of but a single body, finds that it cannot go it alone objectively. In attempting to exercise its claim on all things, it is again and again frustrated and forced, eventually, to seek a compensatory satisfaction in self-righteous, moral alienation from the objective world. The science that focuses on this retreat of Free Mind back into itself is the science of Morality.

Together, Hegel's sciences of Abstract Right and Morality give us an updated recasting of Aristotle's *Ethics*, the conclusion of which is that the individual as person and moral subject cannot realize his individual ends in isolation. Only lately have Right and Morality come into their own as objects of lively if not yet disciplined study in the modern curriculum of the social sciences. But in America, at any rate, they have come in with a vengeance, on the heels of the Negro Civil-Rights movement. It is a matter of newspaper headlines that, after years of fiercely asserting an abstract personal right, the American Negro has experienced an objective frustration that has constrained him to seek a compensatory satisfaction in self-righteous, moral alienation from the objective world. Negroes and the social scientists who study their moral frustration have had to learn the hard way – which is to say, empirically – the ancient truth that Free Mind, whether in a black or a white body, has a better chance of realizing its ends in the objective world if it enters it as a family member.

The "results" of Free Mind's experience in Abstract Right and Morality are the notions of right and wrong, of good and bad, of what ought and ought not to be. And these results are the presuppositions of the further development of the sciences of Objective Mind which are outlined in the *Encyclopedia* and elaborated in the *Philosophy of Right* under the headings Family, Civil Society, and State.

These sciences, which are "social" in the strict sense, provide us with what is unquestionably an updated, Aristotelian *Politics*. Man, Aristotle had tried to demonstrate, is by nature – not by convention – a political animal. And his capacity to speak is perhaps the most distinctive sign of his political nature, in that, while mere voice (such as many animals possess) suffices to indicate pain and pleasure, it requires speech to "indicate the advantageous and the harmful, and therefore also the right and wrong."[15] In words that express Hegel's view as well, Aristotle had thus marked, in this respect, the transition from ethics to politics:

> For it is the special property of man in distinction from the other animals that he alone has perception of good and bad and right and wrong and the other moral qualities, and it is partnership in these things that makes up the family-unit or household and the state.[16]

As in Aristotle, so in Hegel, politics in its broadest sense, as distinguished from the personal ethics and subjective morality of the individual, begins with *economia* – the science of the family unit. From a cultural standpoint, it is regrettable that modern derivatives of the ancient Greek word have not retained its original significance. Our English word "economics," for instance, hardly serves any longer to give us an adequate idea of the original thing. A new content has crept in, gradually crowding out the old, which is now left to fend for itself academically, without benefit of a scientific-sounding name. To identify precisely what he means, and thus avoid cultural confusion, Hegel uses the prosaic designation "die Familie"; but it should be noted that in so doing he is, in effect, following the example of the

---

[15] *Aristotle's Politics*, trans. H. Rackham (Camb., Mass. and London, 1950), p. 11 (1253ª).
[16] *Ibid.*

learned 15th century humanist Leon Battist' Alberti who, in reviving the ancient study of *economia* as Xenophon had perfected it, called his book simply *Della Famiglia*.

In Marriage – first of the three moments of family life distinguished by Hegel – the "I-thou" personal relationship of man and woman, drawn together to perpetuate the species, becomes a "we" relationship with a distinct personality of its own. That "we" is strengthened in its unity through external embodiment in a Family Capital – second moment of the notion – which is not "yours and mine" but "ours." But full objectivization of the bond that unites husband and wife comes only with realization of the third moment – the generation and rearing of children, "in whom the parents can see objectified the entirety of their union. ... For, while in their goods, their unity is embodied only in an external thing, in their children it is embodied in a spiritual one in which the parents are loved and which they love."[17]

Under the rearing of children, Hegel gives us a brief but very suggestive "science of education" which is further developed in the discussions on Civil Society and the State. As a function of the family, education has a negative as well as a positive aspect. On the positive side, its object is to instill ethical feelings that will enable the child "to live its early years in love, trust, and obedience"; whereas, on its negative side, its object is to raise the child out of its original state of dependence "to self-subsistence and freedom of personality and so to the level where he has the power to leave the natural unity of the family." Once educated to freedom of personality (within the "we" experience of family life), the child claims recognition as a person in his own right, and the unity of the original family is on the point of dissolution – an inevitable dissolution that becomes total in the death of the parents.[18]

Dissolution of the family, which may be gradual, eventually leaves the surviving members on their own in the network of "I-thou" relationships that make up Civil Society. They move into Civil Society as individuals, but, if they are products of well-ordered families, they already have in themselves the "we" experience of true community. They are ready in themselves, in other words, for the organic partnership of marriage and the formation of another family unit, at the same time that, as individuals, they are competing and cooperating with their fellows for the satisfaction of their personal needs. The experience of voluntary cooperation in Civil Society coupled with the

[17] *PhR*, pp. 264–5 (note to § 173).
[18] *PhR*, pp. 117–118 (§ 175).

experience of family membership prepares human beings, finally, for fully-conscious participation in the "we" relationship of political community, upon which the objective subsistence of family life and the civil relationships ultimately depend.

In a famous *"addition"* to the *Philosophy of Right*, Hegel observes that Civil Society (*bürgerliche Gesellschaft*) is a distinctly modern development, in the sense that "only in the modern world have all the various elements or determinations of the idea received their due."[19] In this connection, Hegel notes that the ancient Greeks lived their lives almost exclusively as family members and as citizens or dependent subjects of a tightly regulated political community. Public law penetrated deeply into the privacy of family life, leaving virtually no middle ground for a "private" individual or associational existence independent of the characteristic ties of family and state. Separation from the former resulted almost simultaneously in full absorption by the latter. From the point of view of Greek social science, therefore, economics (in its original sense) and the science of politics exhausted the field.

Only in the modern world have family and state come to be separated, objectively, by a vast middle-ground where many human beings born out of wedlock, or separated from their parents in childhood, can manage to live their entire lives without conscious experience of membership in the social orders of family or state. For the ancients, that middle ground was but an abstract, psychological moment of social alienation; whereas, in the modern world, it is precisely there that Objective Mind has fashioned for itself the complex life of Civil Society, which has, in turn, called into being an entire cycle of new sciences whose focus of interest is *more* than economic, in the ancient Greek sense, at the same time that it is also always *less* than political. Defining the limits of this distinctive associational achievement of the modern world, Hegel writes:

Civil Society is the realm of difference that separates family and state, mediating between them, even though in point of time its formation comes after the state, which its own objective existence presupposes as a necessary condition. . . . If the state is represented to us as a unity of persons which is only a contractual arrangement or partnership, then what is really meant is only civil society. Unfortunately, many modern social theoreticians appear at present to be incapable of conceiving any other theory of the state than this.[20]

19 *PhR*, pp. 266–7 (note to § 182).
20 *PhR*, p. 266 (note to § 182).

Cautioning readers against the tendency of his contemporaries to confound state and civil society, Hegel repeatedly stresses that the state no less than the family is an organic union; that its citizens as citizens are not in an "I-thou" relationship with one another, but, rather, like family members, they constitute a substantive "we" that they tend to love and value more than they value their individual existences. In Civil Society, on the contrary,

each member is his own end and everything else is nothing to him. And yet, because each must of necessity enter into relationships with others to realize his ends, those others, who would otherwise be objects of indifference, become indispensable means. Through this utilitarian linkage with others, each member's particularized pursuit of a particular end is universalized, its satisfaction being attainable only in the simultaneous attainment of satisfaction by others. Because the particularity of interests that constitute it are thus inevitably universalized, the whole sphere of civil society becomes an arena of mediation of opposites, where there is free play for every idiosyncrasy, every talent, every accident of birth and fortune, and where waves of every passion gush forth, regulated only by reason [Objective Mind] glinting through them.[21]

Already in Hegel's time, the new science that traced the characteristic acts of mind glinting through the intricate web of human relations in civil society bore the compound name of Political Economy [Staats-ökonomie] – suggesting a fusing, or even a confusing, of the traditional sciences of family and state. Of Political Economy, Hegel writes:

This is one of the sciences which have arisen out of the conditions of the modern world. Its development affords the interesting spectacle (as in Smith, Say, and Ricardo) of thought working upon the endless mass of details which confront it at the outset and extracting therefrom the simple principles of the thing, the Understanding effective in the thing and directing it. It is gratifying to find, in the sphere of needs, this show of rationality lying in the thing and working itself out there; but if we look at it from the opposite point of view, this is the sphere in which the Understanding with its subjective aims and moral fancies vents its discontents and moral frustration.[22]

It is in the competitive self-seeking of individuals in civil society that the personal moral frustration considered in depth by Hegel under the heading Morality actually takes place – a frustration that is relieved, in fact, only through entry into marriage or through the conscious assumption of rights and responsibilities of citizenship. But, while moral frustration is inextricably woven into the fabric of Civil Society, the science that studies the complex web of that fabric is nevertheless, in Hegel's judgment,

---

[21] *PhR*, p. 267 (note to § 182).
[22] *PhR*, pp. 126–7 (§ 189).

a science that does honor to thought because it finds laws in a mass of accidents. It is fascinating to see how action is linked with action, and how such linked actions fall into groups, influence others, and are helped or hindered by others. . . . It has a parallel in the science of planetary motions which, while always appearing complex and irregular to the eye, are nevertheless governed by ascertainable laws.[23]

Hegel expresses great admiration for the achievements of specialists in the "dismal" new science and is not surprised that, absorbed as they are in the excitements of studying a social creation of their own era, many of them should be inclined to ignore the social realities of family life and state that had absorbed the entire interest of their predecessors since the days of Plato and Aristotle. His concern is not to belittle the new discipline, but rather to guard its legitimacy, together with that of the traditional social sciences, by carefully distinguishing the characteristic acts of human association that are the primary object of study in each.

The paragraphs of Hegel's *Staatsökonomie* in which he outlines the "laws" of the internal dialectic of Civil Society have had a tremendous historical impact. His analysis of how that dialectic results in the formation of social classes and special interest groups that compete to universalize their interests fascinated Karl Marx. And, at the point where Marx's powers of concentration apparently failed – which is to say, where the dialectic of civil society results in the formation of "service" institutions for the regulation of civil rights, the "policing" of civil disorders, and for the ultimate resolution of internal conflicts through external expansion – it was Lenin's turn to be fascinated.

Surely worthy of comparison with the scientific achievement of a Kepler or Newton is the economy of thought with which Hegel was able to formulate the "law of social dialectic" in three pages of his *Philosophy of Right*. First he reviews the lessons of the English laissez-faire economists, noting how the untrammelled internal development of civil society results in an over-production of industrial goods and population, and thus in large-scale unemployment. Then he considers the social consequences of such combined over-productivity and underemployment, observing that

when the standard of living of a large mass of people falls below a certain subsistence level – a level regulated automatically as the one necessary for a member of the society – and when there is a consequent loss of the sense of right and wrong, of honesty and the self-respect which makes a man insist on maintaining himself by his own work and effort, the result is the creation of a rabble

---

[23] *PhR*, p. 268 (note to § 189).

of paupers. At the same time this brings with it, at the other end of the social scale, conditions which greatly facilitate the concentration of disproportionate wealth in few hands.[24]

If the wealthier classes, or charitable foundations, attempt by direct means to guarantee the old standard of living of the unemployed, regardless of whether they work or not; or if (despite the fact of over-production) make-work schemes are introduced; the result – according to Hegel – is the same: "The evil to be removed remains and is indeed intensified by the very methods adopted to alleviate it. We have thus the seeming paradox that, despite an excess of wealth, civil society is not rich enough, i.e., its own resources are insufficient to check excessive poverty."[25]

In all the pages of *Das Kapital*, Marx succeeds in adding nothing essential to Hegel's brief formulation. And, as for the Hobson-Leninist extension of the Marxist doctrine in the theory of capitalist imperialism, here is Hegel's brief summation:

The inner dialectic of civil society then drives it beyond its own shores to seek markets, and so the necessary means of subsistence, in other lands which either lack the means of which it has a superfluity, or are generally backward in industries. ... The far-flung connecting-link of the sea affords the means for the colonizing activity – sporadic or systematic – to which the mature civil society is driven and by which it supplies to a part of its population a return to life on the family basis in a new land and so also supplies itself with a new demand and field for its industry.[26]

Hegel, incidentally, insisted that all colonies founded by the modern European states would inevitably gain independence, and that their independence would prove to be "of the greatest advantage to the mother country, just as the emancipation of slaves turns out to the greatest advantage of the owners."[27]

It should be noted here that Marx and Lenin (though the latter in theory only) pursued the line of reasoning of Hegel's contemporaries who confounded civil society and the state. For Marx, the only social reality in the modern world was civil society. The development of capitalism, he held, had reduced the old institutions of family and state to the status of instruments, or tools, for the selfish satisfaction of individual, group, or class-interests in the competitions of civil society.

[24] *PhR*, p. 150 (§ 244).
[25] *Ibid.*, § 245.
[26] *Ph R*, pp. 151–2 (§ 246, 248).
[27] *PhR*, p. 278 (note to § 248).

But Hegel had analyzed that "new economic" view of modern society long before it was explicitly advanced by the authors of the *Communist Manifesto* as a revolutionary revelation; and he had rejected it, even as he rejected by anticipation, the related view of John Dewey, and Arthur F. Bentley which now prevails in the American academy: the view that the patterned activities of classes, interest groups, and "service" institutions in civil society are the sole characteristically political activities, and that political science therefore wastes its time when it looks beyond interest groups, etc., for a higher form of political reality.

In Hegel's judgment, all such Marxist or "systems-analysis" views of society illustrate the error of what has lately come to be called scientific "reductionism." Aristotle had written against such reductionism as applied to politics in the opening pages of his treatise on the subject, where he said that those who insisted that a political community differed only quantitatively from other forms of human association were wrong. Hegel, in fact, explicitly supports Aristotle's polemical demonstration that *politeia* is not an extended family, or an elaborated employer-employee relationship, and certainly not a master-slave or exploiter-exploited class relationship; that it is on the contrary a qualitatively distinct community of free and equal human beings united in pursuit of the highest conceivable earthly ends of free men.

In strictly Hegelian terms, *politeia* is the objective reality Free Mind must fashion for itself if it is to realize all its potentialities – potentialities that cannot be realized in any associations, however large or small, of family-members as such, or civil-society burghers as such, but only in a more perfect union, or *we* relationship, of free and equal citizens.

Hegel thus accepts literally Aristotle's definition of *politeia* as the "government of men free and equal" and of political science as the science of such government.[28] He departs from Aristotle only to deny (but it is a very large *only*) that any human beings are by nature, rather than voluntarily, slaves. He affirms, on the contrary, that, through the extension of Christianity and the development of civil society, it is now possible for all human beings, including emancipated slaves and their descendents, to be educated up to equality in freedom; if not perfectly, as individuals, at least in the form of that politically shared willingness to die rather than endure enslavement, which characterizes the free life of sovereign states, large or small, in the modern world.

[28] *Aristotle's Politics, op. cit.*, p. 29 (1255b20).

But how do the burghers of civil society overcome the tendency of its internal dialectic to "polarize" them into a rich few and a pauperized many? How is the so-called inevitable contradiction of modern capitalist society to be intentionally resolved so as to make a more perfect political union come into being instead? Hegel's answer is: through voluntary association in what he identifies as the "corporations" of civil society. By corporations, Hegel means every possible voluntary association of producers of goods and services, whether on the ownership, management, or wage-earning level. Here is the part of the Hegelian social and political theory that fascinated Benedetto Croce and Giovanni Gentile. It was a theory resembling Hegel's notion of a "corporation" society, to serve as the basis of a "corporate" state, that those philosophers advanced as an answer to the Marxist-Leninist anti-political, revolutionary doctrine. But far more faithful to the Hegelian view in this respect (precisely because of its emphasis on the satisfaction of the individual in the resultant political community) is the corporate ideal of Herbert Croly's *Promise of American life.*

The terms in which Croly argues for the continued "combination of capital," to be accompanied by "completer unionization" of labor, and the development of a "responsible concentration" of political power in government, "in order to maintain the balance," is strictly Hegelian, in form as well as content. And that Croly thesis, which so greatly influenced Theodore Roosevelt, is perhaps most Hegelian where its author concludes: "An organic unity binds the three aspects of the system together; and in so far as a constructive tendency becomes powerful in any one region, it will tend by its own force to introduce constructive methods of organization into the other divisions of the economic, political and social body." [29]

In explaining how membership in business corporations, labor unions, and governmental agencies prepares burghers for integration in the free life of political community, Hegel observes that it is only in the absence of such associations that the polarization of society into a minority of rich capitalists and a majority of pauperized, unemployed workers can occur. "Unless he is a member of a corporation," Hegel writes,

an individual is without rank or dignity, his isolation reduces his productive activity to mere self-seeking. ... We saw earlier that in fending for himself a member of civil society is also working for others. But this unconscious compulsion is not enough; it is in the Corporation that it first changes into a

[29] Herbert Croly, *The Promise of American Life* (Indianapolis, 1965), p. 395.

conscious and thoughtful ethical mode of life. Of course corporations must fall
under the higher surveillance of the state, because otherwise they would ossify,
build themselves in, and decline into a miserable system of castes. In and by
itself, however, a corporation is not a closed caste; its purpose is rather to bring
an isolated trade into the social order and elevate it to a sphere in which it gains
strength and respect.[30]

The corporation thus becomes for its members a kind of family; and
Hegel, in fact, concludes his discussion of Civil Society with the
observation that "as the family was the first, so the corporation is the
second ethical root of the state," the two serving as the only securely
fixed points "round which the unorganized atoms of civil society
revolve."

Yet it would be completely erroneous to assume that political
community, or the state in its proper sense, develops out of the dialectic
of civil society. "Actually," Hegel writes, "the state as such is not so
much the result as the beginning. It is within the state that the family
is first developed into civil society, and it is the Idea of the state itself
which disrupts itself into the two moments" out of which, by scientific
analysis, we seem to "deduce" its existence.[31]

By the time the state in its actuality is made the object of study
in Hegel's *Philosophy of Right*, it is clear that the method of exposition
to that point has been strictly Aristotelian. The whole has been analyzed
into its constituent elements so that the organic connection and dependence of the parts on the whole may be displayed. Aristotle had
said plainly enough that, while individual human beings form and
perpetuate families and states through their common intercourse, the
state is nevertheless, in the order of nature, prior to the family and the
individual. In what is perhaps his most brilliant brief summary of the
dialectic of the progression of sciences in this sphere, Hegel distinguishes
the several sciences according to their objects of study:

We begin with something abstract, namely, with the Notion of Will; we then
go on to the actualization of the as yet abstract will in an external existent, to
the sphere of formal right; from there we go on to the will that is reflected into
itself out of external existence, to the sphere of morality; and thirdly and lastly
we come to the will that unites within itself these two abstract moments and is
therefore the concrete, ethical will. In the ethical sphere itself we again start
from an immediate, from the natural, undeveloped shape possessed by the
ethical mind in the *family*; then we come to the *splitting up* of the ethical
substance in *civil society*; and finally, in the State, attain the unity and truth
of those two one-sided forms of the ethical mind. But this course followed by
our exposition does not in the least mean that we would make the ethical life

---

[30] *PhR*, pp. 153, 278 (§ 253 and note to § 255).
[31] *PhR*, p. 154 (§ 255) and p. 155 (§ 256).

later in time than right and morality, or would explain the family and civil society to be *antecedent* to the State in the *actual* world. On the contrary, we are well aware that the ethical life is the foundation of right and morality, as also that the family and civil society with their well-ordered distinctions already presuppose the existence of the State. In the *philosophical* development of the ethical sphere, however, we cannot begin with the State, since in this the ethical sphere has unfolded itself into its most concrete form, whereas the beginning is necessarily something abstract. For this reason, the moral sphere, too, must be considered before the ethical sphere, although the former to a certain extent comes to view in the latter only as a sickness.[32]

Briefly put, one may say that *abstract right* with its positing of the will in external things, *morality* with its subjective justification, the ethical life of the *family* with its immediate bond of love, and *civil society* with its mediated bonds of need, are moments analyzable out of the actuality of the life of the *state*. The *persons* of abstract right, the *subjects* of morality and conscience, the *members* of families, and the *burghers* of civil society enter the life of the state as *citizens*, to constitute a new whole qualitatively different, as we have stressed, from all other human associations. As to what characteristically unites citizens in a true state, Hegel writes: "Liberty and equality are indeed the foundation of the state." But he hastens to add that they are the foundation which is "as the most abstract, so also the most superficial, and for that reason the most familiar."[33]

The State is the perfection of Objective Mind in the same sense that Free Mind is the perfection of Subjective Mind. Free Mind overcomes the original subjectivity of mind through psychological self-analysis. Similarly, the State overcomes its absorption in the processes of civil society (where classes attempt to use its powers to advance class interests) by the self-constituting processes of rational law.

States have a constituted actuality that can be studied objectively. One can observe empirically how the constitution of one's own state – whether Athens, Sparta, or Rome, England, the United States, or China – actually functions from day to day. A comparative study of such constitutions – comparative "systems-analysis," we would call it today – leads to knowledge of the essential structure of a political community as such. But each state has, of course, an historical development of its own that can be studied in itself as well as comparatively. The Athenian constitution, for example, was originally a despotic rule of one man, but there took place a gradual devolution of power, through a dozen or more political crises, from the rule of one

32 *PhM*, p. 130 (§ 408).
33 *PhM*, p. 265 (§ 539).

through the rule of few and then of many; whereas the Spartan constitution, with its carefully separated and balanced powers, hardly changes at all in a comparable interval of time. Systems-analysis and constitutional histories were the basis upon which Aristotle founded his *Politics* – but only after having reviewed the theories of politics advanced by his predecessors in the field. And Hegel does the same. As T. M. Knox correctly remarks in his notes to the *Philosophy of Right*, according to Hegel,

a study of positive law [systems-analysis] and history must precede the philosophy of right. The philosopher tries to see the meaning of the facts which the historian collects, and to discover the necessity at the heart of their contingency. It is important to notice that Hegel brought to the writing of this book an extensive study of the facts whose inward and moving principle he here professes to expound, and thus he is very far from attempting the deduce the philosophy of the state by *a priori* thinking.[34]

One "scientific" approach to the study of states Hegel very explicitly eschews. And that is the prescriptive approach, the aim of which is to construct a theory of the state as it "ought to be," so that statesmen (or youthful "idealists") may set about reconstituting their actual states on the scientist's model. His own object, he says, is the same as that of the astronomer studying the phenomena of the heavens, which is certainly not to teach men how the heavenly bodies "ought to move." "To consider a thing rationally," writes Hegel, "means not to bring reason to bear on the object from the outside and so to tamper with it, but to find that the object is rational on its own account."[35] This is true not only of the purely observational sciences, but also of those founded on experimentation. The experimenter certainly tampers with things in putting his experiment together; but once the experiment has been "made," his task is simply to describe and formulate the rational law implicit in it, without further tampering.

So it is with the study of the man-made state: its rationality has been built into it in the course of history by the generations of men who made it. The state is infinitely more complex than a man-made experiment in a laboratory, but it is, as we noted before, of the same order. Even in the laboratory, the scientist discounts unessential factors and speaks of "other things being equal." Similarly of the object of study of political science, Hegel says: "The state is no ideal work of art; it stands on earth, and so in the sphere of caprice, chance, and

---

[34] *PhR*, p. 306.
[35] *PhR*, p. 35 (§ 31).

error; and bad behavior may disfigure it in many respects. But even the ugliest of men, or a criminal, or an invalid, or a cripple, is still always a living man. The affirmative, life, subsists despite his defects, and it is this affirmative factor [other things being equal] which is our theme here."[36]

According to its "ratio of truth," the state is known first as rationally constituted in itself (Constitutional Law), then as constituted for others (International Law), and finally as adequately linking its domestic and foreign relations in the unity of its role in World History. The state, Hegel repeatedly stresses, is the actuality of concrete freedom. It is free *in itself* and also *for others*. Its internal freedom is so articulated, constitutionally, as to guarantee maximum subjective freedom (diversity in civil society) with maximum objective freedom (unity of purpose in foreign relations). "Sovereignty" is the historical term for the constituted freedom of a politically united people. In its domestic aspect, sovereignty is the effective unity of the citizens, as producers and consumers of the commonwealth, expressed through the legislative processes; and of the wisdom of the "civil" servants, or public-oriented elites, who in the process of administering the law take notice of the difficulties and unanticipated needs that inevitably arise.

But it is in its foreign-relations aspect that the constituted freedom of a politically united people – its sovereignty – is fully manifest. Hegel's words on this aspect of the subject have a tremendous bearing on the question of knowledge as it pertains to political science; for what is at issue here is the reality of statehood as it has been historically defined. The basis of all Right, Hegel says, is "personality"; and hence the imperative of Right is: "Be a person and respect others as persons."[37] States emerge historically to give every man's personality its due, to realize the freedom of personality in its fullness, equally for all, as far as possible. In the more perfect union of a state, the freedom of personality takes on the individuality of the whole. And Hegel says of it:

Individuality is awareness of one's existence as a unit in sharp distinction from others. It manifests itself on the level of the state as a relation to other states, each of which is autonomous *vis-à-vis* the others. This autonomy embodies mind's actual awareness of itself as a unit and hence it is the most fundamental freedom which a people possesses as well as its highest dignity. ... Those who talk of the "wishes" of a "collection" of people to renounce its own political center and

36 *PhR*, p. 279 (note to § 258).
37 *PhR*, p. 37 (§ 36).

autonomy in order to unite with others to form a new whole, have very little knowledge of what a "collection" is or of the feeling of selfhood which a nation possesses in its independence.[38]

The contemporary world has heard so many voices – especially in the academy – cry out against this traditional notion of sovereignty that it has been a relief in recent years to hear the statesmen of the new state of Israel proclaim it at the top of their lungs, often against the combined self-deluding ignorance of what in the Old Testament is termed the gentiles, or "other" nations. The Israeli people have, of course, saved and planned for almost 2,000 years to make a place for themselves in this world – an objective place where, as Free Minds, they can live and govern themselves autonomously. During that interval, they have enjoyed all kinds of freedoms elsewhere, especially in England, France, and the United States; but for the Jews who think of themselves as essentially Jews, wherever they may happen to live in the world, those lesser freedoms – the freedoms of civil society – have never sufficed. The freedom they have sought, and now hope to realize in Palestine, is that sovereign freedom of autonomous statehood that Hegel characterizes as "the most fundamental freedom which a people possesses as well as its highest dignity."

The realization of freedom in autonomous states that face one another in the world like individualized personalities in civil society makes up, according to Hegel, the course of world history. World history "contains" the histories of individual states, even as the states "contain" the development of their constituent families and groupings of civil society which, in turn, "contain" the lives of their individual members.

The philosophical science of history, therefore, presupposes all that has gone before in the exposition of the sciences of Objective Mind. But here it is the coming to be and passing away of states in their *relations* with one another that is the distinguishably new object of scientific study. The method, however, remains the same; and in his lectures on the *Philosophy of History*, Hegel once again cites the practice of astronomers to justify his own scientific procedure. The astronomer doesn't come to the study of celestial phenomena with a blank mind. He comes to it with a mind full of the best ideas of mathematics and mechanics. Similarly, the serious social scientist doesn't come to the study of civil society, or the state, with a blank mind. And just as the

---

[38] *PhR*, p. 208 (§ 322).

concepts of Mind, Freedom, and Will are presupposed in the scientific study of family life, civil society, and statehood, so the concepts of statehood and related concepts (tribe, people, nation) must be presupposed in the scientific study of the so-called facts of history which cannot of themselves constitute an academic discipline. Against the naive notion of "facts" that can write themselves up into a science on a *tabula rasa,* Hegel observes:

That a particular distinction is in fact the characteristic principle of a people is the element of our study that must be empirically ascertained and historically demonstrated. To do this requires, however, that we bring to the task not only a disciplined faculty of abstraction but also a long familiarity with the Idea. One must have what you may call, if you like, *a priori* knowledge, or long familiarity with the entire sphere of principles to which the specific principle in question belongs – just as Kepler (to name only the most celebrated scientist of this sort) must have been acquainted *a priori* with ellipses, cubes, squares and concepts of their interrelationships, before he could discover from the empirical data those immortal laws which are determinations of that sphere of representations. A person ignorant of such elemental concepts and distinctions will fail to understand – let alone discover – such laws no matter how long a time he spends contemplating the sky and the motions of celestial bodies.[39]

In his extended discussion of methods that makes up the introduction to his *Philosophy of History,* Hegel distinguishes Original History, Reflective History, and Philosophical History, showing how the facts or things of the first are to be adequately linked together with the thoughts or principles of the second in the truth of the third. As Professor J. N. Findlay correctly sums it up: "The Hegelian Philosophy of History therefore builds on the original histories which constitute the source-material for the past, and also on the more reflective histories which subject this source-material to various critical tests. ... It only differs from both [in that] its aim is ... to discover in past States different stages in the developing consciousness of Right, to discover a *line* of development running through all such stages, and to show, further, how events which seem unconnected with this development have none the less contributed to it."[40]

The developing consciousness of Right in history is, of course, the development of freedom. It is in becoming aware of history as the work of Free Mind that the individual mind, first, and then the mind of a people acting together, becomes fully free. The longing for realized freedom is the motive power of human conduct on all levels of the

---

[39] *Hegel's Philosophy of History,* trans. J. Sibree (New York, 1956), p. 64. Translation adapted slightly in accordance with German text (Lasson, 1930).
[40] J. N. Findlay, *Hegel: A Re-examination* (New York, 1962), p. 334.

world of Objective Mind, but particularly on that of universal history. "When individuals and nations have once seized upon the abstract idea of freedom itself," Hegel says, "it has more than any other thing, boundless power, just because it is the very being of Mind, its very reality." [41]

But universal recognition that Mind is free in its essential being has been slow in coming. Whole continents have known nothing of genuine freedom; and even the Greeks and Romans mistook it for something attached to specially privileged races or to be acquired through privileged education. Only with the spread of the Judeo-Christian religion did the idea take root that freedom is the essential characteristic of manhood. Man, Christianity teaches, is intended inherently for the highest freedom – which is oneness with God. And through that teaching, Christianity has realized in its adherents – first in Europe but eventually elsewhere as well – an "ever-present sense that they are not and cannot be slaves"; so that, "if they are made slaves, if the decision as regards their property rests with an arbitrary will, not with laws or courts of justice, they would find their very substance outraged." This will for freedom, Hegel concludes, "is no longer an *urge* demanding satisfaction; it is very character itself – its being, without urgings, become spiritual consciousness." [42]

In the ancient history of the Far and Near East, the political freedom of states (the united willingness of citizens to die rather than suffer enslavement) was a reality only in the head of state: the single person who exercised such freedom in behalf of his subjects. Thus in the Ancient East, as also in its fossilized modern continuations, only *one* person in each free state was actually free. In the history of the classical world, on the shores of the Mediterranean, political freedom was much more widely experienced; *many* in the free states of Athens, Sparta, and Rome were personally free – though not yet all. In modern history, quite uniquely, freedom has at last become a recognized possibility, and is rapidly on its way to becoming an actuality, for *all*. As Hegel foresaw, all the traditionally enslavable peoples of the world – not only in Black America but in Black Africa and Yellow Asia as well – are rapidly becoming genuinely free through their newly asserted, manifest willingness to die rather than suffer enslavement.

[41] *PhM*, p. 239 (§ 482).
[42] *PhM*, p. 240 (§ 482).

III. The political and historical moments of truth

But it is not when political freedom first becomes possible – as in the backward, newly emerging nations of the world – that the truth of the social, political, and historical experience of man can be known. The awakening and flowering of scientific knowledge is itself deeply rooted in the course of history. It has its proper places and times, its propitious moments of truth, in politics as well as history. We noted earlier that the completed system of philosophical sciences has no privileged beginning. But the same cannot be said of the *impulse* to philosophize. An individual may conceivably begin to pursue true knowledge, in a scientific manner with respect to any conceivable object of knowledge whether mathematical or astronomical, biological or psychological, economic or sociological, etc.; but he can in fact do so only if he happens to have been reared in a society sufficiently advanced politically to assure him the leisure without which a scientific pursuit of knowledge is neither desirable nor possible.

In the opening pages of his *History of Philosophy*, Hegel cites Aristotle's words on the subject, agreeing that the desire to know, as an end in itself, becomes a pressing need only when "almost all the necessities of life and the things that make for comfort and recreation have been secured." [43] The possibility of satisfying such a need, even more than its awakening, presupposes the actuality of a politically advanced society with a considerable history behind it. Doubt, or wonder in the Aristotelian sense, which animates the need to philosophize, is not excited into being simply by man's awareness of his natural environment. The hungry man does not "wonder" about the food he needs to eat, any more than he wonders about the "nature" of the beast who attacks him when he is out hunting or about the nature of the pleasure he gets in gratifying his hunger or his sexual appetite. Before the wonder that leads to science can be awakened, the animal cravings must have disappeared, and so must the immediate fears; and in their place, as Hegel expresses it, "a strength, elevation, and moral fortitude of mind must have appeared, passions must be subdued and consciousness advanced to the point that its thinking is free and not self-seeking." [44] It is the point in the cycle of the sciences of Subjective Mind where, as a consequence of self-analysis, Mind is at last free to overcome its subjectivity.

[43] *HPh*, Vol. I, p. 51.
[44] *HPh, ibid.*

Self-analysis of that sort is not possible among primitive peoples. The beginnings of true science are thus reserved for advanced societies; and even in advanced societies, one particular phase of historical development is much more suitable for such beginnings than any other. Hegel emphasizes that, for a genuine awakening of scientific curiosity,

thought must be for itself, must come into existence in its freedom, liberate itself from nature and come out of its immersion in sense-perception; it must, as free, enter within itself and thus arrive at the consciousness of freedom. . . . If we say that the consciousness of freedom is connected with the development of philosophy, this principle must be a fundamental one in the people among whom philosophy begins. . . . Connected with this on the practical side, is the fact that actual freedom develops political freedom, [so that, objectively,] philosophy appears in history only where and insofar as free institutions are formed.[45]

In other words, the mind that can freely philosophize is the same Free Mind which, after experiencing the moral frustration of attempting to press claims of abstract personal right, realizes itself in the actualities of family-life, civil society, statehood, and the universal history of states. Free men constitute states, states make history; and it is in the course of the universal history of states – from the founding of the first historical states in the great river-valley civilizations of the ancient Far and Near East down through the ages of ancient Greece and Rome and of the medieval and modern peoples – that Mind frees itself from temporal things to become Absolute in Art, Religion and Philosophy. In Hegel's words:

It may be said that Philosophy first commences when a race [broadest extension of family-life] has largely left its concrete mode of existence [constituted statehood], when separation and change of class have begun [expansion of civil society], and the community is approaching its decline. . . . This holds good throughout all the history of philosophy. . . . Thus in Athens, with the ruin of the Athenian people, the period was reached when philosophy appeared. . . . In Rome, philosophy first developed in the decline of the Republic. [And] it was with the decline of the Empire that the height and indeed the zenith of ancient philosophy was attained in the systems of the neo-Platonists at Alexandria.[46]

The questioning of experience that results in the flowering of science and philosophy is the same questioning that consumes the social order by undermining its authority. For that reason it can be said that, while in the experience of any one person, wonder may rise to the level of systematic doubt at any point around the great circle of knowledge, historically it has awakened first within the range of the social, poli-

---

[45] *HPh*, Vol. I, pp. 94–5.
[46] *HPh*, Vol. I, pp. 52–3.

tical, and historical consciousness of man. Excited by doubt, Mind invariably brings its quest for truth to focus, first of all, on its own
social environment: which is to say, on the "institutions and forms of
government of the people among whom it makes its appearance; their
morality, their social life and capabilities, customs and enjoyments;
their attempts and achievements in art and science; their religious
experience; their wars and foreign relations; and lastly, the origin and
progress of the states arising to displace them."[47]

When animated by doubt, when pursued questioningly, mind
"subverts" what it studies. That was the charge raised against Socrates
by the Athenian democracy; and it was a valid charge. But, as Hegel
represents it, in condemning Socrates the Athenians were really
condemning themselves. For Socrates was, in fact, the Athenian Mind
itself committed to self-criticism. In every age of intense philosophical
study, the studying mind and the historical actuality which it studies
mirror one another, and are indeed one. On this theme Hegel says in
the *History of Philosophy:* "Mind takes refuge in the clear space of
thought to create for itself a kingdom of thought in opposition to the
world of actuality, and Philosophy is the reconciliation following upon
the destruction of that real world – a destruction which thought has
begun."[48]

Hegel's philosophical sciences of society, politics, and history are
thus mirrors of a dissolving world. Thought consumes its own objectivization of itself in space and time as objectively inadequate.
True philosophy, like true art and true religion, transcends the realities
of politics and history. It is utterly wrong, therefore, to try to make
a secular optimist out of Hegel. What optimism is to be found in his
philosophic system pertains to a sphere beyond history, and therefore
beyond the associational life of family, civil society, and statehood
that makes up the pattern of history.

"Passions, private aims, and the satisfaction of selfish desires are
the most effective springs of action in history," writes Hegel, "because
they respect none of the limitations which Right and Morality would
impose, and because they exert a more direct influence over men than
the artificial and tedious discipline that tends toward order and self-
restraint, law and morality." Yet, when we read the record of history
and note the evil and ruin that such passions, aims, and desires
have wrought, when we contemplate the "miseries that have over-

[47] *HPh*, Vol. I, p. 53.
[48] *HPh*, Vol. I, p. 52

whelmed the noblest nations and polities, and the finest examples
of private virtue," we experience, Hegel writes, "mental torture,
allowing no defense or escape but the consideration that what has
happened could not be otherwise; that it is a fatality which no inter-
vention could alter." It is out of a history that "excites emotions of
the profoundest and most hopeless sadness" that we pass into the
sphere of Absolute Mind. [49] The transition is the flight of Minerva's
owl – which is possible only after the long day's task is done. Philosophy's backward glance on the wreckage of political history is a tragic
theodicy.

One must stress the pessimism of the Hegelian doctrine of Objective
Mind to avoid the popular error that would make of him an idolator
of statehood and the historical process. The state is for Hegel, as for
St. Augustine and the Founding Fathers of the United States, a
necessary evil. Men initially build up the edifice of human society, he
says, to gratify their passions; but they end up "fortifying a position
of Right and Order against themselves." [50] The passionate aims of
individuals are checked and balanced in the rationality of states; and
the self-centered interests of states are checked and balanced in the
hard trials of universal history. That history is by no means a theater
of happiness. On the contrary, its periods of happiness are no more
than blank pages, signifying nothing.

To make a worldly optimist out of Hegel, one must either decapitate
him, denying his doctrine of art, religion, and God-centered philosophy, as Croce and the fascist humanists generally have done; or
turn his entire doctrine upside down, as Marx and the materialist
humanists have done. Right side up and whole, Hegel must rank with
St. Augustine among the profoundest worldly pessimists of Christendom, even as he must rank with Aristotle – *il maestro di color che sanno*
– among the greatest of systematic philosophers who have concerned
themselves with the sciences of society, politics, and history.

[49] *Hegel's Philosophy of History, op. cit.*, pp. 20–21.
[50] *Ibid.*, p. 27.

HEGEL AND THE NATURAL SCIENCES

ERROL E. HARRIS

Northwestern University

I. SCIENCE AND PHILOSOPHY

Hegel is often represented as scornful and contemptuous of the natural sciences. He seems often to ridicule their methods and their achievements and to subordinate them, as forms of knowledge to the speculative "sciences" which, for him, constitute the body of philosophy. This is, at the very best, a half-truth, and is scarcely even true by half; for what Hegel certainly does very frequently ridicule is what he regards as pseudo-science and charlatanry rather than the genuine article, and his taunts are, more often than not, aimed at philosophers with whom he disagrees, and philosophical doctrines about nature which he considers superficial and trivial, than at the practising scientists and their recognized disciplines. Certainly, he did believe and teach, that the empirical sciences belonged to a lower phase of self-conscious reason than philosophy, but such a view is inescapable for any thinker who sees philosophy as the reflective study of human experience, including empirical science; and any philosopher who seeks to deny that his subject includes this reflective task is apt to renounce his own birthright as philosopher. To affirm the reflective (second-degree, or "meta-") character of philosophy, on the other hand, is not to belittle or to despise the natural sciences; for it is only by paying them due respect that any philosophy of science, whether of its method and the concepts it uses (logic) or of its subject-matter (philosophy of nature), is able to attain its goal.

For Hegel philosophy was a single system, not divisible into semi-independent branches labelled Logic, Epistemology, Metaphysics, Ethics and the rest. And this was because he saw knowledge, and, not simply knowledge, but the whole of reality, as a single system. Its unity was not, however, incompatible with diversity, but required and necessarily implied difference, as any accurate account of any feature of his theory must bring out. It follows that a discussion of Hegel's view of natural science will be fruitful only if that is seen in the light and context of the entire system, and only if the structure of the system is rightly understood.

Hegel saw the real as a single continuous dialectical activity, at once absolute, eternally realized as a whole, and perpetually and continuously realizing itself as a process. How these two aspects are reconcilable and reconciled is, fortunately, not my concern in this paper, and it will be sufficient to consider only the second aspect – that of a continuous dialectical process extending from pure being to absolute self-conscious spirit. That this was Hegel's conception of reality is attested by numerous passages in his works. Notably, in the second Preface and in the Introduction to the greater Logic, he maintains, first, that logic is concerned with no merely empty thought forms, devoid of content, but with the thought forms intrinsic to, immanent and inherent in, all forms of experience,[1] and indeed all forms of reality. For he asserts here (as he does also in the *Enzyklopädie*) that the principle of movement in consciousness and thought is equally the principle of all movement and activity in the world.[2] It follows that there is no break between natural movement and the activity of thought. The principle of both is dialectic, and dialectic is a nisus generating a process that goes continuously from one phase to the next – continuously from Being to the Notion.

We must not forget, however, that Being and Notion, while they are *Denkbestimmungen* are not empty formal ideas, but are principles immanent in both "the external world" and experience. Being is the actual world, what is (as well as a category in logic). But its "truth" or reality is the Notion – so Hegel persistently asserts. "The external world is in itself the truth, for the truth is actual and must exist."[3] The truth, however, *qua* truth is known – is for itself (*für sich*) and as such is consciousness or spirit. The knowledge of an object is its notion and the Logic is the science of the Notion;[4] it is the "thinking

---

[1] *Vide Werke*, IV (*Jubiläumsausgabe*, Ed. Hermann Glockner, Stuttgart, 1958), pp. 27ff. and 43–47. A. V. Miller's Translation (*Hegel's Science of Logic*, London 1969) pp. 36ff and 48–51.

[2] *Werke* IV, p. 54: "... *das Princip aller natürlichen und geistigen Lebendigkeit überhaupt.*" (A. V. Miller's Tr., p. 56) and *Enzyklopädie*, § 81, Zusatz 1: "*Es ist dasselbe überhaubt das Princip aller Bewegung, alles Lebens und aller Bethätigung in der Wirklichkeit.*" *Werke*, VIII, p. 190. Wallace's Translation p. 148. (*The Logic of Hegel*, Oxford, 1892).

[3] *Enz.*, § 38, *Zusatz, Werke*, VIII, p. 119, Wallace's Tr., p. 79.

[4] Cf. *Wissenschaft der Logik,Werke*, IV, p. 29. A. V. Miller's Tr., p. 37f.

study" of that dialectical process by which Being generates out of itself the whole gamut of categories up to the Notion; and this answers to the dialectical process (with which logic is continuous) by which the actual "external" world – the world of nature – generates the self-conscious subject of knowledge, both of the world and of itself, as the mind of man.

Natural science is a definite phase in this process and must be seen as such. We must identify it in its proper place in the dialectical series if we are to understand Hegel's view of it and the attitude, *qua* philosopher, which he adopted towards it. The emergence of sentient awareness in the organic world is the point at which nature gives rise to spirit (*Geist*). The development of consciousness proceeds through perception and understanding to reason, and, in its course, produces empirical science. Philosophy is a later phase of this development, for it presupposes the activity of spirit in practical life as well as in theoretical investigation, and logic sets out the thought-determinations (or categories) implicit in all forms of less reflective experience.

The categories of science will, of course, find a place in this logical system; but natural science itself is temporally prior to logic. It is an activity of thought at a less reflective level which takes as its object the natural world as it is observed or perceived. It is a reflection upon, a refinement and an analytic elaboration of, common sense; whereas logic is a further turning back upon itself by thought, and is a reflection upon this reflection. Further, it is only as the self-reflection of philosophical speculation proceeds that the developmental relationships of nature and spirit are brought to self-awareness, and the mind recognizes its erstwhile object (in science) as itself in embryo. Nature as it appears to common sense and as it is investigated by science is mere physical, external, object. Its movements and processes are not recognized as a phase of the dialectical movement generating spirit. It is only when consciousness has reached the stage of self-awareness attained in philosophy, and after it has reflected upon its own activity in common sense and the empirical sciences (which it does in logic), that it becomes aware of the immanence of spirit in nature. It thereupon reverts to nature and re-thinks it as mind in becoming, giving a fresh account of it, not as empirical science has already done, but as *Naturphilosophie*. In this phase, the pronouncements of the natural sciences are not superseded or contradicted, but are seen in a new light, as a preliminary, less self-conscious, awareness of an object now seen to be identical with the knowing subject in the Notion – the truth which is actual and existent. We must, therefore, examine Hegel's treatment of empirical science in the *Phänomenologie* and the *Geistesphilosophie*, in the *Logik*, and in relation to the *Naturphilosophie*.

2. WISSENSCHAFT

First, however, let us consider what Hegel says of *Wissenschaft* and what he understands by the word. *Wissenschaft* is properly translated by "science," but Hegel did not restrict the term to empirical or natural science, nor even to this taken along with mathematics ("exact" science). Primarily, for Hegel, *Wissenschaft* is the Notion, an awareness of self as its own object and as identical with its object – substance aware of itself as subject (or *Geist*) and *vice versa*. Obviously this is the proper province of philosophy. But to be scientific and to be Notion, what is propounded can be no mere abstract universal principle formulated as fundamental, nor yet a transcendent pure thought leaving behind it all concrete content. As Hegel puts it in the Preface to the *Phänomenologie:*

"Among the many consequences that flow from what has been said, these may be given prominence, that knowledge is only real and can only be expounded as science or as system; and further that a so-called fundamental proposition or principle of philosophy, even if it is true, is nevertheless also false, just because and in so far as it is merely a fundamental proposition or first principle."[5]

A mere fundamental principle is in itself abstract and empty, until the system to which it is fundamental has been developed. Only then, as an integral moment within the system, does its true significance appear. Similarly the final conclusion, unless it is seen as the conclusion of the demonstration and in its systematic relations to the evidence from which it is drawn, is merely unintelligible.[6]

---

[5] *Phänomenologie, Vorrede:* "*Unter mancherlei Folgerungen, die aus dem Gesagten fliessen, kann diese herausgehoben werden, dass das Wissen nur als Wissenschaft oder als System wirklich ist und dargestellt werden kann; dass ferner ein sogenannter Grundsatz oder Prinzip der Philosophie, wenn er wahr ist, schon darum auch falsch ist, insofern er nur als Grundsatz oder Prinzip ist.*"

Cf. also: *Die wahre Gestalt, in welcher die Wahrheit existiert, kann allein das wissenschaftliche System derselben sein. Werke* II, p. 27. J. B. Baillie's Translation (*The Phenomenology of Mind*, London, 1910. 1931) p. 85.

[6] Cf. the mathematical equation, representing the form of the physical universe, set out by the modern physicist:

$$(ds)^2 = \left(1 - \frac{\lambda}{3}\, r^2\right)(dt)^2 - \frac{1}{c^2}\left\{\frac{(dr)^2}{1 - (\lambda/3)\, r^2} + r^2(d\theta)^2 + r^2\sin^2\theta\,(d\phi)^2\right\}.$$

Knowledge proper is science, which is fully and systematically developed, elaborated and set out. And the development is the dialectical self-development of the subject matter (*die Sache selbst*). It must be the very nature of the object under scrutiny that impels it to develop, through its own negation, to that ultimate self-knowledge, which is the Notion, and which is *"die wahre Gestalt, in welcher die Wahrheit existiert."* But this is the entire dialectical development, the whole system *aufgehoben*, or sublated, in its outcome.

"The truth is the whole, but the whole is only that essential reality which has fulfilled itself through its development. One may say of the Absolute that it is essentially outcome: that it is only at the end that it is for the first time what it truly is; and its nature consists in just that – to be real, subject, or self-developed."[7]

Accordingly, nothing is truly scientific that is not systematically developed in rigorous dialectical form; and Hegel is very scornful of any exposition, claiming to be scientific, which is merely a collection of disconnected facts, or is an alleged demonstration of a theory based on evidence fortuitously dragged in from some unrelated source (or one the relevance of which is not clearly made out).

In the natural sciences of his day treatises were often written lacking the kind of disciplined rigour that Hegel demanded. They presented their material either as demonstrations, the foundations of which were arbitrarily postulated assumptions, or as mere congeries of facts with little or no systematic correlation. Against this sort of thing Hegel railed unmercifully, though, as I have said, it is more often half-baked philosophy than natural science that is his butt. It does not follow that the empirical sciences, as such and as a whole, failed to meet what he would have considered scientific standards. Scientific procedure as Hegel conceived it is characteristic of the natural sciences and the systematic nature and relations of the categories proper to them is set out and demonstrated in his logic. They do, indeed, form only a part – a limited phase – within the total system, which he insisted must be complete and rigorous throughout and must be elaborated in full. But as a definite and necessary phase of the system the various sciences are not only legitimate and important, but necessary for the adequate understanding and appreciation of reflective philosophy.

---

[7] *Op. cit.*, p. 24: *"Das Wahre is das Ganze. Das Ganze aber ist nur das durch seine Entwicklung sich vollendende Wesen. Es ist von dem Absoluten zu sagen, dass es wesentlich Resultat, dass es erst am Ende das ist, was es in Wahrheit ist; und hierin eben besteht seine Natur, Wirkliches, Subjekt, oder Sichselbstwerden zu sein."* (Cf. Baillie's Tr., p. 81f.)

"It is only after profounder acquaintance with the other sciences," he declares, "that logic ceases to be for the subjective spirit a merely abstract universal and reveals itself as the universal which embraces within itself the wealth of the particular ... Thus the value of logic is only fully appreciated when it has come to be as the result of an experience of the sciences ..."[8]

3. SCIENCE AS A STAGE IN THE DEVELOPMENT OF CONSCIOUSNESS

Whatever else empirical science is taken to be, it is obviously and incontestably a level of development of consciousness. Science is a way of thinking and a form of truth, and so is characteristic of a particular phase of intellectual (or spiritual) maturation. We do not look for scientific thinking among primitive people nor expect it of young children. It is not typical of the untutored mind, of the naive or the unsophisticated. Consciousness must have developed to some degree before it becomes capable of empirical science; and the course of this development is traced in the *Phänomenologie*. "This coming to be of science in general," Hegel says (using *Wissenschaft* in the sense explained above), "or knowledge (*Wissen*), is what this Phenomenology of Spirit sets forth."[9]

Consciousness is shown here to begin with immediate sense-certainty, the direct awareness of a this-here-now; but to be even this it must at once become something more, for no this or here or now can maintain itself except in relation to a that, a there and a then. And though the purport of "this" is particular the term applies indifferently to every this and so is universal – as are "here" and "now." The conflict resolves itself in a here which is many heres, a present which embraces a lapse of several nows, and a this which is a complex of sensuous thises – an individual object. So sense-certainty develops into perception (*Wahrnehmung*), the cognition of individual objects and their mutual spatio-temporal relations. Here again individuality and universality vie with one another. The thing is one but its qualities many, and though it is individual its qualities are each shared with innumerable other things. The merely apparent (qualities) become contrasted with what is veridical, the subjective with the objective,

---

[8] *Wissenschaft der Logik, Einleitung. Werke*, IV, p. 57. Cf. Also *Enz.* § 12. (Cf. A. V. Miller's Tr., p. 58. Wallace's Tr., pp. 19ff.)
[9] *Phänomenologie, Vorrede, Werke* II, p. 30. (Cf. Baillie's Tr., p. 88.)

and perception appears now as one and now as the other. The nisus toward assurance locates certainty in each in turn and finds it in neither, until it seeks truth in a new form of the universal unconditioned by sense. This is a form of essential reality, unsensed, yet imagined as lying behind or beneath the play of sensuous appearance.

The phase of consciousness that thus emerges is what Hegel calls Understanding (*Verstand*). It moves from the postulation of force as the underlying explanation of sensible change, to the idea of a law governing the play of forces. It presents the object as double and self-reflected, as reality and its appearances, as substance and accident, as cause and effect. It analyses and distinguishes and keeps the distincta apart, as if in their mutual dependence they were separable and self-contained.[10]

Findlay calls this "scientific understanding,"[11] though in this context Hegel makes no direct reference to empirical science. In the introduction to the lesser Logic, however, he does tell us that Understanding is an essential moment in all science, empirical as well as philosophical.[12] At one time I thought that, for Hegel, empirical science and understanding were more or less identical and that empirical science was restricted to the level of understanding[13] (which is what Findlay's phrase also seems to imply), but I now think this interpretation is mistaken; first, for the very reason that, in this passage in the Encyclopaedia *Logic*, he insists that understanding is but one moment in all knowledge, be it empirical or philosophic; and secondly because, in the *Phänomenologie* what is patently his account of empirical science is the section entitled *Beobachtung der Natur*, which is an activity of reason (*Vernunft*), a phase of the absolute subject.

To say that *Verstand* is "scientific understanding" is not wrong, because the form of thinking which is characteristic of it is predominant in natural science. But the latter is a *self*-conscious activity which is not always the case with *Verstand* (though it is indeed conscious). In the *Phenomenology*, Hegel tells us that the culmination of the movement of perception (*Wahrnehmung*) is the unconditioned universal, "and it is here that consciousness first truly enters the realm of under-

---

[10] This condensed and elliptical account of Understanding is, of course, very incomplete, and is no adequate summary of Hegel's exposition of its character and dialectic, but I hope it may serve as sufficient for my present purpose – to explain the place of natural science in the development of consiousness.

[11] *Vide Hegel, A Re-examination* (London, 1958), p. 92.

[12] *Enz.* §§79, 80.

[13] Cf. *Nature, Mind and Modern Science* (London, 1954), p. 255.

standing."[14] But he proceeds at once to describe how sensible singleness dissolves in the dialectic of immediate certainty (the "logic of
perception") and becomes universality, and how the interplay of empty
abstractions, singleness as opposed to universality, the essential as
against the unessential (which is nevertheless "necessary") typifies
gesunde Menschenverstand, which J. B. Baillie translates as "sound
common sense."

The world of sound common sense is, by and large, the perceptual
world and *Menschenverstand* is also *Verstand* or "understanding." At
the common sense level the world is not barely perceived it is also
understood, but in abstract and contradictory terms, through which,
Hegel says, the understanding reveals not their truth but its own
untruth.[15] Understanding is as much a feature of common sense as of
science, as the passage in the *Encyclopaedia* implies, and common
sense is largely perceptual thinking. Similarly, empirical science is
based upon observation and includes an important perceptual element.
Verstand signifies a type of thinking present in both but wholly
identical with neither. It is a moment also in philosophical speculation,
which, without it becomes vague and mystifying. In the *Phenomenology*,
the dialectic of understanding constitutes a kind of transition phase
between "sound common sense" immersed in perceptual immediacy
and empirical science – the observation of nature, which is an activity
of reason.[16]

Sound common sense does more than merely perceive the world of
things in space and time; it also offers explanations to itself of what it
experiences – usually implicit and merely "understood," but also at
times explicit. Changes of appearance it sees as the effects of causes,
movements as the products of forces, which are regular in the manner
of their action. For common sense things move only when pushed and
every change is instigated by some agency that initiates it. Hence it
comes to postulate hidden and unperceived influences which express
themselves in perceived events. These ideas are developed and elaborated in natural science, and from natural science are reabsorbed into
common sense. But everything that Hegel includes under *Verstand* in

---

[14] "... *und das Bewusstsein tritt hier erst wahrhaft in das Reich des Verstandes ein.*" *Op cit.*,
p. 105. (Cf. Baillie's Tr., p. 175.)

[15] *Ibid.*, p. 107. Baillie's Tr., p. 178.

[16] Hegel interposes discussions of practical personal relations and moral attitudes, which
constitute equally essential aspects of the dialectic of emerging self-consciousness; for he is
clearly aware that the mind (*Geist*) is no merely cognitive function and that cognition is but
one aspect or moment of its activity and actualization.

the *Phenomenology* is found in the lower phase as well as in the higher. In science, however, it is all made explicit and becomes aware of itself: for itself (*für sich*) and not simply for us (*für uns*), the philosophers, who recognize in the earlier phase factors to which consciousness at that phase pays no heed, or simply takes for granted.

4. OBSERVATION OF NATURE

Empirical science – the observation of nature – belongs to that stage of reason at which consciousness has become aware of itself as identical with its object – the stage of Kantian or Fichteian idealism which realizes that whatever is, is for consciousness, and which establishes objectivity as what conforms to the categories of reason. In claiming the whole world as its own in this way, Hegel reminds us, idealism is merely intuitive and remains oblivious of the process through which it has developed to this stage. This reminder is important, for it underlines Hegel's own realism. The certitude of reason that it is the objective truth has developed not only through the opposition of self to other in the dialectic of master and slave, not only from sense-certainty, perception and common sense, for which the object is external, and to which it appears as immediately presented; but, as we see if we refer to the *Geistesphilosophie*, it draws its roots from still more remote sources in nature. But in the first flush of self-assurance, the subject of reason forgets these obscure and distant origins,

> "... scorning the base degrees
> By which he did ascend ..."

and it is only after subsequent self-reflection, when the mind has made its activity in science its object, and has traced out the dialectic, which has produced it and which moves within it, that philosophy becomes aware of nature as implicit spirit – the potential self-generation of absolute self-awareness. To the philosophical reflection upon nature we shall return below. Here we are concerned with our main subject, empirical science as rational observation of nature.

The confidence of consciousness in its own grasp of, and identity with, objective truth is, however, at this early stage of self-conscious reason, only "for us," who are reflecting upon it philosophically, not for itself. Its own presence in its object is at first only felt, suspected or presupposed in a general way.[17] To know itself as concretely universal it must first have reflected upon its own nature (*in seine eigne Tiefe steigen*),[18] and only thereafter can it return to external reality and find in that its own sensible embodiment.[19] But in its observation of nature reason behaves, as it were, instinctively, unconscious to itself of its own true nature. This unself-consciousness of self-conscious reason is no stark paradox. It is conscious of itself as seeking universality (its own nature) in its object, but it is not yet aware of itself as expressed and embodied in that object, because it has still to reflect upon its own universal nature in philosophy (especially logic).

Accordingly, reason seems to return to intention (*Meinen*) and perception (*Wahrnehmung*). Again, this is no paradox or genuine regression, for in the dialectic the proximate object of each phase of consciousness is always the prior phase, and we constantly find Hegel apparently going back on his tracks to cover what seems to be old ground in a new way. So here the objects of reason are common sense and understanding – the perceptual world as understood by sound human intelligence (*gesunde Menschenverstand*). It is precisely the world as understood by common sense that the natural sciences investigate, and their method of investigation is by observation (sense-perception). Nevertheless, the return to sense-perception is not a return to mere naivety. Observation is not just a matter of "tasting, smelling, feeling, hearing and seeing"; for the sensuously apprehended object has already been determined, in the perception, by thought (distinguishing, correlating and identifying mutually opposed elements); and for scientific observation the object must have universal significance. For natural science, therefore, though the medium of investigation is sense-observation, it is not simply fortuitous perception, but is directed by the questions raised and the explanations sought. "Reason sets out to know the truth, to find as a concept what for intention (*Meinen*) and perception (*Wahrnehmung*) is a thing."[20]

Into the detail of Hegel's treatment of the sciences in the *Phenomenology* we need not enter. Throughout he views the scientific enterprise as a phase in the continuous effort of the mind to become aware of

---

[17] *Zuerst sich in der Wirklichkeit nur ahnend oder sie nur als das Ihrige überhaupt wissend, schreitet sie in diesem Sinne zur allgemeinen Besitznehmung des ihr versicherten Eigentums ..."* *Ibid.*, p. 190. Baillie's Tr., p. 281.

[18] "Plumbed its own depths" – as in the Logic. *Ibid.*, p. 191. (Cf. Baillie's Tr., p. 282.)

[19] In *Naturphilosophie*.

[20] *Phän.*, p. 190. (Cf. Baillie's Tr., p. 281). *Meinen* might better be translated as "ostension".

itself as self-conscious notion; and he describes the objects and concepts of natural science as partial and halting pre-figurations of this self-knowledge, which in various ways, characteristic of the stage reached, fail to achieve the goal pursued. Reason in its observation of nature discovers, not what consciousness itself is (though that revelation is the ultimate outcome of its persistent effort), but what things are. It regards all its objects externally, as things unaffected by its observation, and adopts the observational attitude towards both nature and mind, as well as towards their mutual relation (the expression or manifestation of the latter in the former). Hence we have the gamut of the sciences developing itself, from physical science (observation of the inorganic) to biology (observation of the organic) and thence to psychology (observation of self-consciousness itself in relation to external actuality) and to the sciences which deal with the anatomical expressions of the mind (physiognomy and phrenology). Every stage of advance is stimulated by contradictions which appear and become intractable in the current phase.

Empirical science moves from the early stage of promiscuous observation, indiscriminate collection and minute description,[21] to classification in terms of distinguishing marks (or common characteristics). But that proves unreliable, for the mark is subjectively selected and what is required is an objective criterion. Hence a law is sought linking characteristics more systematically. But this turns out to be only an hypothesis, its truth only probable, whereas it was taken as necessary. Reason then seeks to establish its necessity more firmly by devising experiments to determine what is essential and what is not. At this stage there emerge imponderables and theoretical entities which, though supposed to be observed entities, are actually unobservable, and the universal is emancipated from its immersion in sense.[22]

Organism, the object of biological science, Hegel sees as new and further development of the concept as it appears to observing self-consciousness. Biology, in Hegel's day, was just beginning to develop as a systematic discipline and he outlines and criticizes the concepts it was striving to develop. He notes the looseness and banality of its classifications,[23] the vagueness of the "laws" governing the influence of environment on the organism, and the externality of the "teleolo-

---

[21] Cf., *ibid.*, p. 193f. Baillie's Tr., p. 285f.
[22] *Ibid.*, p. 200f. Baillie's Tr., p. 292.
[23] "... animals that belong to the air have the nature of birds, those belonging to water have the nature of fish, animals in northerly regions have thick furry pelts, and so on ..." *Ibid.*, p. 202. (Cf. Baillie's Tr., p. 294.)

gical" relation postulated to explain it. He himself has a much sounder conception of teleology as self-maintenance, identified as purpose, of which the aim is the organism itself. His whole conception and exposition of the notion of organism is far in advance of his time. He is well aware of the distinction between merely chemical process which "gets lost in its environment" and the organism which maintains itself by adaptation to, and self-assertion against, its surroundings.

This inner nisus to self-maintenance he sees expressing itself, in the three main living functions that contemporary biology distinguished, as sensibility, excitability (*Irritabilität*) and reproduction, each of which is manifested in anatomical structure (nervous system, musculature, intestinal structure, etc.). But none of these are separable entities, or are exclusively devoted to a single function, for the whole organism functions in each of them. They are moments of an organic process of which the distinction between inner and outer aspects is purely formal. The anatomical organs are what they are strictly only *qua* functioning. As merely material structures they belong only to the cadaver, which is not the living organism as properly known and conceived. Structure and function are but moments of the living reality, which alone gives them intelligible meaning.[24]

There are, in Hegel's treatment of the organic, many more examples of his penetrating insight into the nature of life, and he attributes the relative failure of contemporary biological science to grasp the true concept of the organic, to the persistent tendency of observation to reify and set in mutually external relation what are essentially inseparable moments of a dynamic concrete universal.

There is, however, no contempt or disrespect for empirical science as such in Hegel's criticism. He sees it as a necessary phase in the development of consciousness, but one inadequate to full self-knowledge. It occupies a relatively low level of self-consciousness, at which external nature is explored in the pursuit of that universality which belongs essentially to self-conscious mind. Empirical science, therefore, is, as it were, the first step towards the discovery of mind in nature. Its limitations are the natural consequences of its attitude to its object

---

[24] Cf. *Ibid.*, p. 216: "Since the being of an organism consists essentially in universality or reflection into self, the being of its totality, like its moments, cannot consist in an anatomical system, but their actual expression and externalization are rather present only as a movement running throughout the embodied frame; and what is extracted and fixed as a single system, presents itself essentially as a fluid moment. So that it is not that actuality which anatomy takes it to be that should rank as its reality, but only its being as process, in which alone the anatomical parts have a meaning (*Sinn*)." (Baillie's Tr., p. 309–10). Compare J. S. Haldane, *Organism and Environment* (Yale, 1917), pp. 102–4.

– that of observation – and the inescapable peculiarities of that level of consciousness.

But observant reason does not restrict itself to the investigation of inorganic and organic nature, it adopts the same attitute to mind itself and seeks to observe consciousness as well, both in its own process and in its material manifestations. Hence it produces two new pairs of sciences for which Hegel had little or no respect. The first pair concern themselves with subjective aspects of mind, the second with its external anatomical signs. On the subjective side is the traditional formal logic, which Hegel regarded as a sort of "natural history of thought" – a treatment of the laws and forms of judgment, as derived from an external observation of its operation, so that they appear, not as a self-generating dialectical progression, but as "a collection of disconnected necessities," fixed and unchanging, merely "a found, given, i.e. merely existent content."[25] Here Hegel contents himself simply with emphasizing the inadequacy and invalidity of "these so-called laws of Thought," reserving more detailed exposition for the *Logic*, and passes to psychology, the second empirical science of the mind. This is the observation of the process of consciousness, the habits, customs and ways of thinking of consciousness in action. As before, observant reason finds only a collection of faculties, traits, passions, and the like, the unity of which in a single individuality it fails to grasp. These it catalogues as it might species of insects or mosses, and with less right, for they are not (as are the latter) fortuitous and mutually independent particulars.

If biology was in its infancy in Hegel's day, empirical psychology was embryonic, and we can understand his dismissal of what he felt was (in his own terms) far from scientific. His contempt for formal logic sprang from another source – his belief that genuine thought and its true logic was dialectical, in which the distinction of form from content was relative and at best provisional, such that, if sharpened to a sepa-ration, it falsified the nature of thinking altogether.

For the last two sciences, which Hegel treats at some length in the *Phenomenology*, he had least respect of all. These are the "sciences" of physiognomy and phrenology. In his day they were taken so seriously that Hegel could not afford to neglect them, but he is never taken in by their pretentions, and ridicules their pronouncements with ribald contempt. He tries, however, to rationalize their actual

[25] *Ibid.*, p. 234. (Cf. Baillie's Tr., p. 330.)

occurrence as sciences and to show why observing consciousness turns to the physiognomic and cranial characteristics of the individual in search of "a law of relationship between self-consciousness and actuality, or the world set over against it." For all their ineptitudes, there is some point to these pseudo-sciences. It is the life-process, the nisus towards self-consciousness itself that has evolved the bodily form. And, in each individual case, the body is the medium through which whatever the person does is effected and expressed. It therefore constitutes "a sign" of his personality and his characteristics. Hegel always insists that every psychical act and capacity has its physical embodiment, so the expressive organs of face and hand cannot, for him, be wholly irrelevant, in their form and articulation, to the characteristics of the person to whom they belong and who uses them to express his personality.

But the alleged "sciences" Hegel castigates as bogus. Their so-called laws are guess-work and empty "fancying" (*Meinung*) and really say nothing at all: mere chatter, on the level of the housewife's assertion that it always rains on washing day.[26] This last stage of observing reason is, he says, its worst, and it underlines the necessity for a complete reversal of outlook.

5. SCIENCE AND LOGIC

Hegel described the *Phenomenology* as his voyage of discovery. It was his first major philosophical reflection upon the entire range of human experience. It may serve us, therefore, as a guide to the more detailed elaboration of his system in later works. In the section to which we have been paying attention he is outlining the process by which consciousness at the level of reason constructs new ("scientific") objects out of the materials already formed at the lower level of perception and common sense. In the third part of the *Encyclopaedia*, the *Philosophy of Spirit*, we are told that consciousness derives its objects from the more primitive stage, in soul, of sensation (*Gefühl*). It does so by determining the sensory content as sensible, existing, material things.[27] The multiplicity of presentations, at this stage, is ordered and reduced to unity at the next, by the imposition upon it of laws and universal principles by the intellect.[28] So the stage which is characterized by

---

[26] *Ibid.*, p. 249 and p. 261. Baillie's Tr., pp. 348–49 and 361.
[27] Cf. *Enz.* §418 and §448.
[28] *Ibid.*, §422.

empirical science, is one at which, by such organization, reason constructs its data out of the material of the preceding phase. Contemporary philosophers of science are, today, rediscovering this truth about the methods and procedures of science and are coming to admit, in opposition to the empiricism which has so long held the field, that there is no theoretically neutral body of observable evidence available to the scientist, but that he reads his observed data in terms of the scientific theories already established and accepted. [29]

The *Phenomenology*, at its conclusion brings us to Absolute Knowledge, "the reconciliation of consciousness with self-consciousness – i.e. the stage at which spirit is conscious of its own actual self-consciousness. This is essentially the philosophical stage and so, in a way, the stage of the *Phenomenology* itself. "All that remains to be done now," Hegel says, "is to cancel and transcend this bare form [of objectivity]; or rather, because the form appertains to consciousness as such, its true meaning must have already come out in the shape or modes consciousness has assumed" [30] (which in this work he has already reviewed). But, while this, the culmination of the "voyage of discovery," is a return upon itself, Hegel contemplates, and in the *Encyclopaedia* carries out, an explicit, scientific elaboration of this final phase. Its content (he says here) "is the spirit which traverses [the whole range of] its own being, and does this for itself, *qua* spirit, by the fact that it possesses the shape of the notion in its objectivity." [31] And this he regards as going beyond what he has done in the *Phenomenology*. Spirit having attained the notion, he tells us, unfolds its existence in its own medium ("the aether of its life") as Philosophical Science, setting forth the moments of its dialectical process "as determinate notions" and not, as does the *Phenomenology*, "as determinate modes or shapes of consciousness." [32]

The first part of this philosophical science is logic, which sets out the moments, or categories of the notion, corresponding to the gamut of forms of consciousness, as pure concepts and "exhibits them ... in accordance with their immanent opposition." Logic is concerned, for the most part, with categories of the purely cognitive forms of consciousness (e.g. perception, understanding, science, etc.), and constitutes a

---

[29] Vide N. R. Hanson, *Patterns of Discovery* (Cambridge, 1958), T. Kahn, *The Structure of Scientific Revolutions* (Chicago, 1962), E. E. Harris, *Hypothesis and Perception* (London, 1970), *et al.*

[30] *Werke*, II, p. 602. (Cf. Baillie's Tr., p. 789.)

[31] *Ibid.*, p. 611. (Cf. Baillie's Tr., p. 798.)

[32] Cf. *Ibid.*, p. 617. (Cf. Baillie's Tr., p. 805.)

further phase of reflection upon those activities which operate at a prior and less self-conscious level. As perception and common sense serve as objects to empirical science, so empirical science serves as object to logic; and, of course, in doing so brings with it the lower forms of awareness as implicit objects. This must not, however, be understood as excluding other branches of knowledge (e.g. mathematics, or theology), for, as we are about to note, the application of the logical categories is universal and is not restricted to any special department of experience.

The correlation of the three parts of the Logic, the Doctrine of Being, the Doctrine of Essence and the Doctrine of the Notion, with the three main phases of experience, the immediacy of perception, mediated scientific knowledge and speculative philosophy, has some very rough justification, but is much too facile and is really inaccurate and misleading. The dialectic in its movement grows like a fugue, and in so advanced a stage as philosophical logic the whole range of less reflective experience is *aufgehoben* or involved. Hegel declares that each category of the logic is a (provisional) definition of the Absolute. [33] In other words, each category presents the whole of reality in one special aspect (or moment), and Hegel finds illustrative material for almost every category from a wide range of diverse experience and from several different branches of knowledge. One cannot, therefore, identify any special group of categories as those belonging exclusively, or even mainly, to the empirical sciences.

For instance, while it is true that perception and common sense, accepting their objects as immediate, conform to the categories of Being, who would wish to deny that, for instance, becoming (change, transition, evolution), quality, quantity, repulsion and attraction, magnitude, number and measure, were concepts essential to the empirical sciences, let alone mathematics? On the other hand, identity, difference, thing and its properties, inner and outer, possible and actual, all categories treated by Hegel under Essence, are categories of common sense just as much as they are categories of science. Nor can science, at least in its methodology, dispense with the categories of the Subjective Notion: and those of the Objective Notion, though they might be taken as typical of certain forms of metaphysics (materialism, holism, finalism, for instance) are clearly concepts derived from and operative in the special sciences. One may say that Hegel's logic as a whole is a logic of the empirical sciences, but also,

[33] Cf. *Enz.*, §85.

at the same time, much more; for it is also a logic of levels of thought both below and beyond empirical science. In it natural science is *aufgehoben*, is preserved while it is also surpassed, abolished and annulled. It is preserved in as much as the logical categories are its categories; it is annulled and surpassed insofar as the logician knows the categories as at once *Denkbestimmungen* and principles of the real (definitions of the Absolute). For logic subject and object are one, whereas for science the object is external and merely observed, treated from the outside, classified, analysed and the like, by an observer and theorist who does not recognize it (or at best very dimly) as the embodiment of the logical principles in terms of which he is thinking.

Desirable as it may be, it is hardly possible in an essay such as this to discuss in detail the special relevance of various logical categories to the empirical sciences. It is sufficient to point out that on numerous occasions Hegel uses instances from science to illustrate his exposition. He is particularly fond of calling attention to electrical and magnetic polarity as an analogy to, yet an inadequate exemplification of, dialectical opposition, as well as, in particular, a special case embodying the category of difference in the form of positive and negative contrariety.[34] In the larger *Logic* he uses the notion of gravity and its relation to a house standing upon its foundation, to a falling body and to the trajectory of a projectile, as illustrative of the category of ground.[35] But, of course, he is far from confining himself to scientific examples, for, as we have said, the logic reflects upon the whole range of human experience, and art, religion and philosophy provide instantiating material as well as science.

Sometimes Hegel adjudicates between the attitudes of these different fields of knowledge, as, when he is discussing the correlation of force and its expression, he vindicates the scientific attitude against that of the more bigoted form of religion – the demand to specify and explain natural phenomena in terms of laws, as against the dogmatic assertion that it is all the work of an omnipotent God.[36]

6. SCIENCE AND THE PHILOSOPHY OF NATURE

As the *Phenomenology* culminated in Absolute Knowledge, which was philosophy, and is forthwith elaborated in the *Encyclopaedia of*

[34] Cf. *Enz.*, §119.
[35] *Werke*, IV, p. 578. A. V. Miller's Tr., pp. 463–64.
[36] *Enz.*, §136, *Zusatz* 2.

Philosophical Sciences, so philosophy in its logical phase culminates in the Absolute Idea, effecting another *enroulement sur soi-meme* (to borrow a phrase from Teilhard de Chardin). This logical phase of philosophy is the mind's reflection upon its own cognitive experience in common sense, science, art, morals and religion. In each and all of these it is confronted by an object, which is really itself in its prior phases summed up as a whole in the one immediately preceding. But the object is not recognized as such but is seen as an other set over against the subject. Yet in each of these cognitive forms in different ways the mind discovers its own principle in and as its object. This discovery, however, at the stage in question is only *für uns* – for us who are reflecting upon it philosophically – not *für sich*, for itself. At the philosophical level, however, we who are reflecting are identical with it (the knowing mind) and the identity of object with subject is grasped *an und für sich*. The identity of subject and object aware of itself as such is the absolute idea – the ultimate realization of logical reflection in and as the notion (*Begriff*).

But logic realized the identity only in the form of notion, only as idea, the true significance of which is that the idea is no mere idea but is the truth of the world of nature – "the truth is actual and must exist." Philosophy, therefore, returns to nature as revealed in science and gives a new reflective account of it as the implicit idea – the idea in the form of externality or other-being – the manifestation of spirit as the world in space and time.

The philosophy of nature, the second phase of philosophy, is therefore a further phase of self-consciousness, taking as its object (as before) itself in prior phase (absolute idea). As the second main division of philosophy (absolute knowledge), it stands in opposition to logic, an opposition which is resolved in the philosophy of mind. But, *qua* philosophy, the *Naturphilosophie* has this reconciliation already implicit in it, because it *is* philosophy – it is mind reflecting upon its own experience, and so it is in itself a reconciliation of opposites, namely, the logical idea, on the one hand, and the observed world of science on the other.

Whereas the scientist sees the world as a congeries of external phenomena, linked together by causal laws, the philosopher of nature sees in it the immanent idea, sees nature as mind implicit or potential. His task is to understand what nature is as a whole and he asks himself the question: What is nature? – a question that the natural scientist either does not raise, or, if he does, he seeks the answer in the details, which are endless, and fails to see the wood for the trees.[37] The difference between *Naturphilosophie* and empirical science is, therefore, one of point of view, the former is synoptic and self-reflective, whereas the latter is as we have already seen, observational. In the philosophy of nature the activity of reason is full blown while in natural science it is only "instinctive" and largely intuitive.

Naturphilosophie, in consequence, is not a high-falutin attempt to supplant natural science or to do its work over again more adequately. It must accept the pronouncements and discoveries of natural science as the source of its material. It cannot supplant it because it cannot dispense with it. "Not only must philosophy be in accordance with the experience of nature, but the emergence and formation of the philosophical science has empirical physical science as its presupposition and condition."[38] Hegel's intellectual integrity with respect to science is, in fact, marked. Contrary to what is often alleged of him, he makes no attempt to dictate to the sciences or pontificate on what their results should be. The old libel, that he declared, on *a priori* grounds, that there could not be more than seven planets, has long since been exposed as false and whoever invented it had certainly not read the *Naturphilosophie*, from which it is apparent that he knew of the existence of Uranus and several of the planetoids.[39] Nor is the more plausible accusation that the philosophy of nature is an attempt to deduce the details of the physical universe from *a priori* principles, any better founded. Hegel repudiates and disapproves any claim of this sort. He treats the accusation (which was made against him in his own life-time) with the contempt it deserves in his reply to Herr Krug, who demanded that he should deduce, from his principles, the existence of his pen.[40]

What Hegel does in his philosophy of nature is to accept the scientific knowledge of his own day as material from which to construct an "idea of nature" – a world-picture or *Weltanschauung* (in a somewhat narrower sense than that usually understood in German) – that shows the world of nature to be an exposition, in spatio-temporal, material form, of the Idea proper. As such it will both be a self-complete,

[37] Cf. *Naturphilosophie, Einleitung, Werke* IX, p. 33. A. V. Miller's Translation (*Hegel's Philosophy of Nature*, Oxford 1970) p. 3.

[38] *Enz.*, § 246.

[39] *Vide Werke* IX, p. 149. A. V. Miller's Tr., p. 82 – nor even Hegel's Inaugural Dissertation of 1801: see Bernard Baumont, "Hegel and the Seven Planets," *Mind*, LXIII, 1954, pp. 246–248.

[40] *Enz.*, § 250, footnote.

internally coherent whole and it will have a dialectical structure. There will be immanent in it that movement of thought which, in consciousness, led up to absolute knowledge, and, in logic, to the absolute idea. Consequently, we find in Hegel's conception of nature two features which were not especially characteristic of the science of his time, and there results a tension and oscillation in his treatment of it, between faithfulness to established scientific theory and speculative venture, which does credit both to his intellectual integrity and to his philosophic penetration.

(i) The holistic cast of his thought leads Hegel to realize that the truly fruitful aspiration of the scientist is towards the construction of a coherently systematic theory, which expresses itself as the belief in the harmonious and ultimately rational character of the physical world. Thus he applauds Kepler's faith in the *harmonia mundi* (which has more recently been voiced in no less insistent tones by Einstein), and defends Kepler's view of planetary motion against Newton's as conceptually sounder. There is undoubtedly an element of nationalistic partiality in his obvious preference for Kepler, "the German," over Newton, "the Englishman"; but he eulogizes Kepler especially for his "absolute faith that resaon must be [embodied] in" the facts of planetary motion, and there is a sound epistemological principle implicit in Hegel's appraisal, which most other philosophers of science fail to recognize. It *is* the urge to find a reasonably unified system that leads scientists to their discoveries and is the motive power of scientific advance. Copernicus states it explicitly as his reason for advancing the heliocentric hypothesis. In their dismissal of Kepler's early astronomical theory, correlating the orbits with the regular solids, for instance, commentators usually fail to observe that it was this venture in geometrical organization that led him to make the important scientific move of measuring planetary distances from the Sun's centre (the "true Sun") instead of (as had been done previously) from the centre of the Earth's orbit (the so-called "mean Sun"). It is, perhaps, Newton's profession of radical empiricism, at least as much as his nationality, that Hegel finds distasteful, but he does not give Newton credit for those scientific speculations, especially in the last book of the *Opticks*, which are by no means consistent with his admonitions elsewhere against the framing of hypotheses.

In defending Kepler's conception of the movement of the planets, Hegel stresses the fact that their motion is a single curved movement, and he inveighs against Newton's analysis of it into two rectilinear movements, one tangential to the curve and the other radial. The protest is against the rigid divisions and separations of the Understanding. His point is that the two elements in the planet's motion are not two separate and accidentally combined forces, producing separate rectilinear courses, neither of which is actually pursued, and which could not actually be combined to constitute an elliptical curve. "The motion of the heavenly bodies," he says, "is no such hither and thither drag (*Hin- und Hergezogensein*), but free movement; they go on their way, as the Ancients said, like the blessed Gods."[41] So poetic, and apparently wild, a description of the astronomical facts is apt to be laughed to scorn by the hard-headed scientist. Yet Eddington made this quotation a text on which to elaborate his own version of the movement of the planets in the new light of relativity theory in the twentieth century.[42] This, he maintains, justifies precisely that view of planetary motion which would vindicate Hegel's contention.

On the other hand, Hegel's prejudices in favour of the German astronomer led him altogether to suppress the fact that Kepler too believed that the planet was pushed and pulled. He thought the circular tendency of its motion was the result of a thrusting power of solar light as the Sun turned on its own axis; and that the elliptical shape of the orbit, along with the deceleration of the planet at aphelion, was to be accounted for by a certain inertia or "laziness" on the part of the planet itself.

Yet surely Hegel is not wrong to insist that what must here be conceived is not a collection or a bundle of forces, but a single movement along a geodesic determined by the total configuration of the system.[43] And that is exactly how present-day astronomers would wish to describe the fact.

(ii) The second characteristic of Hegel's view of nature, which produced the kind of tensions mentioned above, is the immanence of the dialectical movement, on which he insists. The processes of a dialectically structured world should be essentially teleological and evolutionary. But in his day the conception of evolution had not yet been accepted by biologists as scientifically established. It was only in the year of Hegel's death that Darwin sailed in the *Beagle* to the Gallapagos Islands.

Yet, what is remarkable about Hegel's treatment of the scientific

---

[41] *Enz.*, § 269, *Zusatz*, *Werke*, IX, p. 123. (Cf. A. V. Miller's Tr., p. 65.)
[42] Cf. *The Nature of the Physical World* (Cambridge, 1948), pp. 147–151.
[43] Cf. *Enz.*, 269.

detail is that he never allows his philosophical insight to dictate what the scientist ought to find or what nature ought to reveal, but he adheres closely to the scientifically accepted theories of the day, even though that philosophical insight constantly prompts him to statements and interpretations which foreshadow later development in science. His faithful adherence to what in his time was held to be scientifically respectable led him to reject the notion of biological evolution, convenient though it would have been to him to accept it. At the time when he wrote it was, at best, a very speculative hypothesis, which had indeed been put forward by Erasmus Darwin (Charles' grandfather), Geoffroi St. Hilaire and Lamarck, but which lacked the support of empirical evidence. [44] The geological evidence of fossils which had already been discovered he explains away – not, like Professor Scheuchzer of Zürich, as "the damaged skeleton of a poor sinner drowned in the Deluge" – but as the results of an "organic-plastic" impulse immanent in the physical elements, which produces likenesses of living forms which are not themselves organic.

On the other hand, he takes over from Cuvier the hypothesis that the early history of the Earth was marked by a series of cataclysms (without accepting the explanation this provided of the fossil record), and that of spontaneous generation which was current before the experiments of Pasteur proved it false.

This conscientious adherence to what science had established and refusal to postulate as empirical fact what had not been observed, leads to a discrepancy between Hegel's logical and metaphysical insights, on the one hand, and what he accepts as scientifically supported fact, on the other; and this he attributes to "the weakness of nature" (*die Ohnmacht der Natur*), its inability, as the merely self-external and repetitive manifestation of spirit, neatly and precisely to exemplify the categories and moments of the Idea.

But he is unshakably convinced that the Idea is immanent in every natural form and process and that the dialectic is "the principle of all movement and all activity." "Nature," he says, "is only implicitly the

[44] It is not my intention to suggest that Hegel would necessarily have endorsed every aspect of every theory (supposing he could have known of it) that has come to be accepted since his day. He would no doubt have rejected, or at least criticized, the more mechanistic aspects of Darwinism. That the sole agencies at work in evolution are chance variation and natural selection is not held, even today, by all biologists. Nor is the belief necessary to an evolutionary conception of nature that biological evolution can be explained wholly and adequately in these terms. To conceive the process as a dialectical progression is more illuminating and more fruitful. (See my argument in *The Foundations of Metaphysics in Science*, especially Chapters XII and XIII).

Idea, therefore Schelling called it 'petrified' and others 'frozen intelligence.' But God does not remain stony and dead; the stones cry out and raise themselves to Spirit." [45] The idea that nature is in some sense at least potentially alive and evolutionary is deeply embedded in Hegel's thought, and, for all his scepticism of biological evolution and his rejection of the view that the forms of nature and the species of plants and animals actually develop one from another, he cannot refrain from expressing the evolutionary concept if only in poetic form. The history of the Earth, he tells us, goes back beyond any existence of life and consciousness, to ages when its dormant spirit was merely, as it were, in gestation (*in sich selbst gährend*); when its life was "the movement and dreams of one that sleeps, until it awakens and achieves its consciousness in Mankind." [46]

This conviction of the immanent dialectic in nature enables him to see, at times, in the forms and phenomena of nature, what the science of his day had not yet discovered, but what has since become sound, scientific doctrine. What the thinking of the understanding regards as separate and mutually independent, reason sees as moments of a single unity. So Hegel, in nature-philosophy, can transcend the abstract "absolutes" of Newtonian mechanics to assert the inseparable interdependence of space and time, and their essential union in motion. He maintains that position in space apart from motion and succession in time, is meaningless, [47] anticipating the ideas on which, in our day, the Theory of Relativity has come to be founded. Similarly, he foreshadows twentieth century conceptions of matter when he alleges that the structure observable in the solar system is equally inherent in all matter down to the least detail. [48] Again, his doctrine of light as the realization of space anticipates relativity theory. Light, he says, is the pure actual (*daseiende*) power to fill space. Space itself is "mere abstract subsistence or implicit being, while light is the actual being in itself, or that which is in itself and, therefore, pure presentness – the power of universal actuality, to be outside itself, as the possibility which coalesces with everything, that which is in community with everything that remains in it." [49] Compare this with E. A. Milne's statement that space is not *per se* an object of perception, but only a locus for perceived objects.

---

[45] Enz., § 247, *Zusatz; Werke* IX, p. 50. (Cf. A. V. Miller's Tr., p. 14f.)
[46] *Enz.*, § 339, *Zusatz* 2; *Werke* IX, p. 463. (Cf. A. V. Miller's Tr., p. 282.)
[47] *Werke* IX, pp. 78f. and 87ff. A. V. Miller's Tr., pp. 34–35 and 40–41. Cf. Findlay's comment, *Hegel, A Re-examination*, p. 275.
[48] Cf. *Werke* IX p. 151. A. V. Miller's Tr., p. 83f.
[49] *Werke* IX, p. 157. (Cf. A. V. Miller's Tr., p. 87f.)

Observation of objects in space implies a causal chain linking the object with the percipient, namely light. Space without light has no physical geometry and so no physical properties, thus it is the spreading light wave that creates physical space. [50]

Had the scientific knowledge which is available to us in our time been at Hegel's disposal, how much more powerful a case he could have made for the system which he advocated! He might then have had second thoughts about *die Ohnmacht der Natur*, and have found more reliable evidence of dialectical process in the whole range of natural phenomena than was open to him at the turn of the 18th century. The science of today accepts without demur the conception of nature as a continuous process from radiant energy (or even prior to that, from space-time) to elementary particles and from these to atoms, molecules and crystals. The dividing line between the inorganic and the organic has been blurred and the original evolution of life from the non-living is accepted (if not yet explained). Within the living kingdom the evolution of species is the theory universally held, and the continuity of physiology with conscious experience is widely taken for granted.

In this continuum of developing forms there are evident dialectical relationships, quite apart from those (like the polarity of the magnet) which Hegel noticed, and more integral to the developmental process. Radiant energy stands at least in *prima facie* opposition to matter, as active to inert, yet in the elementary particle the two are united. Each can pass away into the other, and the particle exemplifies both at once according to Bohr's principle of complementarity. The inorganic is opposed to the organic, as dissipating to self-maintaining – processes of increasing entropy as opposed to steady-state open systems – yet chemistry and organism are united and reconciled in metabolism. In the ontogenesis of the vertebrate three stages have been distinguished forming a typical Hegelian triad. The first, in which the fertilized ovum divides and segments without differentiation; the second, in which cells differentiate and different groups develop functionally in different and virtually independent ways, though always mutually complementary; and the third, in which the whole system is united and co-ordinated by the development of nervous and vascular systems.

These are but isolated examples, typical of contemporary scientific discovery, and indicative of a new view of nature as a continuous

[50] E. A. Milne, "Fundamental Concepts of Natural Philosophy" *Proceedings of the Royal Society of Edinburgh*, Sec. A., Vol. 62, 1943–44, Pt. I.

dialectical process that is essentially Hegelian in character. For Hegel saw the universe as a single dialectical whole, in which the dualisms and pluralisms of past philosophies (many of which are still with us) were resolved, while the multiplicity of forms which they recognized was preserved and rendered intelligible as moments in, and successive dialectical phases of, a single burgeoning process.

REFLEXIVE ASYMMETRY:
HEGEL'S MOST FUNDAMENTAL
METHODOLOGICAL RUSE

J. N. FINDLAY

Boston University

PREFATORY NOTE

The paper here printed was given to the Philosophical Seminar of Freiburg University in Western Germany in June 1971. It was not intended to be an essay in heavy scholarship, but a philosophical interpretation and defence of some of Hegel's basic logical principles in modern terms and a modern context. Hence the absence of detailed documentation: those familiar with the Logic will know that what are being dealt with are whole stretches of the Dialectic, long studied at close quarters and now seen from a considerable distance. Its most important suggestions from the epistemological angle of the present volume are the following:

(1) That the basic categories in the light of which the world is to be understood fall into three different groups: (a) the Descriptive Categories or Categories of mere Being, in terms of which items and facts are distinctively characterized, placed, numbered and measured but never seen as requiring explanation; (b) the Explanatory Categories or Categories of Essence, in which we are forced beneath the descriptive surface and postulate permanent simple natures, forces, laws and such-like which explain surface variety – such explanation always leads us on to something else and never achieves finality; (c) the Self-Explanatory Categories or Categories of the Notion, in which explanation becomes circular and explanans and explananda identical. Universals functioning in thought, organisms in nature, and cognition and volition in the mind's intercourse with the world function in this self-explanatory way: they make everything alien into an instrument, a presupposition or a form of themselves.

(2) That the Descriptive Categories logically demand completion by the Explanatory Categories, and the latter by the Self-explanatory Categories. And within each group of categories there is a logical line leading from more incomplete, superficial to more complete, deep-going categories. But this logical line is not understood by those using the categories in question, who think them all independent, and often do not advance beyond lower ones. Only the logician sees them all, and the requirement of later by earlier ones.

(3) That Hegel's transformation of lower categories into higher ones does

not introduce a dangerous instability into the realm of logical meanings. Even in the ordinary logic of modality, a meaning is transformed by the modalizations with which we qualify it, and yet in a sense remains the same. "The imagination of probable rain" in a sense conserves, but also sublates, the ordinary sense of "rain."

(4) That Hegelianism is an extraordinary monism which perpetually postulates and yet perpetually "sublates" and modalizes otherness. Everything demands a context of others which, at a higher level of discourse, are identified with the original item. Identity is in fact only fully meaningful as at once positing and sublating otherness. It is only as this becomes fully lucid and is made into a principle that one enters the sphere of the Self-explanatory Categories.

(5) Neither "thinking" nor "reality" is as such ultimate: what is ultimate is the living universality of the Absolute Idea which is itself in them both. Knowledge is a categorial pattern which is not the last thing in the logical development of the Absolute Idea, which latter must accordingly transcend transcendentalism. But the Absolute Idea in a sense "leaves everything as it is," only "bracketed" in its all-explanatory self-explanatoriness.

(6) It is helpful to characterize the modalizing movements of the Logical Idea as "ruses" (*Liste*). (Cf. *Die List der Vernunft.*) This guards against any settling down into the one-sided clarity and fixity of meaning of a definite "solution." Circular movement is the only legitimate form of philosophical rest.

The aim of this paper is to suggest that while there are innumerable distinct ideas or principles at which Hegel arrives in the course of his systematic exposition – the primacy of spirit, the Bad and True Infinites, the Concrete Universal, the Passage of Quantity into Quality, etc. etc. – and innumerable distinct methodological devices by means of which he is able to move from one stage of his argument to the next – the collapse into immediacy, the discovery of a difference without a difference, the conversion of an identification of *A* with *B* into an identification of *B* with *A*, etc. – all these distinct ideas and devices can be regarded as specifying a single *idée mère* which is also a sovereign methodological ruse. I shall call this *idée mère* or sovereign ruse that of Reflexive Asymmetry or Self-repulsive Attraction, but it is also what is less dynamically conveyed by the phrase Identity-in-Difference, as also by talk of Self-specifying and Self-individualizing Universality, etc., etc.

In speaking of this central feature of Hegel's performance as a ruse, I am only half-suggesting that there is something underhand or sophistical about it. There are, of course, many sophistically tricky passages in Hegel, as there are in Socrates or in Kant or in many other of the greatest philosophers, places where some important insight is

too ill-worked out to be put forward in its genuine, inchoate form, but
has to be veiled in an appearance of clarity and rigour, so that one may
pass on to the next more important, relatively clear issue. After all,
the truth is the whole, and those who refuse to consider it till they can
circumambulate it on a perfectly paved circuit never see it at all. Not
all have the gift of Plato of being ironically yet profoundly playful
when they cannot as yet be well-worked out and clear. I am not,
however, when I talk of Hegel's ruses, talking of the numberless small
deceits by which he covers up an obscurity in meaning or a slide or gap
in argument: I am rather talking of deceits which are, on his view, part
and parcel of the Cunning of Reason, which represent a certain
twistedness or deviousness in the very make-up of the Absolutely
Real itself. For on Hegel's view Dialectic is no adventitious art which,
by winnowing away falsehood, leads us to the unshaken heart of
well-rounded truth: it is, in retrospect, seen to be and to have always
been, the unshaken heart of well-rounded truth itself.

   Dialectic, however, appears to involve a mutability in conceptual
contents and an infection of them by other conceptual contents, which
is readily thought to render ordered discourse impossible. Sensible
things, as the early Plato was wont to suggest, may certainly pass from
illustrating one conceptual content to illustrating another, or may
illustrate them both in a confused manner, but conceptual contents
themselves admit of no such transitions or external mixtures, and the
modern philosophy that has been broadly called "analytic" adheres
steadfastly to this position. Hegel, however, and on his view the mature
Plato of the *Parmenides, Sophist,* etc., could see a distinction between
the in-itselfness or intrinsicality of each conceptual content, which is
as durably unchangeable as any analyst would like it to be, and what
such a content *becomes* when put into contexts necessary for the
completion of its sense, contexts which in one sense leave it exactly
as it is, yet in another sense transform it utterly, and in effect leave
not a jot of its original meaning standing. How this can be is indeed
hard to understand, and the Hegelian notion of *aufheben,* variously
translated by "superseding," "overcoming," "abolishing," "abro-
gating," "annulling," "transcending," "transforming," etc., yet always
involving the difficult double sense of both a laying up or a preserving
as well as a discarding or a laying aside – a doubleness of sense seldom
preserved in the translations – is certainly one of the most tantalizing
in philosophy. But what we have when conceptual contents enter into
transforming contexts can perhaps be most simply elucidated by

considering what happens when simple assertions are *modally* transformed, when they are put, as it were, into modal or other "brackets," when we pass, e.g., from simply asserting it to be raining to asserting the *possibility* that it should rain, or to asserting that, *in the opinion* of this one or that, it is raining.

The change which here occurs, though not exactly like what occurs in the Hegelian dialectic, has certainly occasioned almost as much difficulty to certain logicians. Obviously when we compare the fact of rain with the mere possibility or believed eventuality of rain, we have in a sense exactly the same content. There is no iota of meaning that occurs in a situation where it rains that is not exactly repeated (with of course some addition) in a situation where it is a mere possibility or a mere conceivability that it rains: a hundred actual Thalers, as Kant pointed out in a similar context, do not differ in content from a hundred merely possible or conceived Thalers. But, viewed in another light, the modal transformation makes all the difference in the world, for possible or conceived rain is not a particular sort of rain at all, not, certainly, the sort which requires us to have recourse to a rain-coat or an umbrella, and in the same way to have only a hundred conceived or possible Thalers in one's pocket is not to be richer by the same sum changed into some novel currency, but to be poorer by exactly the same sum, stated in our actual currency.

Now what Hegel invites us to consider is that contents of any sort, while in themselves having the necessary invariance which Plato attributes to his εἴδη, none the less not only *can* be, but also *must* be, incorporated in contents which are in a sense their developed selves, but which yet so utterly transform them that what we have in the end, while absolutely conservative of what we originally started with, is so entirely different that we readily take refuge in contradictions: preserved in being abolished, abolished in being preserved, the same in utter otherness and utterly other in being the same, and so on. And what we are also invited to consider is that this process of conservative transformation can be reiterated indefinitely or at least for a large number of successive stages, so that what we have at an advanced stage of the series is both an unimaginably transformed version of its earlier stages, particularly of its very early ones, and also a wholly conservative version of those earlier stages and of any transformed version of them at later stages. And Hegel also invites us to consider that while this incorporation of contents into bracketing contexts is something that *we* perform and perform in time, and while its exe-

cution in time is an important and necessary mode of its being, yet the
incorporation of such contents in transforming contexts is also
something that is what it is without relation to time or to our manner
of conceiving it. The content A, its bracketed and transformed version
(A) ..., its doubly bracketed and transformed version $((A ...) ...,$
and so on, are all incorporated in a later or perhaps final unity,
which we can then contemplate as a unity without running through
its serially arranged members one by one.

Hegel also invites us to consider that this bracketing or conservative
transformation of contents in wider contexts takes place on three
planes, as it were, to which the three sections of his systematic work
are devoted. It can be studied, and also has its operation and being, on
the plane of pure essentialities, of Platonic abstracta divorced from
sensuous concretion, in which it will have no relation at all to time,
though notions analogous to temporality may well have a place in it.
It can be considered and also has its being on the plane of reality, in
which it manifests itself in the unchanging order of natural forms in
space and in the developing order of spiritual and social forms in time.
It can finally be considered and also has it being on the plane of that
subjective acquaintance that can get better and better acquainted
with it in time: this "getting better and better acquainted with the
whole order of bracketings in time" can itself be considered in time
and as a sort of temporal series, but it can also be considered in a single,
total historical perspective in which, of course, it ceases to be in time.

Hegel has various other opinions which his use of the method of
bracketing transformation is meant to establish: that the series of
bracketings has a natural terminus, or dies down into a certain
stationariness in which further bracketings would merely coincide with
former ones and thus make no difference, that it can proceed only along
one single, unramifying route, and that the subjectivity which runs
through the whole series also appears in its *finale,* and so yields us an
ultimate idealism or spiritualism, whether in essentiality or in reality
or in personal discovery. These final Hegelian opinions have much
less mandatory acceptability than the methods by which they are
reached, and it is plain that Hegel does not invariably endorse them,
and certainly does not always follow them in his practice.

I have, however, only given this extremely condensed, slightly
offtarget account of what Hegel understands by the dialectical nature
of thought-contents, thinking and reality, because I wish it to be seen
as something eminently acceptable in principle, and not at all unlike

what happens when a series of modalizations is continuously carried
out. When we consider the series formed by a simple assertion, the
negation of the same, the assertion of the possibility of its negation, the
necessity of this possibility or the knowledge that someone has of this
necessity, we have a series in which the original sense of an assertion
is preserved with rigour, and is in fact the necessary foundation of the
whole series, but which none the less gets progressively transformed
by the modal transformations which are heaped up on it and are
themselves modalized in further bracketings. The Hegelian transformations are of course different in character and more interesting than the
simple series we have been considering: they are held to be mandatory
and not facultative, they at times involve bracketings of numerous
terms in a single context, as when an infinite series becomes a simple
variable, or reciprocal bracketings of one term by another (as when
essence posits accident and accident essence), and they tend towards
a final stationariness where further bracketing will make no difference.
But by and large they involve nothing more destructively self-contradictory than is met with in the ordinary logic of modality.

I am not, however, concerned with the generalities of the Dialectic
but with one special ruse that is constantly operating in it, and which
gives it its predominantly triadic rather than merely dyadic character.
This ruse as I said I propose to call that of Reflexive Asymmetry, and
I propose to introduce it by recalling what interested me vastly many
years ago, when I first read Russell's *Principles of Mathematics* in regard
to the issues raised by closed as opposed to open series. Russell tells
us that series are generated by relations that are asymmetrical,
transitive and irreflexive (and also "connected" – which is not,
however, important for our purposes), relations that imply a radical
difference of position among their terms so that if A stands in such a
relation to B, B does not so stand to A but in a differently converse
manner, and they also imply a carry-over from A to C if A has them
to B and B to C; it seems a mere consequence of such asymmetry that
they invariably relate something to something *else* and never to itself.
As asymmetry is normally defined, this consequence obtains, but there
are types of series that make it doubtful whether it should be thought
of as obtaining. Thus the relations left of and right of, and the relations
west of and east of, certainly seem to merit the name "asymmetrical."
They place their terms in a different relative position and as it were
alienate them from each other, and yet anyone who has sat at a round
table knows that by the very relation that arranges guests round the

table, he is both seven places to the right and seven places to the left of himself, and likewise fourteen and twenty-one and so on places to the right and left of himself, and so in a sense occupies an infinite number of distinct places and fulfills an infinite number of distinct roles in relation to himself. And New York is 25,000 miles West and East of New York, and likewise any multiple of that mileage to the East and West of itself, all of which as it were pluralizes and 'others' New York from New York. If a simpler example is needed, need I go further than the mirrors in an old-fashioned barber's shop – one wonders whether such mirrors may not have featured in Hegel's early haircutting experiences in Stuttgart – which generate innumerable *reflexions* of what can be established to be the same small boy himself. Now formal logicians make short work of closed series: they find ways to break down closure and to turn closed series into open ones in which no term occurs twice. Hegel, however, employed as his central philosophical ruse the generation of open series which he then proceeded to close, so that they became, as his phrase is, *zurückgebogen*, turned back to self. They lead back to self even more ineluctably than do ordinary closed series since there are no intercalated terms between self and self which are not also variants of self. We may say, in fact, that Hegel operates on two extraordinary axioms: (I) that all cases of diversity, otherness, are "really" cases of asymmetrical self-relatedness, that one can only be *other* than anything if one is also, at an immediate or remoter remove, identical with it; (II) that all cases of self-identity entail some form of otherness, one can only be identical with anything if one is also other than it, and in fact only identical with oneself if one is also other than, distanced from oneself. One is tempted to say that Hegel works on a new principle: that all diversity is really only diversity of role, and that there is really only one single thing diversified by taking up innumerable asymmetrical roles in relation to itself.

One must not, however, make the matter too simple since we do not wish to deprive the ordinary notion of diversity of all its force, nor to bring all things together in an undifferentiated identity – the night, as Hegel famously phrased it, in which every cow is black – which is not even a significant identity since there is nothing to oppose it, and since even the difference of role, which is brought in to diversify it, will vanish in the maw of the same or some higher identity. Diversity, otherness, as the sheer exclusion of a thing from a thing, or of an experience from an experience, or of an abstract moment from an abstract moment, may be something that must in the end be itself transformed in an ultimately valid conception, but it cannot be so transformed unless it has a certain resistant significance, and so by contrast must also be the case in regard to the sheer exclusion of sheer diversity which for many is what they wish to understand by identity. Hegelianism in fact believes that such sheer diversity, and the sheer exclusion of such diversity which counts as identity, have a necessary first-order place in experience, meaning and reality, the place preempted by the Understanding, the sheerly othering factor in mind, meaning and the world. This is so much the case that no experience, no notional meaning and no reality can in fact *be* without being set among what at first pass for sheerly other experiences, notional meanings or realities, by contrast with which it alone is precisely what it is. And at the level at which the matter first presents itself, the others which surround it are not given as simply itself in another guise, or as itself squintingly seen apart from itself; if this were the case, the whole masquerade would lose all sense and all substance, and would have absolutely nothing in it from which truth and reality could be elicited. The matter does not, however, stay at this point of sheer diversity and sheerly contrasted identity, but gets bracketed or sublated for Hegel in what is now describable as a "deeper" identity, which can be said to underlie and to have been active in all such othering. This description is itself taken from a "deeper" standpoint which sees what must have been there "all along," though it did not declare itself "at the time," and it conserves, while sublating, the sheer diversity and sheer identity at first presented, as necessary to this very sublation. And so much are this sheer diversity and sheer identity *not* merely negated, that they necessarily break out again at a higher stage of the argument. The "deeper" identity which has shown itself in and through the original sheer diversity and contrasted sheer identity, is now itself in the position of logically requiring a sheer diversity with which it may be sheerly contrasted, and this logically leads to the emergence of another still deeper identity which can now be held responsible both for the self-repulsion which led to the second diversification and for the new identification which has overridden it. And so the game proceeds, and one is never in a position of sheerly outlawing sheer diversities, but only of overriding them in profounder identities.

The identity in which Hegelianism believes has accordingly as many levels as the sheer diversities that it overrides. The abstract identity of something like the smell of camphor or an entity of physics or the ratio of three to seven, an identity not very variably specified in context, is the most empty and superficial form of identity, the identity of the morning star with the evening star is somewhat less of the surface, the identity of a man in youth with a man in age is yet more genuine, and so is the identity of a man's mental with a man's bodily or cerebral being, an identity which can be worked both ways and not merely in the one way favoured by a confused modern materialism. Beyond this we get to even more genuine identities which the hard-headed and tough-minded like to call "metaphorical": the identity of a man's spirit with the spirit of those who are his associates in a culture or in the common life of reason, and the identity of man's understanding with the natural world in whose workings it discovers a reflection of its own concepts and manners of thinking. If it be protested that to discover all these deep identities is merely to obfuscate issues, let it be replied that issues are much more obfuscated if we assume there to be sheerly diverse, and therefore mysteriously related entities wherever differences can be predicated. Such a view has dirempted the flow of time into an infinity of infinitely separated phases among which it is not clear how continuous progression is thinkable, and it has dirempted the continuous growing of effects out of their causes into a sheer succession of occurrences between which no rational nexus can be discerned. The belief that sheer diversity is logically impossible, and that diversity is thinkable only to the extent that it can be subordinated to unity, at least prompts us to look for unifying explanations, whereas the belief in the logical possibility of wholly unsubordinated diversity makes it unnecessary and unreasonable to look for unifying explanations at all. We shall not, however, argue for Hegel's type of self-pluralizing monism or self-unifying pluralism against those who do not desire comprehensive intelligibility in thought or the world.

Hegel's remarkable notion of self-othering identity can of course be traced back to his immediate predecessors, in particular to Fichte and Schelling. The Fichtean Ego is not anything that first is there and then is self-conscious; it is there only in being conscious of self, in differentiating itself into a subjective and objective aspect which then are identified. And Fichte assumes that there are no other objects for the Ego but the Ego itself: what it sees as an object projected in front of itself is in fact only its own energy bent back upon itself and returning to the centre from which it streamed forth, and having a seemingly alien character which is none the less always being overcome in the process of theoretically understanding it and in practically remoulding it. Theory and practice are in fact the palpable demonstration of the non-absolute character of the subject-object diversity. By this strange, self-departing self-returningness Fichte manages to give some sense to the intractable obscurity which surrounds the accommodation of objectivity to subjectivity in the system of Kant. Schelling in his *System of Transcendental Idealism* largely repeats these notions, but in his remarkable, early nature-philosophical papers and System of Identity writings carries their logic yet further in that he makes them be two-sided, objectivity and subjectivity being the *two* fundamental differentiations of the one basic Identity, *either* of which can be regarded as logically embracing the other, so that a whole range of universal "potencies" and individualities arises, each involving a differently ordered hierarchy of subjectivity embracing objectivity or of objectivity rising to subjectivity. (I am very far from understanding Schelling satisfactorily.) But in Hegel the notion of self-repelling self-coalescing unity assumes a more general, strictly logical form, and is as much illustrated by the way qualities fight against and also accord with other qualities, or forces solicit and are solicited by other forces with which they join in a joint expression, as it is by the relations of subject to object or of object to subject. This change to the logical is undoubtedly due to the influence, in the early years of the last century, of the later dialogues of Plato, and particularly of the Platonic *Parmenides* in which Hegel saw "the greatest work of art of the antique dialectic and the true revelation and positive expression of the life of God" (*Phenomenology*, p. 57). There one had the Idea of Absolute Unity which, while holding itself aloof in its own being, none the less was able to reveal as contained in itself, the whole range of logical, mathematical, spatial and temporal ideas. And Hegel also saw in the Platonic *Timaeus* an account of the way in which the One and Selfsame is not merely "othered" in the range of the Ideas but also in the whole range of the instantial world. I am not, however, proposing to investigate fully the origins of Hegel's basic conceptions, but to argue how interesting and explanatory and above all how self-consistent they are. They are superior as explanations since they do not end in a dualism or a pluralism in which no term explains the presence or character of the others nor yet in a featureless monism in which no differentiation is understandable. Hegel's Absolute requires the sheer diversities and oppositions which by explaining it also transforms and negates. And the identity towards which it works is not the mere neutrality which is equally revealed in different fundamental ways as in the thought of Schelling, but always has a resultant character in which one form of being or thought subordinates or brackets all the others.

Having sketched Hegel's fundamental logical ruse of positing a sheer diversity necessary to give sense to a sheer identity, and then taking the former back into the latter so that a transformed identity now gives sense to the transformed set of its own differences, I shall now try to show in principle how this ruse operates in the three departments with which Hegel concerned himself, the Logic, the Phenomenology of Spirit and the *Realphilosophie*. (I include in the last-named both the Nature-philosophy and the Philosophy of Spirit, which form a continuous treatment.) But I shall concentrate on the Logic because I regard it as the centrally important section of Hegel's mature thought.

The Logic of Hegel continues an enterprise with which his predecessors Kant, Fichte and Schelling had also concerned themselves: the Deduction of the Categories, meaning by the Categories a set of basic formal notions from which the concrete specificity of sense and the intuitive apartness of Space and Time and even the detailed nuances of our subjective life had alike been abstracted. These concrete realities were, however, represented by categorial deputies: thus there is a Category of Quality which corresponds to the qualities of sense, a Category of Becoming which represents the dialectical seriality of which temporality is the concrete existence, a Category of Cognition which is the peculiar formal pattern of Subject-Objectivity of which actual knowledge is the illustration, and so on. Hegel's Deduction of the Categories is, however, dialectical to an extent to which the work of his predecessors only distantly approximated. For he was not content to range categories side by side as coordinate notional approaches, but rather to treat them in depth, certain categories being regarded as more immediate and more of the surface than others, and the more superficial categories having no other destiny but to reveal their roots in the deeper categories by which they were "superseded," but in which supersession their original sense was still, in "bracketed" fashion, conserved. This deduction of the categories was not, however, clear to the people who used the categories in their thinking, or who saw them embodied in the realities before them or around them. For them the categories (if they think of them) are largely an assemblage of independent notions: they do not need to think of the dialectical principles which order them into a series of increasing profundity, but we, the logicians, see those principles, and in the final categories of the system the principles in question are themselves made into explicit categories. They have been the powers behind the scenes, but they now take the centre of the stage. We shall not be far wrong in seeing in these powers behind the scenes the reflexive asymmetry of which we have been talking.

The Logic as is well known falls into three parts: the Doctrine of Being, the Doctrine of Essence and the Doctrine of the Notion. I have long found it helpful to call these three parts the Theory of the Descriptive Categories, the Theory of the Explanatory Categories and the Theory of the Self-explanatory Categories respectively. In the Doctrine of Being Hegel deals with the kind of categories that might be employed in describing the character and lay-out of the objects on one's desk without ever raising any question Why? regarding them: they are accordingly of almost exclusive interest to traditional and modern formal logicians or to wholly dedicated empiricists. They are the categories involved in recognizing distinct subjects and finding distinct qualities which mark them off from one another, in going so far as to notice absences and gaps among them, in considering them singly or in groups, and in generalizing their diversity in indefinitely many numerical and quantitative manners without ever delving below the surface or even admitting that there may be more to them than such surface existence. But Hegel also detects a profound dialectic at work beneath the merely descriptive categories which those who use them would be the last to suspect.

Thus the logician sees, as the ordinary thinker does not, that the subjects we pick out as indubitably there, without bothering as to their further qualities and relations, would be nothing whatever if not given as manifesting some determinate quality, and as set in an environment of indefinitely many other subjects otherwise qualified, in distinction from which each is whatever it is, and that, in this relation to otherness, quality necessarily becomes an insignificant surd merely serving to bring out numerical distinctness and multiplicity and quantitative range. He also sees how each numerical and quantitative determination only is what it is in a setting of indefinitely many other numerical and quantitative determinations into which it can be said to "send itself forth," and also how this infinite welter only makes sense if broken up by firm qualitative nodes, so that certain ranges of quantity and quantitative ratio correspond to definite qualities which alter dramatically when those ranges are exceeded. Only by such an association of the discrete πέρας of quality with the wholly continuous ἄπειρον of quantity can either category make sense at all. Hegel here teaches the immensely interesting, challenging doctrine that there is something inherently necessary in the connection of primary with secondary qualities in which science believes: qualities make no ultimate sense, and are not truly knowable, unless capable of being placed in a continuous quantitative scheme, but quantities in their turn make no sense and are wholly empty distinctions unless bent round into ratios which form the basis of qualitative distinctions. Hegel's arguments in this section repeatedly show us points of apparent simplicity multiplying themselves in ungovernable diversity, and then again gathering up such diversity into a higher sort of differentiated simplicity.

Surface-description never, however, really evades the reference of items to environing others which in their turn make similar references without end. We require to put a stop to this bad infinity by moving into a new dimension of depth where an invariant language of delimited disposition or underlying "nature," takes the place of a varied language of actual existence. The variable surface-qualities and quantities of things imply, or to use Hegel's term "posit,'" an unchanging underlying essence of which they are the manifestations, while the unchanging essences of things imply or posit changing qualities and quantities which are their manifestations. The function of the "essence" located under the surface of being is not idly to duplicate the variations of the surface but to gather them together into a unity in which they repose calmly together because they are only alternative *possibilities*. The important point in Hegel's treatment is that he believes that such a confinement of surface variety within a limited range of possibilities, is not a factual but a logically necessary requirement: nothing can *be* in that indefinite multiplication of alternatives in which the modern theory of chances tries to believe. Variety, even infinite variety, can only be within the firm bounds of a "nature" that contains it, and that has that genuine unity which makes us recognize it as "simple." Modern science, of course, always looks for invariant simple natures expressed in terms of musts and coulds underlying a vast variety of actual qualifications and quantifications: it is, however, ashamed to use the Aristotelian categories of essence and accident, and so has genuine difficulty in explaining why the characters of things must fall within definite, simple limits at all. But for Hegel there is no shame in explaining the sleep induced by opium by its *virtus dormitiva:* the reduplication of what actually happens in the tranquil, virtual, severely restricted medium of what can or could or would happen is a condition alike of intelligibility and of actual existence.

The thing with its various essential and accidental properties is, however, unable to sustain itself except on a background of indefinitely many other things with other properties with which it contrasts. Such a thing then becomes eroded, as a result of arguments too complex to be gone into, from being a genuine focus of properties and forces, into being a mere meeting-place where they congregate together, and from which they then flit on to other similar meeting-points in accordance with certain laws. We move into a world of infinite relativity where there are no things but only "phenomena" of an electrical, thermal or other general sort, nesting in each other's interstices and governed by characteristic laws. This welter of law-bound phenomena, however, leads us back to a sort of unitary Spinozistic Substance whose invariant nature is manifest in these changing phenomena and in the laws binding them together, and which restores the integrity of the thing by being undividedly present, with all its implied relativity, in each single thing. Substance so concentrated in centres must, however, pluralize itself in an indefinite number of distinct substances, each of which actualizes itself in modes which in their turn touch off other modes in the same and other substances in endless series. All this is naturally interpreted as in time, but the notion of a fixed openness to alternatives in varying conditions, and the actualization of a given alternative in given conditions, are notions which have a formal generality which extends beyond the temporal.

Hegel then performs one of his celebrated bending-back acts in which the open chain of causal dependence is twisted back to become a closed series in which there is a perfect reciprocity between cause and effect, the various substances having modes which, in virtue of the single common nature and necessity pervading them all, alike act upon and are acted upon by each other, and pass away in a continuous joint outcome which is the "truth" of all of them. Necessity is then said to have melted away into freedom, by which is meant that we have achieved a mutual gearedness of explanatory item into explanatory item which at a higher level of integration will yield us the self-explanatory freedom which is here only foreshadowed. (I may say that my desperate abbreviations of complex dialectical trains in the Logic cannot be said to have brought out more than their very general drift or gist.) What it is important to note is that in this whole second section of explanatory categories we have explicit playing about with categories which were at work beneath the surface in the first section and will be even more explicit in the third section: the deeper identity of qualitative and quantitative actualities which are sheerly diverse has been brought out in the concept of essence which explicitly contrasts with surface diversity. And the asymmetrical reflexivity which underlies the whole Hegelian system has then led things, with their separate essences, to become mere knots in a system of mutual interrelation in which each has its essence as it were in the other, and then to swing back to a more pervasive essentiality which, in all the interaction and mutual evocation of thing by thing, remains underlying and selfsame.

What the whole development of the Logic is, however, headed for is a passage both from the non-explanatoriness of surface-description and from the explanation-by-another that we have in the sphere of essence, to a stage where what explains assumes identity with what is explained, and we have accordingly a self-explanatory situation. This has been the mechanism working behind the stage-scenery and stage-changes all along, but it now itself assumes a fully illuminated central position on the stage. There have been philosophers before Hegel who have thought in terms of the self-existent and the *causa sui*, but it is arguable that Hegel is the first philosopher who has employed these notions successfully, since his self-explanatory principle leaves nothing outside itself and only explains itself as a result of having explained all, and gathered all into itself.

This part of the Logic is that of the Notion or *Begriff*, which now takes the place of the being of the descriptive categories as well as of the deeper-lying essence of the explanatory categories. The change to the *Begriff* does not mean that subjectivity, in the usual sense, is now taking the stage, despite the fact that the treatment of the self-explanatory categories is also called the Subjective Logic. What it means is that Universality is now the operative notion, and that things, particulars are now, as in Plato, being treated as mere shadows and parasitic reflections of what is Universal rather than *vice versa*. The change is essential, for only something universal can preserve its identity in and through apartness and mutual exclusiveness, and in fact requires apartness and mutual exclusiveness of species and instances in order to be the pervasively dominant universality that it is. This is, of course, the lesson of the Platonic *Parmenides*, where the First Part shows up the absurdity of attributing to universals the division, multiplicity and derivative status of their instances, while the Second Part shows, with even greater magnificence, the absurdity of giving a merely separate, aloof status to the Principle or Principles which underlie(s) the whole realm of distinct ideas. Hegel's *Begriff* is not a specific universal, but rather the Principle of Universality as such, but it lives inseparably in all distinct universals, and is even more livingly and inseparably present in the rich individualizations which, in their incorporation of many specific universals and their relativity to all others, become like Leibnizian monads envisioning a total world. And Hegel like Plato believes in the activity of the Universal of Universals: it can be said to "generate" its Species which, in their turn, are the only "true causes" of what falls under them. For if the true substance and being of everything is to be found in what is Universal, and if the specific and instantial is merely parasitic upon it, then to what shall we ascribe the action responsible for whatever happens or is, but to the Universality from which it flows? And if even Mind and Spirit are to be regarded as special cases of detached, active Universality, then what bounds can be set to the power of the Universal? It is only if we believe in a *second* world of self-sufficient particular instances in which the real action proceeds, that we can, like Aristotle, and others, cast doubt on the real causality of the Universal.

Hegel develops the life of the *Begriff*, the Principle of self-specifying, self-individualizing active Universality, in a fascinating study of Judgements and Syllogisms on which some British logicians, e.g. Bosanquet, have based much fine work. He passes on, however, to the region of Objects, the individualities which compose a concrete world, and which are no longer existent surface-things, or the essences behind these, but entities whose whole being consists in an incredibly diversified, deeply unified type of universality. Despite the uncomprehending strictures of existentialists, there is for Hegel no Universality more meaningful and more rich in internal logic than the individualized universality of the man Socrates or of a work of art like *Romeo and Juliet*. Such individualized universals can be conceived in the likeness of the surface things from which they are descended, in which case they become the individual units of a mechanistic system, individuating a universality which is largely abstract and external, and which leaves its individual units abstractly external and "indifferent' to one another. But such mechanistic individualization involves an implicit gearing of the units into one another, which becomes more explicit at the level of chemico-physical individuality, where separate sorts of individualization have a peculiar mutual affinity and a deep identity revealed in their periodical vanishings into a compound product. But such imperfectly dominant universality becomes more fully explicit in the profounder dominance of purpose or teleology, where countless apparently unrelated individualities and processes combine to realize an End which is their common Notion. On Hegel's view, the Universe and all that is in it are and must be a teleological system: it includes and must include elements of the mechanistic and the physico-chemical, but all these are necessarily twisted and used by a universal, immanent teleology, which is not so much concerned to press on to a goal beyond itself as to be, ever more fully, its own eternal goal. Hegel at his parents' knees was no doubt filled with a boundless belief in the power of divine providence: the providential power, without the divinity behind it, became his ultimate philosophical thought. It is the Idea, the All-Notion, which has created the world and which will redeem it in the ultimate self-lucidity which is Spirit.

The asymmetrical reflexivity which Hegel identifies with his self-explanatory Absolute, now makes itself evident in three culminating forms, the three phases of the Idea. Life is the first of these phases, the one which exhibits asymmetrical reflexivity and absolute teleology in the form of surface-being. In Life every function and organ represents the whole organism totally operative: none has a fixed character and behaviour that is not twisted and modified by the self-maintaining *nisus* of the whole, and none works on the other in a rigorous legal way which is not liable to be twisted by the needs and uses of the organism: mechanism and chemistry have a say in the life of the organism but never the last word. Hegel holds, even more audaciously, that everything that impinges on the organism from without is necessarily jolted out of its own rhythms and caught up into the rhythms of the organism, so that the whole of nature is really bracketed in what is organic. A readiness to subordinate itself to the organisms in their midst and to do practical homage to them is in fact built into even the least organized natural substances, so that organisms, though perhaps fully occupying only a small segment of the universe, really dominate and pervade the whole. They have a titular sway even over the lifeless spaces of the moon, since even there all is ready for organic incorporation in proper circumstances. (Needless to say, not an example culled from Hegel.) It is for the sake of organisms that everything in the organic world can be held to exist, and that in a plain, logical sense of the word: nothing can be said to exist for the sake of what is unorganized, nor can the latter be said to make *use* of anything, since it can have no intrinsic ends for which anything can be used, or for the sake of which it can be. And organisms in virtue of the self-directed teleology which pervades their individuality necessarily expand themselves into other individualities of the same species, or into other species of the same genus, in all of which Life as active universality affirms its continuous identity.

The teleology of Life is, however, carried to a yet further culmination in the even more overriding teleology of conscious and self-conscious Subjectivity which here for the first time enters the logical scene. Conscious subjectivity is, logically speaking, the status of a Universality loosened and detached from immediate connection with concrete individuality, but going forth from such detachment into a yet more intimate and ultimate union with the individuality from which it has thus detached itself, the union, on the one hand, of Theoretical Cognition, where detached Universality *discovers* itself in the mundane universality that surrounds it, and, on the other hand, of Practical Volition, which *imposes* its organizing pattern on the world around it. Cognition and Volition are not two accidental properties of certain accidental existences in the universe: they can be seen with the eye of Logic, to concentrate the whole meaning and truth of the universe in themselves, and, even though perhaps only lately come upon the universal scene, to be that without whose ultimate presence nothing whatever would have the remotest thinkability or logical viability. It is important to note that it is not as some universal idealistic presupposition that thought and will here enter the categorial picture: they enter it as logical forms into which alone the logical forms that have preceded them can be intelligibly gathered up and which embody, with the utmost poignancy and clarity, the essential principle of the whole series. A quality has been what it was in and through the opposing qualities that showed it up, and a force has been what it was in and through the other forces and occasions which elicited it, but Cognition and Volition find their very selves in their others in a manner which these other categories only vaguely adumbrate. Cognition confronts the confusions of sense, the random variety of existence, the continual flux of appearances and educes from it all patterns of order and simplicity which are its very self, while Volition confronts all these and in addition the diversified recalcitrance of things and persons, and imposes on them all a common pattern of order and mutual accommodation which again is its very self. It is only by thus confronting an apparently alien, objective world around us, and then through Understanding and Practice removing its alien character, that our conscious life can *be* at all, and it is likewise only by being destined to be thus consciously understood and remoulded that the natural external world can be there at all. The natural world, on this Hegelian view, is not "there for us" in the purely "dreamt up" sense envisaged by Kant and Fichte, and more recently by Husserl, but it is "there for us" in the teleological sense that it is but a ruse in the all-explanatory, absolute strategy of which conscious subjectivity is the final expression. The astonishing, apparent ὕβρις of this conclusion must not blind us to its logical basis: it is in virtue of the sovereign capacity to subordinate otherness to itself which is found in no other category that Cognition and Volition occupy a supreme place among categories and in the real world.

The self-explanatory categories then culminate in what Hegel calls the Absolute Idea, which is simply the notion of reflexive asymmetry realized in the form of a self-lucid consciousness, one which sees itself as the self-active universality in all forms of otherness that confront it, and in and through all the stages of objectivity and subjectivity that have led up to it. In it the power of "the Other" has been wholly done away with, but it is important to realize that this is only true *in a teleological sense*. Hegel's Absolute Idea is *not* the conception of a thing or state or consciousness from which all tensions have been eliminated, in which all problems have been solved, all gulfs bridged, all conflicts brought to a reconciliation and all refractory elements harmonized and domesticated. It is rather the conception of a consciousness which *leaves everything as it is* but which yet brackets it all in an infinite acquiescence, having seen it all to be part and parcel of the eternal, rational strategy which is itself.

It will not prove possible, within the limits of the present paper, to show how the *idée mère* and sovereign ruse which governs the Logic is also at work in the much misunderstood, preparatory *Phenomenology* and in the completing *Realphilosophie*. In the former we see conscious subjectivity, not at all magisterial and demiurgic as in Kant, Fichte and Schelling, but humbly seeking to know itself and to penetrate the alien forms of objectivity and subjectivity that surround it, coming at length to realize that what it truly is, and what the world and the society around it truly are, are both nothing but the active universality of conceptual thought which will be fully set forth in the Logic. In the *Realphilosophie*, on the other hand, we see the self-externalization of the self-active *Begriff* at work in the murkier medium of nature and finite spirit. Both of these works have a dark richness which is not to be found in the Logic, and which lends them their special attraction, as well as showing up the extraordinary range and depth of information which Hegel commanded, both in the field of history and the humane enterprises, and also in natural science. But with such dark richness goes an increase in arbitrariness and contingency, which Hegel may have disavowed in his programmes, but which is none the less evident in his practice. There is nothing at all shameful in this arbitrary, contingent element, since the contingently specific and individual is as much a facet of the Absolute Idea as the necessary and universal.

The present paper can attempt no detailed justification of the form taken by self-explanation in the philosophy of Hegel. For many the descriptive categories suffice completely, and for many the unending explanation of one thing in terms of others is not felt to be absurd and self-frustrating but all that can be rationally desired. For some, however, the notion of the self-explanatory and absolute still has its allure, and for these it can be argued that Hegel has provided better provender than anyone else. We may also emphasize, at our close, the logical realism which makes Hegel so remarkable, and which puts him so close to the Plato of the *Parmenides, Sophist* and *Timaeus,* and so far from his Germanic predecessors with their metaphysical dramas of subjectivity. For Hegel, not only all that is specific and individual in the real world but also all that is achieved in the detached universality and shared spirituality of conscious experience is the expression of a Logical Idea which is more fundamental than either and which embraces the possibility of both in itself. I do not, however, imagine that my special reverence for the first member of the Hegelian Trinity of Idea, Nature, and Spirit will be acceptable to everyone.

PHENOMENOLOGY: HEGEL AND HUSSERL

QUENTIN LAUER

Fordham University

At a time when the philosophy of Hegel is awakening renewed interest among scholars both on the European continent and in the Anglo-Saxon world it would seem not only desirable but even imperative to institute a comparison between one of the most influential movements of our own age, the phenomenological movement, and that part of Hegel's philosophical endeavor for which he is, perhaps, best known, his *Phenomenology of Spirit*. The comparison, of course, is of interest, not simply because in both instances the same term, "phenomenology," is employed, but, more significantly, because in both the same sort of appeal is made to human consciousness, to experience, as the key to philosophical knowledge. It would, assuredly, be claiming too much to say that the two types of phenomenology greatly resemble each other in their approach to experience, but it is to be hoped that, even in their differences, they can be seen as somehow complementing – or, perhaps, illuminating – each other.

In allowing these two types of phenomenology to confront each other it would undoubtedly be of major interest to see Hegel's endeavor against the background of the outstanding figures of the contemporary phenomenological movement, both those who have to some extent been influenced by Hegel, such as Merleau-Ponty, Sartre, even Heidegger and, perhaps, Ricoeur, and also those who have been influenced either not at all or only negatively by Hegel, such as Husserl, Scheler, Schütz, and Gurvitsch. Since, however, such an undertaking could be carried out only within the framework of an extended monograph, we shall confine ourselves here to the more modest task of coming to terms with the meanings which Hegel and the most illustrious of "contemporary" phenomenologists, Husserl, give to the undertaking called "phenomenology."

In view of the fact that both Hegel and Husserl make common cause against both the sceptical phenomenalism of Hume and what both consider to be the "empty formalism" of Kant's response to Hume, it can seem strange that Husserl, in the vast corpus of his published and unpublished writings, should for the most part have ignored Hegel and, in the few notices he does give to Hegel, should have criticized the latter severely for having retarded the impulse to "scientific" philosophical thinking. One could, of course, put the whole thing down to the difference of temperament in the two men – and this is not without significance – seeing in Hegel the all-embracing universal spirit who will leave no avenue of human knowing, no facet of human experience, untried, and in Husserl the painstaking scientific spirit – the erstwhile mathematician – who will not move forward in the vast uncharted wilderness of philosophical investigation until he has perfected the method which will assure him that what he knows, be it ever so little, he knows "scientifically." It is difficult to escape the impression that Hegel was impatient (he wrote the *Phenomenology of Spirit* in six months) to press within the covers of one book the vast erudition which he had accumulated through years of voracious reading and profound meditation, and that Husserl had the unremitting patience of the experimental scientist, willing to spend years eliminating the influence of those variables that could throw doubt on the results of his investigations. It is just as inconceivable that Hegel could spend a lifetime perfecting techniques that would enable him to pile apodictic certitude upon apodictic certitude in raising the edifice of universal science as it is inconceivable that in investigating consciousness Husserl should range through Greek tragedy and Judaeo-Christian revelation, stoicism and the Enlightenment, the Ancien Régime and the French Revolution, experimental science and phrenology, or morality, jurisprudence, art and religion. Hegel and Husserl are alike, it is true, in their contention that no sphere of reality is closed to rational investigation, but they are utterly unlike in that Hegel actually endeavors to come to terms with the totality of reality, while Husserl limits himself to establishing the method which will enable others to achieve a scientific knowledge to which no limits can be assigned.

Tempting as it is, however, to delay on the differences of fundamental attitudes which produced such radically different results, we must take a closer look at the results themselves to see if they reveal similarities as well as differences, to say nothing of complementarities. Before the unpublished manuscripts of Husserl were made available to the scholarly world, it was customary to locate the major difference between

Hegel and Husserl in their approach to history. Hegel, we were told made history – not merely the history of philosophy but also the whole of human history, world history – integral to the process of philosophizing, whereas Husserl philosophized in an historical vacuum. Husserl's 1911 essay. "Philosophy as Rigorous Science,"[1] was, it is true, available, as were the first two parts of *The Crisis of European Science and Transcendental Phenomenology*,[2] both of which undertook a somewhat historical investigation of the progress of philosophical thinking. Since the former, however, presented only a somewhat truncated record of abortive attempts to make philosophy "scientific" – and thus, incidentally, properly speaking philosophical – and the latter used a relatively brief segment of European intellectual history, from Galileo to Kant, as illustrative of the need for a genuinely transcendental phenomenology, if philosophy were ever to fulfill its role of being scientific, little damage was done to the "historical vacuum" thesis. With the publication, however, of Husserl's *Erste Philosophie*, with its "Critical History of Ideas"[3] and the remainder of *Krisis*, and with the availability of other late manuscripts, still unpublished, the thesis has had to be reexamined. The result of the reexamination has been to show that for Husserl, even in his late years, world history continues to have no philosophical significance whatever, and the history of philosophy from Plato to Husserl – with notable gaps – records only the vicissitudes of the scientific ideal in philosophy, not the process of philosophizing. The difference between Hegel and Husserl, then, here too remains acute. For Hegel the history of philosophy is integral to the philosophical enterprise; for Husserl it serves as illustrative material in his efforts to establish the scientific ideal. Hegel took all "significant" philosophers – and they are legion – seriously; Husserl took Plato and Aristotle, Descartes and Leibniz, Locke, Berkeley, Hume, and Kant seriously.[4] Given his conviction

---

[1] "Philosophie als strenge Wissenschaft," *Logos* I (1911), 289–341 (English translation by Quentin Lauer, in *Phenomenology and the Crisis of Philosophy*, New York: Harper and Row, 1965, pp. 71–147).

[2] Parts I and II, *Philosophia* I (1936), 77–176 (contained in *Die Krisis der europäischen Wissenschaften und die transzendentale Phänomenologie*, ed. W. Biemel, The Hague: Nijhoff, 1954).

[3] *Erste Philosophie* (1923–24), 2 vols. (ed. R. Boehm). The Hague: Nijhoff. Part I, *Kritische Ideengeschichte*, 1956; Part II, *Theorie der phänomenologischen Reduktion*, 1959.

[4] This tendency to accord significance to historical positions only when they manifest a demonstrable relationship to transcendental phenomenology is admirably illustrated in Husserl's preference for empiricism over rationalism, because the former makes clear "the historical tendency toward a thoroughly necessary and true philosophical method, the phenomenological" (*Erste Philosophie* I, p. 187).

that the *unum necessarium* in philosophy is that it be scientific, it is understandable that he should have taken these men seriously. That he should have ignored the whole neo-Platonic and Scholastic contribution, that he should merely mention in passing Bacon and Hobbes, Spinoza, Fichte, and Hegel, that he should have acted as though Rousseau and Schelling, Marx, Kierkegaard, and Nietzsche, had never existed is somewhat less understandable. The procedure, however, does permit us to see how he could be so cavalier in his treatment of Hegel, and it points up strikingly the difference between the two phenomenologies.

HUSSERL'S CRITIQUE OF HEGEL

Apart from a remark in Vol. I of the *Logical Investigations*[5] that Hegel had denied the principle of non-contradiction – a remark which is not documented – and a reference to Hegel's abortive desire in the Preface to the *Phenomenology*[6] to make of philosophy a "foundational science," we find Husserl's complaints against Hegel summarized in *Philosophy as Rigorous Science*. Here without further ado he lumps Hegel's philosophy with "romantic philosophy"[7] which either denies the ideal of scientific philosophy, "however much Hegel insists on the absolute validity of his method and his doctrine,"[8] or makes it impossible of attainment. In view of Hegel's own vigorous – sometimes almost vicious – criticism of Romanticism this can, of course, seem strange, but it is explained by Husserl's further remarks in the same context. Hegel's "system," he goes on to say, "lacks a critique of reason, which is the foremost prerequisite for being scientific in philosophy."[9] Lest this criticism seem to be written in ignorance of Hegel's own burlesque of Kant's own demand that knowledge be validated by a knowledge of the faculty of knowing – like learning to swim before going into the water[10] it should be noted that the "critique" which Husserl finds lacking in Hegel is one which guarantees the objectivity of the concepts one employs.[11] To put it in the somewhat more

---

[5] *Logische Untersuchungen*, Halle 1900–1901. Second (revised) edition, Halle, 1913 (further editions unchanged). Vol. I, p. 141. English translation by J. N. Findlay (New York: Humanities Press, 1970), Vol. I, p. 158.

[6] *Krisis*, pp. 204–205.

[7] *Philosophie als strenge Wissenschaft*, pp. 292–93 (transl., pp. 76–77).

[8] *Ibid.*

[9] *Ibid.*, p. 77.

[10] Hegel, *Geschichte der Philosophie*, vol. III (ed. Glockner, 19), p. 555.

[11] *Formale und transzendentale Logik*. Halle: Niemeyer, 1929, p. 160. English translation by Dorion Cairns (The Hague: Nijhoff, 1969), p. 180.

contemporary terms of the philosophy of science, Husserl is accusing Hegel of failing to give an adequate justification of the concepts he forms within a pre-structured "system." In terms of phenomenology this means that Husserl sees in Hegel's dialectical method a means of introducing more into his conclusions than is warranted by the experience to which he appeals.

Paradoxically enough, however, the main thrust of Husserl's objection to Hegel's philosophy is historical. Whatever Hegel's scientific intentions may have been, the results of his efforts, according to Husserl, were "either to weaken or to adulterate the impulse toward the constitution of rigorous philosophical science,"[12] an impulse which Husserl had seen at work from Plato to Kant and for which in his own day he looked in vain. Although Hegel called what he was doing "science," with the progress of the natural sciences it was more and more discredited, and its place was taken either by a "naturalism" coming out of the eighteenth century, which sought to turn philosophy into a positive (exact) science, or by a scepticism which would turn philosophy into a *Weltanschauung* laying no claim to being strictly scientific at all. By the same token, Hegel's "historical relativism," which recognized no philosophy as valid once and for all time, simply did away with the need of one absolutely valid scientific philosophy and opened the door to one *Weltanschauung* after another, each of which is relatively justified for its own time.[13]

This last objection is particularly interesting because it goes right to the heart of the difference between Hegel and Husserl in their conceptions of what philosophy is. As Husserl sees it, philosophy is a sort of Platonic idea which, even though it may take centuries or millennia to realize, is eternally one and the same, unchangeable. If it is realized in his own day with the transcendental phenomenological method, that is nothing but the realization of the ideal which has always been the same[14] – what philosophers have thought down through the centuries makes no difference whatever for the ideal.[15] For Hegel, on the contrary, philosophy is concrete thought, concrete philosophizing. There is no antecedent ideal; it comes into being in the historical process of its development. This is not to say that each

---

[12] *Philosophie als strenge Wissenschaft*, p. 293 (tr. p. 77).

[13] *Ibid.*

[14] What bothered Husserl perhaps most about Hegel was that the latter produced a reaction which became a refusal of any and all transcendental philosophy (cf. *Krisis*, pp. 196, 199, 201).

[15] Cf. *supra*, n. 4.

individual philosophy is valid for its own age, only to lose its validity in a succeeding age. Rather it is to say that philosophy is a living reality whose life is the process, and which is scientific to the extent that it is inseparable from its process. Individual philosophies are not philosophy; they are "moments" in the development of philosophy, which is one, not because it is an ideal to be realized but because it is constantly in the process of becoming, corresponding to a reality which is constantly in the process of becoming.[16] Husserl can look at history and find there only abortive attempts to achieve the antecedent ideal which is achieved only with the elaboration of a method which makes "scientific" philosophizing a possibility. Hegel can look at history and find there a philosophy constantly on the march, which is in danger of becoming unscientific only if it stops marching. Thus it is that Hegel's much-controverted contention that philosophy ends with himself must, it would seem, be taken figuratively, in the same way as Hegel's remark, "If one is to begin philosophizing, one must first be a Spinozist."[17] Just as the latter remark does not mean that philosophy is complete with Spinoza, so the former does not mean that there will be no philosophizing after Hegel. The meaning is simply that it is impossible to go back beyond Spinoza or beyond Hegel – and still do philosophy! Husserl's contention, on the other hand, that philosophy begins with transcendental phenomenology, in the sense that what preceded it was not philosophy – only an impulse to become philosophy – must, it would seem, be taken quite literally.[18]

Given such an enormous difference between two conceptions of what philosophy is, or of what philosophy does, it may seem strange to speak of significant similarities in the two types of endeavor. It should seem less strange, however, if we recognize that even where the differences are most pronounced they are not necessarily contradictions. Husserl is primarily concerned with the rigor, the apodicticity of philosophical knowing, convinced that once this has been secured no limit can be put on what is to be known. Hegel's primary concern is with what philosophical knowing knows, confident that faithfulness to the content of consciousness will result not only in a universal knowledge but also in a method which makes universal knowledge available. Husserl will make the validity of the method, antecedently assured, the criterion for the

---

[16] Hegel, *Einleitung in die Geschichte der Philosophie* (ed. J. Hoffmeister, Hamburg: Meiner, 1940), pp. 118–34 (transl. in Quentin Lauer, *Hegel's Idea of Philosophy*, Fordham University Press, 1971, pp. 83–91).
[17] Hegel, *Geschichte der Philosophie* III, p. 376.
[18] *Phil. als str. Wiss.*, pp. 290–91 (tr. pp. 73–75).

objectivity of the knowledge attained. Hegel will make the unbroken chain of objectivity in knowing the self-regulating guarantee that the method it progressively reveals delivers the truth of reality. What both are convinced of, however, is that genuine philosophical knowing has a content and that the progressive appropriation of this content is a goal which man can justifiably set for himself. It makes little sense to say with Kojève[19] that the method of philosophical "meditation" is the same for both Hegel and Husserl – what they meditate on is simply too different – but it does make sense to say that they are pursuing similar goals by different paths and that both recognize the need of avoiding the pitfalls inherited from previous philosophers, whether from Descartes or Locke, Hume or Kant.

If one were to draw up a table of the similarities and differences between the philosophies of Hegel and Husserl, it might well be that the differences would outnumber the similarities – or at least outweigh them in significance. At the same time, however, one would be forced to recognize that the differences are genuinely intelligible – and illuminating – only if seen in the light of the similarities. At the risk of becoming prolix, then, it might be well to examine both similarities and differences, in the hope that they will both illumine each other and throw light on the larger enterprise which might be called the phenomenological endeavor.

THE DEMANDS OF REASON

Although it would be a mistake to call either Hegel or Husserl a "rationalist," in any narrow sense of that term, it is clear from the beginning that both are very much alike in their extraordinary confidence – itself non-rational perhaps – in the autonomy of human reason and in its capacity to come to terms with reality. Neither will, in theory at least, put any limits to reason's field of competence – above all not limit it to determining the rules of its own functioning. "Infinity," then, is characteristic of reason. But here, immediately, a difference is discernible. For Hegel a capacity for the infinite bespeaks an infinity on the side of reason that is more than potential, but this it can be only if it is ultimately identifiable with concrete infinite reason, infinite or "absolute" Spirit.[20] For Husserl human reason is

---

[19] Alexandre Kojève, *Introduction à la Lecture de Hegel*. Paris: Gallimard, 1947, p. 447 (English translation by J. H. Nichols, Jr., New York: Basic Books, 1969, p. 171).

[20] For documentation on this cf. two articles by the present author: "Hegel on Proofs for God's Existence," *Kantstudien* 55 (1964), 443–65; "Hegel on the Identity of Content in

faced with an infinity of rational tasks, and it is equal to those tasks, in the sense that no task is outside the competence of rational investigation – provided that all investigations are rational in the sense in which he means rational.[21]

By the same token, then, both Hegel and Husserl seek an adequate guarantee of rationality in human thinking, and both see the need of a philosophical science, if this is to be achieved. What each means by "science," however, particularly when applied to philosophy, is quite different. Hegel sees science in the unbroken character of the chain of implications issuing from an indubitable beginning, whether it be the beginning of experience in the *Phenomenology of Spirit* or the initial affirmation of being in the *Science of Logic* – to begin is to begin a process, and the necessity of the process is science.[22] Husserl, on the other hand, has submitted the very notion of science to a phenomenological analysis and has come up with an eidetic intuition of the "essence" of science. Philosophy will be science if it conforms to this essence.[23] Like Hegel, of course, Husserl recognizes that the *manner* in which philosophy is scientific will not be the same as the manner in which the "exact" sciences are scientific – its subject matter does not permit that – but it will be equally scientific.[24] Thus, both Hegel and Husserl agree that without phenomenology, the study of consciousness as the unique locus of givenness, there can be no science. But here a striking difference enters in: for Husserl phenomenology *is* the science of philosophy, because it is at once the unique and the universal method of philosophical investigation; whereas for Hegel, phenomenology is properly speaking a preparation for philosophy (corresponding, in a sense, to Kant's *Critique of Pure Reason*),[25] because it is the progressive revelation that reason is in truth spirit, whose progressive self-revelation is philosophy. Thus, although for both Hegel and Husserl the implications of phenomena are manifested in a reflection on consciousness,

---

Religion and Philosophy," in *Hegel and the Philosophy of Religion* (The Wofford Symposium), The Hague: Nijhoff, 1970, pp. 261–95.

[21] *Phenomenology and the Crisis of Philosophy*, pp. 163–64.

[22] In both the Preface and the Introduction to the *Phenomenology of Spirit* Hegel makes abundantly clear what this means.

[23] Cf., for example, the First Cartesian Meditation; *Philosophie als strenge Wissenschaft*, pp. 289–91 (transl., pp. 71–75). This ideal, toward which history tends, is called the "Grundforderung der Apodiktizität" (*Krisis*, p. 274).

[24] *Ideen* I (*Ideen zu einer reinen Phänomenologie und phänomenologischen Philosophie*, ed. W. Biemel, The Hague: Nijhoff, 1950), nos. 73–75. (English translation, *Ideas*, by W. R. Boyce-Gibson, New York: Macmillan, 1931.)

[25] Hegel, it is true, does not institute a "critique of reason," but in the *Phenomenology* he seeks to trace the process which becomes reason and thus to assure rationality.

Hegel will draw out those implications in rich profusion – in a logic which necessarily passes beyond the "essence" which reflection reveals, in a philosophy of nature which studies spirit's external self-manifestation, and a philosophy of spirit which knows spirit itself in the workings of the human spirit – while Husserl will get very little beyond the discovery that the "transcendental subjectivity" which the epoché and reductions have revealed is the "a-priori source" of all objectivity. Whether the phenomenologist opts for the method of Husserl – with its conceptual rigor – or that of Hegel – with its socio-historical ramifications – he cannot fail to contrast the tremendous issues of total human experience which crowd the pages of Hegel's writings with the painfully detailed "clarifications" of the individual phenomenologist's somewhat banal experiences which emerge from Husserl's voluminous life work. The difference here may very well be due, once more, to the fundamental divergence in approaching the rational problematic. Both Hegel and Husserl agree that reason is consciousness functioning at its peak and that philosophy is reason's highest accomplishment. In Husserl's view, however, this bespeaks a constantly renewed effort to raise consciousness to the level of reason as it confronts each and every task, which means beginning over and over again. Hegel, on the other hand, sees a need of tracing consciousness from its incipient, immediate, abstract form through all the stages of concretion to its perfection in reason (the work of phenomenology) so that then philosophy can begin. Because there is no need to go through the procedure again and again, once reason has begun to philosophize it can keep moving. The danger that the Hegelian mode of philosophizing may become slipshod is, of course, greater, but it has advantages which are too obvious to enumerate. It is one thing to elaborate a method for the investigation of consciousness, another to investigate it. Husserl spends so much time on the former task that he has little opportunity for the latter; Hegel gets on with the show – and the show is most interesting.

RATIONALIZING EXPERIENCE

Perhaps one of the most vigorous reactions to Kant among his immediate followers, a reaction which is shared by Husserl and his followers, was a rejection of the Kantian "dualism" of sense and intellect and its attendant postulation of the non-phenomenal "thing-in-itself." By separating sense and intellect, it was felt, Kant put reason in the position of supplying a rational form for experience but of being unable to rationalize the content of experience. Thus the very heart of reality, that which was somehow "behind" its appearances to consciousness, became for philosophical reasoning simply an "unknown X," and the a-priori forms of sense, understanding, and reason were left with only a phenomenal content. Both Hegel and Husserl are quick to dispose of this unknown and unknowable reality, and both for the reason that an unknowable reality would not be real; a "thing-in-itself" simply would not be a *thing*. Both, then, will rationalize experience in such a way that reason can be "conscious of being all reality." In order to do this, however, Husserl will appeal to an eidetic intuition of the very "essence" of reason, whose function it is to "constitute" its objects in the mode of necessity – thus permitting an a-priori constitution even of the contents of experience.[26] An experience so rationalized will have its own "logic," and this will be discoverable in an intentional analysis of transcendental subjectivity, which is the a-priori source of any and all content for consciousness. Given any conscious act, say the perception of tree, Husserl will be able so to analyze the act that he will know not only the essence of the perception but also the essence of the tree which is its object. What is important, then, is not the individual act of perceiving nor the individual tree perceived, but the essential contained in the act, i.e., what perceiving a tree *must be* and what a perceived tree *must be*. In all this one has the lingering suspicion that Husserl is concerned neither with trees nor the perceiving of trees but only with what one must *mean* when one speaks of trees or of the perceiving of trees.[27] In any event, it is here that the difference between Husserl's and Hegel's approach becomes glaringly apparent. Apart from the fact that Hegel devotes little time – and that only at the very beginning of the *Phenomenology* – to such experiences as that of tree, or of color, shape, geometric figure, and the like – all of which are constants in the Husserlian gallery of experiences – he is even less concerned with "essences," be they of conscious acts or their objects. In the dialectic of "Force and Understanding," it is true, he speaks of a search for hidden essences, but only as a stage along the way, a stage which must be superseded if phenomenology is to get anywhere. It is true, too, that in the *Logic* the "Doctrine of Essence" constitutes approximately

---

[26] *Formale und transzendentale Logik* (Halle: Niemeyer, 1929) has "rational constitution" as its principal theme. Cf. *Ideen* I, nos. 144, 149.

[27] The intentional constitution of essences and the constitution of meaning are scarcely to be distinguished - especially if there are *necessary* meanings.

one third of the whole work, but here too the movement is such that it must go beyond essences (or, perhaps, meanings) if it is to get to reality, which is reason's concern. The point is that in no sense does Hegel feel that he has reconciled experience and reason by discovering the abstract essences either of experience or of what is experienced. For him experience will be rationalized if he can trace the whole process from its minimal beginnings in sensation to its maximal grasp (*Begriff*-concept) in absolute knowing and show that they are inseparable because no step along the way has been left out. Hegel is very little interested in what the act of consciousness must be if it is to be valid; he is very much concerned with what the total process of consciousness is – if the process is really total it will be self-validating.

It could be argued, of course – and perhaps it should – that Husserl has the advantage over Hegel in all this of being much more carefully consistent in his use of language and of concepts – if, indeed, it is true that absolute terminological rigor promotes rather than stultifies philosophical discourse. Aside from the fact that Husserl does not always – he cannot – submit his own terminology and conceptual structures to the painstaking analysis he advocates, it is true that it is easier – if slightly less rewarding – to follow his meaning than it is to follow Hegel's. It may also be true that, if philosophical importance is measured by the validity of our cognition and not by its significance, Husserl again has the edge. It is not true, however, that Hegel is less rigorous in describing a movement whose scope is so vast than is Husserl in detailing an analysis whose scope is so limited.

PHILOSOPHICAL SCIENCE

This brings us back to the task of describing similarities in the Hegelian and Husserlian positions, similarities which both illumine and are illumined by manifest dissimilarities. In his own day Hegel was unremitting in his opposition to the non-rational intuitionism of the romantics, convinced as he was not only that philosophy could not be unscientific but also that it constitutes the highest form of science – not in the sense that its certitudes were the most certain but in the sense that its truths, which could be genuinely known, were the most significant for man. Husserl, as we know, shared Hegel's conviction regarding the scientific character of philosophy – he saw it as essential to philosophy that it be scientific, such that an unscientific, romantic philosophy simply would not be philosophy. Nor is the meaning which each gives to the term "science" – *Wissenschaft* – so very different; it signifies the purity of the knowledge in question, as opposed to mere opinion or conjecture, and it calls for strict methodical procedures in its acquisition. The difference between them, then, lies less in the kind of knowledge each aims at than in the emphasis they put on the manner of approaching it. If, says Husserl, philosophy is the highest form of rational endeavor – a supposition which, for him, does not seem to require any discussion – then it cannot be inferior to any other form of rational endeavor, certainly not inferior in rationality. At the same time Husserl is convinced that the positive sciences have achieved a very high degree of rationality: they are "sciences" in the strict sense of the term. Philosophy, then, cannot be less scientific in its area of competence, the area of universal "essential" knowledge, than are the particular sciences in their limited areas of competence. Philosophy must, in fact, be in a sense *more* scientific than the other sciences, since one of its tasks is the validation of those concepts which the particular sciences employ without being able themselves to validate these concepts.[28] If, then, other disciplines are to be authentically scientific, the concepts they employ must be susceptible of thoroughgoing verification in a higher discipline called philosophy. Thus, for Husserl, the very essence of philosophy is revealed in the necessity of an ultimate guarantee of scientific knowledge as such. If philosophy is not scientific, there is no science.[29]

Hegel, as we have seen, will not yield to Husserl one bit in his demand that philosophy be scientific – the knowledge it affords is knowledge in the strictest possible sense of that term, it is "absolute knowing." In his approach to "philosophical science," however, Hegel will not take his cue from the scientific character of the positive sciences or of any other discipline. He will see in the sciences, it is true, as well as in morality, jurisprudence, art, religion, and history, so many manifestations – in addition to philosophy – of reason's operation in the world of man.[30] He will even seek to integrate all of these in the universal whole which is his "system," without which science is meaningless, but his approach will be to follow the self-development of consciousness as it progressively manifests and corrects its own deficiencies until it eventually becomes absolute (i.e., unconditioned) knowing – and this last will be the culmination of the scientific process,

[28] Cf. *Erste Philosophie* I, p. 13.
[29] *Philosophie als strenge Wissenschaft*, 298 (transl., p. 85).
[30] *Einleitung in die Geschichte der Philosophie*, pp. 155–56 (transl., p. 99).

philosophy. Hegel, will, it is true, be guided in his quest by his antecedent conviction that man is most truly human when he is most truly
rational, that whatever is specifically human in man's endeavor has
the mark of rationality on it, but he will let rationality reveal itself in the
process, not decide ahead of time what it *must* be. Ultimately Hegel
will, like Husserl, say that reason is the autonomous source of its own
"absolute knowing," but this is a discovery he will make in the course
of tracing the development of consciousness, and he will devote more
than two thirds of his *Phenomenology of Spirit* to articulating the
implications of this discovery. The result will be a reason which bears
little more than a family resemblance to the reason analyzed by Husserl.

It seems scarcely necessary to describe in detail – for those who are
not totally ignorant of Hegel's philosophizing – his approach to knowing
through an objective consciousness which does not make sense, even
to itself, until it becomes self-consciousness, a self-consciousness which
does not really grasp the self of which it is conscious until it becomes
reason, a reason which runs the risk of bogging down in its own
particularity if it does not move on to identify itself with the truly
universal spirit, the ultimate source of all being and all truth. All this
is too well known already, and any attempt to describe it, short of
rewriting the entire *Phenomenology* runs the risk of trivializing it. To
go back over certain facets of the development, however, may help us
to see why the results of the Hegelian phenomenology differ so much
from those of the Husserlian.

Husserl, we know, was permanently suspicious of Hegel's dialectical
method, both because he considered it an arbitrary construction of
questionable implications and because he saw it as an imposition from
without not demanded by the contents "given" in consciousness. It is
difficult, of course, to answer either of these objections – Husserl was
not the first to raise them – but it is Hegel's contention that, if we
follow him faithfully (facing "the labor of the negative") [31] we shall
see that every implication is inevitable – hence "given" – once we
accept the initial position, which cannot but be accepted. It is also
Hegel's contention that the method is not imposed from without but
that it is merely a description of the process through which consciousness goes in discovering its own inadequacies, negating these inadequacies, and thus reaffirming itself at progressively higher levels. Like
Husserl, Hegel is concerned with the assurance that reason be ade-

---

[31] *Phänomenologie des Geistes* (ed. J. Hoffmeister). Hamburg: Meiner, Preface, p. 20
(translation by J. B. Baillie, New York: Macmillan, 1949, p. 81).

quately rational in its functioning. Unlike Husserl, however, he refuses to believe that the apodictic certainty of its knowledge will guarantee its rational adequacy. It is not the certainty of knowledge which constitutes its rationality; rather it is its grasp of reality in its total interrelatedness. Husserl can institute a phenomenology which piles up – and even relates – bits of certain knowledge; and given enough time – and enough phenomenologists – it will get around to investigating society and history, law and morality, art and religion. In this view phenomenology is phenomenology antecedent to any concrete investigation it undertakes; it is a sort of blueprint for future investigations. For Hegel phenomenology is a "science of the experience of consciousness," and it is not complete as phenomenology until it somehow embraces the totality of consciousness – which is why, after beginning as a "science of the experience of consciousness," it realizes itself only as a "phenomenology of spirit." Hegel is determined, then, that his philosophy be rooted in experience, but not merely in his own experience – even as paradigmatic – nor, for that matter, in the experiences of philosophers, privileged as those experiences may be, but in the whole of human experience. It may, of course, be questioned just how successful even Hegel's *Phenomenology* can be in coming to terms with the totality of human experience, but its attempt to do so is a testimony to Hegel's conviction that to attempt less is to condemn reason to being inadequately rational. [32]

SELF-CONSCIOUS REASON

If then, we take as a sort of least common denominator of any phenomenology, whether it be Hegel's or Husserl's or that of any of the latter's followers, that it will appeal to no data except the data of consciousness, that it will not seek to go "behind" experience to what is not experienced for an explanation of experience, we are still faced with a tremendous difference between the experiences to which Hegel and Husserl appeal. This manifests itself most strikingly perhaps in the approach each takes to consciousness of self. Like Kant, who saw in the original transcendental unity of apperception the basic condition of all consciousness, both Hegel and Husserl see all consciousness as mere empty abstraction if it is not ultimately identified with

---

[32] What has always fascinated readers of the *Phenomenology of Spirit*, even those who disagree with it, is the extraordinarily broad range of experiences it seeks to integrate into the process of experience.

consciousness of self; consciousness can find its guarantee only within itself, not outside itself, where nothing is to be *found* – to find it would be to find it in consciousness. For Husserl it is not consciousness which discovers within itself the need to become self-consciousness; rather it is the philosopher who sees that the necessity of apodictic certainty – if his philosophy is to be science – dictates that he seek apodictic evidence where it can alone be found, in the original source of all objectivity, transcendental subjectivity.[33] It is not too easy to say what this transcendental subjectivity is, since, it is neither the individual subjectivity of the philosopher (although it does seem capable of being multiplied)[34] nor the concrete totality of subjectivity, since his method, at least at this level, does not give him access to that.[35] One is tempted to surmise that the exercise of the epoché and the reductions has permitted Husserl to eliminate whatever is idiosyncratic to individual subjectivity and has thus provided him with a sort of subjectivity as such – which can stand for any and all subjectivity. Such a subjectivity can well manifest the necessary laws of subjective constitution and thus provide a guarantee for what is subjectively constituted. It can at the same time be sure that no other individual subjectivity – if there be such – can see things differently and be right.

That Hegel, in his search for a subject which will ultimately find in the consciousness of itself the consciousness of all reality, does not come up with such a "transcendental subjectivity" is due largely to the point of view from which he approaches the whole question. He has begun his study of consciousness with the simplest, most direct, most immediate form of objective consciousness, sensation. Sensation alone proves to be inadequate to its own sense object and must introduce the mediation of reflection in a perception which somehow fixes the object as a thing. This in turn can find no satisfaction in the abstract "thingness" of its object and so turns to understanding for an explanation of what appears to it. Understanding proves to be the last step in objective consciousness, since it is forced to look outside consciousness for an explanation of what is in consciousness. The next step resembles what we find in Husserl's procedure. Consciousness realizes that by continuing to look outward it has gone down a dead-end street which promises no further satisfaction in that direction.

[33] Cf. First Cartesian Meditation; *Ideen* I, pp. 72–73; *Formale und transzendentale Logik*, p. 237; Cairns, pp. 268–69.
[34] Cf. *Erste Philosophie* I, nos. 14, 20.
[35] We get a hint of this in the notion of pure "Ich-Pol" (*Krisis*, pp. 188–90).

Unlike Husserl, however, Hegel does not immediately turn inward – seeking means to purify the inward view – he seeks a relation to the objective which will mediate the return to the subjective, and this he finds in desire; it is desire which begins to mediate the consciousness of self as the subject of conciousness. It is in following the development of this sort of consciousness that Hegel realizes that the self will never find itself merely by itself; a condition for the discovery of self becomes the discovery of a community of selves, and the voyage of discovery is already a tortuous one; not until the end of the *Phenomenology* will the self find its true self.

It is true, of course, that Husserl too institutes an elaborate procedure – both negative and positive in its elements – for arriving at a pure transcendental subject which will be the guarantee of all knowledge, and the knowledge of which can be called an "absolute knowing." The difference, however, is enormous, which could have been expected, considering the goal that each has in view. Because Husserl is more concerned with the apodictic certitude of the knowledge he can attain than he is with the extent of that knowledge, his aim is to find in self-consciousness the guarantee of any knowledge, however trivial it may be. Since Hegel's aim is the attainment of knowledge which is truly knowledge only if it is total, he cannot be satisfied with anything less than absolute Spirit's absolute knowledge of itself, a knowledge which cannot stop short of the interrelatedness of all knowing and of all that is known. Thus it is that, even though both men recognize that the investigation of a subjectivity which would be merely individual can produce only abstract results and that the mere universalization of such a subject will not concretize its original abstractness, Husserl will recognize the need of coming to terms with intersubjectivity only after he has completely laid the foundation for genuine subjective analysis, whereas Hegel will insist that a self outside the framework of mutually interrelated selves is meaningless and can guarantee nothing, not even itself. It is all very well to speak of the autonomy of reason, as both Hegel and Husserl do: for Hegel this autonomy is to be won in dialectical struggle – embracing the whole socio-historical dimension of man – not simply discovered in a process of eliminating whatever would make for contingency and, hence, uncertainty in cognition.[36]

---

[36] There is, of course, danger of undue negative emphasis, if one looks only to Husserl's "epoché" as the suspension of any "position" which would make for contingency. The "reductions" are not negative but positive; they make it possible for transcendental

Husserl, as we have said, recognizes that an absolutely valid knowledge makes sense only if it is known to be absolutely valid for any possible subject. This could simply mean that it does not make sense to speak of a knowledge which would be valid for one subject and not for another – only if reason is genuinely one does it make sense to speak of knowledge at all. If that is all it means, however, it would be enough to institute a method to validate absolutely one's own knowledge, since by definition such a knowledge has to be universal. The point is, and Husserl saw this clearly, that unless there is some way of determining that others do *de facto* know in this way, "absolute" knowing can be only abstractly universal. Husserl, therefore, finds himself forced to say that the laws of intentional constitution he has established are operative in all subjects and that there are other subjects. Without going into the intricate details of intersubjective constitution, which occupied Husserl's thoughts for many years – without ever giving him complete satisfaction [37] – it seems safe to say that the constitution of other subjects is simply the extension of self constitution and that the essential in any subjectivity has already been discovered in the discovery of subjectivity as such. It is not an intersubjective investigation which is what is essential to subjectivity; rather it is the subjective (solipsistic) [38] investigation which reveals what is essential and, therefore, true of any subject whatever.

Hegel's procedure is entirely different. For him intersubjectivity is no special problem, not because it is not a problem, but because it is not distinct from the problem of self-consciousness itself. To attempt to separate the consciousness of self from the consciousness of other selves and then to seek in the former an explanation of the latter would be, for Hegel, to involve oneself in a Humpty-Dumpty situation, trying to put together what never should have been put apart. A community of selves, for all of whom knowledge must be the same if it is to be truly knowledge, is for Hegel not an after-thought dictated by the need of concretizing the universality of knowledge. The community of selves is a prerequisite for any meaningful self-realization. From the initial confrontation of master consciousness and slave consciousness, through the gradual development of slave consciousness to a consciousness of being free, down to the ultimate realization that the only frame-

---

subjectivity to reveal the riches contained in its self-consciousness. Still, it is only if the negative function of eliminating contingency is constantly operative that positive discovery in subjectivity can attain to any kind of certainty at all.

[37] Cf. Fifth Cartesian Meditation; *Ideen* II (ed. M. Biemel, The Hague: Nijhoff, 1952).

[38] Cf. Fourth Cartesian Meditation, no. 41; *Erste Philosophie* II, pp. 65–66, 174.

work within which self-consciousness can be legitimately achieved is the totality of consciousness called "spirit," consciousness in isolation, whether as individual or "essential" consciousness, has no place in Hegel's *Phenomenology*. One can readily see why history has such monumental importance for Hegel, whereas for Husserl it is only incidental to the philosophical enterprise that the impulse toward scientific philosophy has a "history." Because he is convinced that development is integral to the very intelligibility of that which develops Hegel is incapable of *doing* philosophy in any but a historical perspective, and the history he considers is always a concatenation of real events, whether the subject under consideration be consciousness, morality, law, art, religion, or philosophy itself. The one exception to this within his "system" is logic, which, because it is concerned with logical implications apart from temporal dimensions – "the presentation of God as He is in His eternal essence before the creation of the world or of a single finite spirit" [39] – can be, if not completely a-historical, at least not historically conditioned. This, too, may serve to illustrate the difference between Husserl's and Hegel's views of the philosophical enterprise. In view of the emphasis which both put on the content of thought – as opposed to merely the activity of thinking – it is no surprise that both seek to institute a new logic, which will be adequate to the content of thought, to the being which reveals itself in thought. For Hegel this will mean a dialectical logic capable of doing justice to the processual character of the being which reveals itself. For Husserl it will mean a transcendental logic, which will establish the laws for the intentional constitution for all content of thought.

For Hegel, then, phenomenology will bring consciousness to the level of absolute knowing, which is then capable of looking into itself and discovering all that pure thought reveals. Logic is justified because it has been preceded by a phenomenology. For Husserl the logic and the phenomenology are not to be distinguished, both are transcendental, both are constitutive of their own content. When the phenomenological method has been perfected to the point where the "laws" of transcendental constitution have been firmly established, phenomenology *is* logic, transcendental logic. [40] For this very reason there is a risk, in instituting a comparison between the Hegelian and the Husserlian

[39] *Wissenschaft der Logik* (Hamburg: Meiner, 1963), Vol. I, p. 31 (translation by A. V. Miller, New York: Humanities Press, 1969, p. 50).
[40] What *Formale und transzendentale Logik* seeks to do is to justify an ultimate confidence in the "constitutive" function of transcendental subjectivity—provided that it adheres to the "logical" rules established for it (cf. p. 14); Cairns, pp. 15–16.

phenomenologies, of falsifying the issue. Because it is an introduction to philosophizing and not philosophy itself, Hegel's *Phenomenology* leaves untouched some of the questions raised by Husserl; Hegel takes them up only later in the *Logic*. Thus the whole question of the cognition of essence constitutes both the culmination of Hegel's "Objective Logic" and the transition to "Subjective Logic" or "The Doctrine of Concept." Here we see both that the knowledge of essence is not the goal of the Hegelian enterprise and that much of his teaching on subjective knowledge, corresponding to Husserl's transcendental subjectivity, belongs to the *Logic* and not to the *Phenomenology*. If, however, we were to make a comparison not between phenomenologies but between the whole philosophical endeavor of the one and the other, we should run the risk of being unfair to Husserl. In the interests of perfecting a method which would assure scientific rigor in philosophical thinking Husserl deliberately limited his investigations to the kind of considerations which would illustrate the fecundity of the method and left to others, who would employ the method he perfected, the larger issues which abound in Hegel's system. To put the whole question of the difference between the two men somewhat succinctly – and, perhaps, too simply – both sought to rationalize being thoroughly: Husserl by narrowing the notion of being to that which can be intentionally constituted in reason; Hegel by broadening the concept of reason so that it embraced the totality of human experience integrally interrelated. It is the difference between a concern for what reason can reveal and a concern that it be reason that is doing the revealing.

COMPLEMENTARITY OF THE TWO APPROACHES

If this long comparison of Hegel and Husserl is to be fruitful for our own philosophical thinking and not trail off in a sterile catalogue of similarities and differences, we are now faced with the task of indicating, however briefly, the ways in which the two approaches can complement and thus, perhaps, fructify each other. When we look at the two men we can admire at one and the same time the infinite patience of a Husserl, who is willing to spend a lifetime laying the methodological foundations without which, he is convinced, it is senseless to even dream of a philosophical science, and the majestic impatience of a Hegel, who simply refuses to so linger over the foundations that the philosophical edifice remains incomplete. Our own impatience with

Husserl, as he returns again and again to the task of determining conclusively the essence of the various modalities of consciousness, may be tempered as we realize that the rapidity with which Hegel – particularly in the early sections of the *Phenomenology* – takes us from sensation to perception to understanding leaves us with the uncomfortable feeling that we do not quite grasp what is happening. There is much to be said for Hegel's refusal to leave any facet of human experience unexplored – which does not permit him to linger – but this could, and perhaps should, be tempered by a painstaking effort to reconstruct the most basic of experiences. It is not out of the question to see that what Hegel, as well as Husserl, is doing is engaging in a kind of re-constitution of naïve experience. It might, in fact, not be amiss to say that a more conscious theory of intentional constitution could have made Hegel more aware of just what he was doing. Even if we are to look upon the Husserlian method of intentional constitution as primarily geared to assure consistency of *meaning*, we might also say that a more meticulous care in the determination of meaning could make Hegel somewhat less difficult to follow. At the same time it should be noticed that, had Husserl put less emphasis on the question, "What must experience be," and more on the further question, "What does experience reveal," his writings might be both more readable and more fruitful.

Husserl realizes, as well as does Hegel, that the fruitfulness of the phenomenological method lies in its ability to spell out the implications of original experience. We can, however, ask whether the Husserlian method might have proved even more fruitful, had he been willing to recognize that the implications which are not immediately available *in* experience but are mediated through thought as it *thinks* experience are integral to the total process of experience. Here it is, perhaps, that the suspicion arises that Husserl's insistence on the certainty of the philosopher in *seeing* is an obstacle to his grasping the significance of *what* he sees. The detailed (and repeated) efforts of Husserl to assure that nothing goes wrong might well give way to a more fruitful confidence in the self-corrective character of experience and thought, if we are faithful to their inner dialectic. There is, it is true, no substitute for methodological rigor, but exclusive insistence on method is found to leave philosophy standing still.

From the methodological point of view one cannot help being struck by a certain similarity between Hegel and Husserl in their insistence that philosophy can be legitimate only if it is willing to come to terms

with its own beginnings. Hegel, it is true, will not return to the beginning again and again, as Husserl insists one must do if one is not
to wander off into uncertainty, but it does not seem farfetched to say
that we can detect in Hegel's method something resembling the Husserlian epoché and something resembling the reductions. When Hegel
insists on beginning his *Phenomenology* – his voyage through the
process of experience – with the simplest of experiences, thus eliminating
both what might be foreign to experience and what could be considered
too quick a leap into thought, it takes no great stretch of the imagination
to liken this to an epoché. By the same token, Hegel's sedulous sticking
to the ordered series of implications growing out of this original experience could be looked upon as not unlike the method of reductions.
Had Hegel himself made us more aware of such elements in his
methodology – if indeed he himself was aware of them – our own task
in following him might have been an easier one. In any event, it is not
out of the question that we could be helped in doing a sort of Hegelian
phenomenology by such a consciousness of what is implied in sticking
to experience.

It is scarcely subject to question that no one prior to Husserl,
including Hegel, ever made such gigantic – and detailed – efforts to
analyze thoroughly the reality of consciousness, the essential *ways* in
which we can be conscious. One of the reasons which impels Husserl
to do this is his determination not to go, in the process of "objective"
analysis, beyond the evidence afforded by consciousness. Nor is it
always clear, even to those who have read Hegel most carefully, that
the latter does not sometimes advance beyond this sort of evidence –
or at least it is not always clear that he shows adequately that he
does not. Perhaps it is too much to ask that Hegel should show a
Husserlian concern for this sort of analysis, but it should not be out
of place to point out that such a concern need neither alter nor compro-
mise the Hegelian enterprise. At the same time it should not be unfair
to ask whether Husserl's unshakable confidence in the universality
of his method, i.e., as the unique method which will provide the results
he desires, does not prevent him from seeing that the universality of
the method is of little value, if no appeal is made to the universality
of experience. One can, perhaps, see some justification for Husserl's
limitation of the historical problematic to the tracing, among a carefully selected list of philosophers, of the impetus to scientific philosophizing, which is satisfied only when transcendental phenomenology
appears on the scene. One is still entitled to ask whether an intuition

into the requisites for philosophizing which does not in any way take into account the actual philosophizing that has gone on – even among the selected few who are considered – is not at best arbitrary. A discovery of the essence of rational thinking which ignores what rational thinking has been doing for 26 centuries – or which denies that it has been rational thinking – would seem to rule out a very important testimony to the activity of thinking spirit. One might find in the Hegelian effort to tie philosophical thinking in with the activity of infinite reason (spirit) a concretely universal point of view for which Husserl has no substitute. It is not, of course, clear how Husserl could permit this to be done without altering or compromising the "purity" of his own endeavor, but one can wonder how "universal" that endeavor can ever become, if it is not thus concretized. In this connection it might not be amiss to point out that a phenomenological theology – Husserlian style – is scarcely conceivable, since God does not "appear,"[41] whereas for Hegel, although God may not appear as an object, He quite definitely does manifest Himself in the very activity of thinking spirit, with the result that, for Hegel, a philosophy which stops short of God is but a truncated philosophy.[42]

It has been suggested earlier that Husserl's "constitutive phenomenology" will be particularly significant, if we see its primary function as that of constituting "meanings." There is no doubt that it can be employed to clarify what we "mean" when we speak. What it claims to do, however, is to tell us not only what we *do* mean but also what we *must* mean when we speak, and since Plato's time it seems to have been rather clear that the establishment of "essential" meanings is not likely to be successful – let alone make sense – in a non-dialectical framework of investigation. Here it is that the Husserlian phenomenology might have its perspectives broadened by an infusion of Hegel's dialectical method. To be even more specific it might be suggested that the Husserlian notion of "subjective constitution" could be rendered more intelligible if it were seen in the framework of a Hegelian subject-object dialectic.

By itself, of course, the dialectical method cannot be a guarantee of the faithfulness of the phenomenological investigation. In fact, if all it is is a method it can guarantee nothing at all. If, however, it is, as

---

[41] Cf. *Ideen* I, pp. 121–22.

[42] Once more the reader is referred to the documentation supplied in the present author's *Hegel's Idea of Philosophy*, "Hegel on Proofs for the Existence of God," and "Hegel on the Identity of Content in Religion and Philosophy."

Hegel contends it is, the method dictated by the movement of consciousness itself, then faithfulness in the examination of actual phenomena will result in a method that is dialectical. Here then is the place to ask whether Hegel or Husserl really examines consciousness more effectively. Husserl begins with an ideal of apodictic certitude,[43] which can be achieved only if the philosophical investigation sticks to the data of consciousness. This passes over to a determination of what the philosopher would necessarily discover if he examined consciousness, i.e., what is essential to an "act" of consciousness of this or that kind. There is, however, a question as to whether the antecedent ideal of apodictic certitude does not prove an obstacle to actual examination of consciousness, since any "act" which is examined will, by the fact that it is actual, also be contingent. Hegel, on the other hand, is not bothered by contingency, above all not by the contingency of any act of consciousness. He is not bothered by contingency because he is convinced that in the overall framework of the process of consciousness it is no obstacle at all to rationality; and he is not bothered by the contingency of any act of consciousness, because he never examines an act in isolation from the process. Thus, while both men are determined to establish the rationality of consciousness, Husserl will do this for "acts" of consciousness, precisely as acts, while Hegel will do it for the whole process, by tracing its movement from beginning to end and showing that its implications are inescapable. There are times, of course, when Hegel's conclusions would be more plausible, if he commanded a methodology which made more rigorous claims on our assent. But there are also times when we should find the results arrived at by Husserl more convincing, if he could show us how they fit in to an overall process which is concrete consciousness. Perhaps what we should ask of Hegel is that he take more methodological pains to show us where he is going and how he gets there, while asking of Husserl to show us that he is going anywhere at all, and that it's worthwhile going there.

---

[43] No amount of phenomenological investigation, it would seem, can reveal just why this kind of certitude is a prime value – for life.

HEGEL AND HERMENEUTICS*

THEODORE KISIEL

Northern Illinois University

Some of the most recent developments under the banner of "hermeneutics" have made explicit appeal to various facets of Hegel's thought, suggesting that its current *Wirkungsgeschichte* goes beyond Marxism and existentialism pure and simple, while still including these in sublated forms. Such direct appeals are to be found in both the hermeneutical phenomenology of Hans-Georg Gadamer and its incorporation in the most recent efforts of the Frankfurt school of ideology critique, particularly in the work of Jürgen Habermas and Karl-Otto Apel, who together constitute the hard core of what has been called the "hermeneutical-dialectical approach to metascience" (Radnitzky). Moreover, inasmuch as the aim of the latter approach is a "philosophical anthropology of knowledge" and hermeneutics as such remains centered on the problem of *Verstehen*, one might expect that a rereading of Hegel in the light of these recent developments should reveal something of what is still alive and operative in his thought with regard to the so-called "problem of knowledge."

THE HERMENEUTICAL WIRKUNGSGESCHICHTE
OF HEGEL'S THOUGHT

But the problem of knowledge here no longer remains within its classical epistemological boundaries. It must now be glimpsed in its permutations: for Gadamer and his most proximate influence, Heidegger, epistemology devolves into an ontology; for Habermas and Apel, the philosophy of knowledge finds its basis and justification in a philosophy of society.

But both developments are already found more or less explicitly

* The following essay was prepared during a stay in Germany made possible by the Alexander von Humboldt Foundation.

in Hegel. Habermas, for example, points out that Hegel's contribution to the theory of knowledge was precisely to jar the problem loose from the paradigm of a fully developed self-consciousness reflecting in solitude, which dominated the epistemological tradition from Descartes to Fichte, and instead to pose the question of the *becoming* of self-consciousness in its context of interaction with other self-knowing individuals.[1]

Epistemology from Descartes on claimed a radical starting point free from presuppositions in the self-reflection of the *Cogito*. The radical doubt developed into a critical procedure which sought to justify the conditions of possibility of knowledge before putting any confidence in already acquired knowledge. This claim of providing its own ultimate foundation, as the demand for a "presuppositionless" beginning, reputedly assumes nothing but its intention to doubt radically. In reality, the critical consciousness is an advanced moment of development which Hegel in his *Phenomenology of Spirit* aims to bring to the fore. "The critique of knowledge is not master of the spontaneity of an origin but, inasmuch as it is reflection, remains dependent on something that has preceded it."[2] Reflection is such that one must already have known in order to be able to know explicitly. Knowledge-critique obfuscates this circle of a reflection that remembers, and thus, in its endeavor to investigate the possibility and faculty of knowledge prior to actual knowledge, exposes itself to the aporia of a knowledge *before* knowledge. "But the investigation of knowledge cannot take place except as knowing; to 'investigate' with this so-called instrument means nothing else but to know it. The desire to know *before* one knows is as absurd as the wise intention of Scholasticus, who proposed to learn to *swim before he ventured into the water*."[3]

The modern critique of knowledge is therefore permeated by a false consciousness which Hegel proposes to demystify. From the very first sentence of his Introduction to the *Phenomenology of Spirit*, Hegel is already pursuing a kind of ideology critique of modern epistemology. Here, the more specific presuppositions of the critique of knowledge

---

[1] Jürgen Habermas, *Technik und Wissenschaft als "Ideologie"* (Frankfurt: Suhrkamp, 1968)p. 13.

[2] Jürgen Habermas, *Erkenntnis und Interesse* (Frankfurt: Suhrkamp, 1968) p. 16.

[3] *Encyclopedia of the Philosophical Sciences*, § 10. See also *Hegel's Lectures on the History of Philosophy*, trans. E. S. Haldane and Frances H. Simson (New York: Humanities Press, 1968) vol. III, pp. 428ff. Though references to Hegel are generally only to extant English translations, wherever these are available, translations of direct quotes have usually been modified in accordance with the direction of this essay.

then in vogue are unmasked. Reinhold, for example, proposes to reduce philosophy to a logic, an organon which studies the instrument of knowledge before knowledge itself. Aside from the difficulty that a knowing instrument would shape and therefore alter what it knows, the organon theory of knowledge also presupposes a division between the knower and the known that suggests at least the following presuppositions: a distinction between theoretical and practical reason, a fixed and stable knower as subjective norm, and a specific kind of knowledge as cognitive norm, namely, natural science, which, in the famous words of Kant, "must compel Nature to reply to its questions, not content merely to follow its leading strings."[4] All of these presuppositions are to find their proper place in the "history" of consciousness that Hegel here proposes to elaborate.

Habermas finds in the suggestions of the Jena period preceding the *Phenomenology of Spirit* a much more acceptable structure for this developmental history than that which emerges in the more absolutistic accounts of the later period. Instead of the encyclopedic division into subjective, objective and absolute spirit, Hegel in the Jena lectures bases himself on the dialectical paradigms of work, speech and interaction, which represent not only stages in the development of spirit, but also principles of its *Bildung*. Spirit is to be taken in a demystified way, as when we speak of the spirit of a team, people, or epoch, which are formed precisely through work, language and social interaction. Structurally, spirit is the organization of means, and the medium *in* which and *by* which the individual I educates itself, which means at once to come into its own and to participate in the universal that spirit is. Through the concrete universal of spirit, the I is at once particular and universal. The grammar of the "I" itself suggests this, inasmuch as it is the most singular word in any language, and yet applies to all of us. "When I *say* 'I,' 'this individual I,' I am *speaking* generally, about all I's; everyone is what I *say*, everyone is I, this individual, I."[5]

On the basis of the tripartite schema of work, language and interaction as dimensions of dialectical mediation which socialize and humanize man, Habermas and Apel have developed an "anthropology of knowledge" which seeks to ground the natural, human and the so-called critical social sciences respectively in three types of cognitive

---

[4] *Critique of Pure Reason*, B XIII.
[5] *The Phenomenology of Mind*, trans. Sir James Baillie (New York: Macmillan, 1961) p. 154. My emphasis.

interest: the technical, the hermeneutical and the emancipatory.[6] Just how deeply this anthropological topography finds its roots in Hegel is manifest from the fact that the third, and for the ideology critics the most important, dimension is usually referred to as the medium of *Herrschaft* (dominion, mastery) and therefore bears an evident relation to that most influential of Hegelian themes entitled *Herrschaft und Knechtschaft* in the *Phenomenology of Spirit*. Against a scientistic restriction of what constitutes valid knowledge, ideology critique seeks to establish a critical social science which will bring to bear all the resources of science and human knowledge upon the aporias of the master-slave dialectic still prevalent in an "industrialized advanced-capitalistic society."

But if its aim is "interaction free from domination," or more positively, interaction in which self-domination prevails, it is nevertheless admitted that both interaction and work are "symbolically mediated," so that language, the hermeneutical dimension, literally stands in the middle of the scheme and is presupposed by the other two dimensions of humanization.[7] Moreover, language is not only the medium of social communication, through which work relations and political interactions are mediated, but also the medium of tradition and, most important of all, of revealing the world. Hence Gadamer begins with the hermeneutical experience of e.g. an interpreter confronting a text in such a way that a mediation between present and past takes place ("the happening of tradition")[8] in and through the medium of language, and ends with the endeavor to develop a hermeneutical ontology within the horizon of a language considered first of all and most of all to receive its determinations from the world that it discloses. In turn, the world is revealed only in and through language. Human experience even in its most immediate forms is linguistic through and through. It is in language that Gadamer finds the true contemporary heir of the Hegelian thinking concerning spirit, inasmuch as language is "infinite like spirit and yet finite like every happening."[9]

[6] For a detailed account in English of these themes, see Gerard Radnitzky, *Contemporary Schools of Metascience* (New York: Humanities Press, 1970) vol. II, and my "Ideology Critique and Phenomenology" in *Philosophy Today* XIV (1970) pp. 151–160.

[7] Habermas, *Technik und Wissenschaft als "Ideologie,"* pp. 46, 42, 32. The essay we have been following is entitled *Arbeit und Interaktion*.

[8] Theodore Kisiel, "The Happening of Tradition: the Hermeneutics of Gadamer and Heidegger," *Man and World* II (1969) 358–385.

[9] Hans-Georg Gadamer, *Kleine Schriften I: Philosophie – Hermeneutik* (Tübingen: Mohr, 1967) p. 148.

LANGUAGE AS DIALECTICAL MEDIUM

Though the discussion of language is dispersed throughout the Hegelian opus and is never dealt with in any sustained fashion, so that it seems to appear somewhat peripheral for the march of consciousness to spirit in the fullness of its concept, there is nevertheless some warrant for bringing it more into the center of the picture than the older schools of Hegelian interpretation have been inclined to do. And inasmuch as it appears so quickly at the very beginning of the movement of consciousness in its "sense certainty" in the *Phenomenology of Spirit* as well as in the *Logic*, one may even be justified in identifying language as the very medium of the Hegelian dialectic.[10] Moreover, the fact that every major philosophical movement of this century has ultimately centered itself on the topic of "language" makes inevitable the task of reinterpreting Hegel's idealism for the twentieth century problematic precisely in this direction. Nowadays, the critique of knowledge is largely a critique of language, the condition of possibility of knowledge and of thinking.

If this is so, then there are no concepts without language. Language is the home of the concept, the place of the universal. That this is within the spirit of Hegel finds confirmation in the chapter on "Sense Certainty" in the *Phenomenology of Spirit*. Here, it is precisely language which is invoked to counter sense certainty's direct but opaque intuition of the immediate, in the night in which all cows are black; it is language which is introduced from the start to sustain the mediation of the immediate through the entire breadth of experience from sense certainty to the self-transparency of thought thinking itself. The brunt of the argument against the claim of sense immediacy to be the richest kind of truth is that *it cannot be said*. To say the immediate is to mediate it and therefore to lose it in its pure simplicity. To say the singular "this," "here," "now" and "I" is to relate them to others of their kind and therefore to universalize them. The singular of sense certainty is accordingly known and expressed only through universals, aimed at and intended only through the mediation of language, which is the "more truthful" here.[11] The *knowledge* of the immediate thus proves to be the most abstract and poorest of truths which depends

[10] Jean Hyppolite, *Logique et existence: Essai sur la logique de Hegel* (Paris: PUF, 1953) p. 6.
[11] *Phenomenology of Mind*, p. 152. One is reminded here of the Aristotelian-Thomistic tradition concerning the knowledge of singulars.

on the more basic truth of the universal concept. But the immediate as such is unsayable, i.e. inconceivable and therefore unknowable, the absolute limit of knowledge and therefore the very opposite of the absolute knowledge that Hegel seeks. And what cannot be said is the most untrue. "Consequently, what is called unspeakable is nothing but the untrue, irrational, merely intended."[12] "But if language only expresses the universal, then I cannot say what I merely intend. And the ineffable, feeling, sensation, is not the most excellent and true, but the most meaningless and untrue."[13] It is rather language, the medium of mediation and *eo ipso* universalization, which is the place of the truth of the immediate. Language, by introducing mediation and thus universalization, is, in relation to the singular, precisely the power of the negative that holds Hegel spellbound, that "speech which has the divine power of immediately reversing the intention [toward the singular] and making it into something else."[14]

To assert the above situation in its somewhat more cosmological implications, the physical world of nature does not stand over against the "ideal world" of language as an extralinguistic and prehuman world. Rather, nature for man is already *aufgehoben* in language. The task for the "becoming consciousness," which already finds itself in a language that speaks of the world, is therefore not to tear itself away from nature, *"but rather to find the reality for its ideality"*[15] precisely within language. To talk of a nature as a given without man, as of a This of sense, is only to formulate a limit concept that results from a complex and derivative reflection occurring within a given language.

That language stands at the beginning of all of Hegel's work as the most immediate dimension of spirit is strikingly reinforced by the Preface to the second edition of the *Logic*, written shortly before Hegel's death, which acknowledges that "the forms of thought are first of all set out and laid down in language."[16] But the task of logic as Hegel sees it is precisely to purify the instinctive, unconscious and sometimes confused categories contained in the natural logic of a

[12] *Ibid.*, p. 160.

[13] *Encyclopaedia*, § 20.

[14] *Phenomenology of Mind*, p. 160. Also *Philosophische Propädeutik*, § 20: "Die Sprache ist Ertödtung der sinnlichen Welt in ihrem unmittelbaren Dasein, das Aufgehobenwerden derselben zu einem Dasein, welches ein Aufruf ist, der in allen vorstellenden Wesen wiederklingt."

[15] *Jenenser Realphilosophie* I, ed. Johannes Hoffmeister Philosophische Bibliothek vol. 66b (Leipzig: Meiner, 1932) p. 235. Cf. Theodor Bodammer, *Hegels Deutung der Sprache* (Hamburg: Meiner, 1969) pp. 19, 171.

[16] *Hegel's Science of Logic*, trans. W. H. Johnston & L. G. Struthers (New York: Macmillan, 1961) vol. I, p. 39.

language, and thereby "to elevate the spirit through them to freedom and truth."[17] Fortunately, certain given languages have an incipient wealth of logical possibilities which put them at an advantage over other languages for such a purpose. For example, Hegel finds in his own German language a wealth of words which at once possess not only various but in fact opposed meanings, and therefore already contains *in limine* the speculative spirit essential for the kind of logic he seeks to develop.

But if language already possesses a natural logic, then reason has already been at work in the development of language long before any systematic reflection on its categories was attempted. Hegel himself refers to the philological evidence of his day which showed that even the most primitive languages already possess a highly elaborate and consistent grammar, in which thought is already unconsciously at work revealing its categories.[18] Such acknowledgements dovetail with a favorite theme of contemporary hermeneutical phenomenology and are already present in the linguistics of Hegel's day (Hamann, Herder, Wilhelm von Humboldt): the "already there" of language as a contextual immediate that provides man with a preunderstanding from which he develops all of his more reflective meanings. How much Hegel diverges from phenomenological hermeneutics is manifest from the starting points that he expressly avows: not the thick immediate of the comprehensive linguistic situation, but the thin immediate of sense in the *Phenomenology of Spirit* and the abstract immediate of empty Being in the *Logic*. But the degree to which he is aware of this highly developed "thick immediacy" can be measured, for example, by his arguments against Jacobi. Against the immediate knowledge of an inner revelation of an indeterminate which is "beyond me" that Jacobi made central, Hegel insists that immediate knowledge is always the result of learning and the long series of mediations of culture. We may e.g. know America immediately, but we arrive at this knowledge through second-hand reports of others which prompt us to travel there and thus experience America in its immediacy. The opposition between immediate and mediated knowledge is accordingly without justification. "Immediate knowledge is thus everywhere mediated, and philosophy does nothing but bring this to consciousness."[19]

[17] *Ibid.*, p. 46.
[18] *Reason in History: A General Introduction to the Philosophy of History*, trans. Robert S. Hartman (Indianapolis: Bobbs-Merril, 1953) p. 77.
[19] *History of Philosophy, op. cit.*, vol. III, p. 422.

And yet the immediate mediation of language is explicitly excluded from examination. The unconscious of language is not really a theme of philosophy for Hegel, precisely because it is unconscious. If history is the progress of consciousness in freedom, then the reason unconsciously at work in language is not yet history and is consequently relegated to a prehistory.[20] The theme of the historicity of language thus finds no legitimate place in Hegel's world history and history of philosophy. The problematic of language as an ever-operative background and thus itself historical is left an unfinished task, taken up only recently by, among others, Gadamer. The origin and development of the speculative spirit of the language in which Hegel finds himself remains largely an unexplored presupposition for him. Instead, he turns his attention to the further development of the rational already implicit (*an sich*) in the natural logic of language, in particular the movement toward its culmination in the Absolute of a pure logic through the "progress of culture in general and the sciences in particular" which "gradually bring to light higher relations of thought."[21]

For reason is more than language. Hegel was well aware of Hamann's thoughts on this subject. "Hamann places himself in the middle of the problem of reason and proposes its solution. But he formulates this in the framework of language."[22] With this "but," Hegel sets himself off from Hamann's approach to the problem, summarized in the maxim "Reason is language, *logos*." For Hegel, reason is only *in* language, but cannot be taken *as* language. Language may then be the medium *in* which dialectic takes place, but it is not really the motor *by* which the dialectic moves. Though Hegel affirms that language precedes all history and first enables it, it must be remembered that a "condition of possibility" is not a "principle."[23] The principle of history and dialectic is rationality becoming conscious of itself, and the rationality of language is unconscious.

Thus in the *Logic*, what interests Hegel is not really language or even its natural logic, whose categories function only instinctively, but the "higher relations of thought" developed from it through "the progress of culture in general and the sciences in particular." The *Logic* therefore does not really start from language but rather takes its point of departure from the notion of Science already developed in the

[20] *Reason in History*, p. 78.
[21] *Logic* I, p. 40.
[22] "Hamann's Schriften," *Sämtliche Werke*, ed. Hermann Glockner.
[23] Bodammer, *op. cit.*, p. 275.

Phenomenology of Spirit. The reference to language in the Preface to the second edition thus appears almost as an afterthought; in fact, the Preface itself was written long after the text itself. And it is precisely in the *Logic* that Hegel seems furthest from phenomenological hermeneutics. Instead of the acceptance of a finite beginning intrinsic to the doctrine of the hermeneutic circle, which affirms that we have already been begun in finding ourselves in our linguistic situation, Hegel situates himself in the immanent circle of reflection and asks for an absolute beginning in philosophy. The relation between the natural logic of language and the absolute logic of reflection appears more as an abrupt leap rather than a smooth transition. In relation to unreflective language, the reflective logic is to be a "reconstruction,"[24] seemingly a total one, if we recall the abstract methodic beginning in the indeterminate and therefore "unsayable"[25] immediacy of Being, "an empty word,"[26] bearing only an extraneous relation to the natural logic of language. And deep within the *Logic*, he asserts:[27]

Philosophy has the right to select from the language of common life, which is made for the world of sensuous representation, those expressions which seem to approximate the determinations of the concept. It therefore cannot be a matter of showing, for a word selected from the language of common life, one that can also in common life link the same concept with that for which philosophy uses the word. For the common life has no concepts, only representations; and to know the concept of what is otherwise representation, that is philosophy.

The transition from ordinary language (the language of representation) to philosophical language (the language of concept) is perhaps most clearly seen in Hegel's doctrine of the speculative sentence, which takes its point of departure from the ordinary predicative proposition. And if the analytical logic (*Verstand*) of the metaphysics prior to Hegel is viewed as a continuation of the natural logic of the subject-predicate sentence, then the movement of the speculative sentence may be considered as an overcoming of all previous metaphysics. Even though previous philosophy spoke of the concrete totalities – God,

[24] *Logic* I, p. 48. Hegel's attitude toward starting points finds its parallel today in the constructive logic of Paul Lorenzen, who accepts the finite starting point in ordinary language emphasized by hermeneutics but at the same time proposes to begin anew to "methodically reconstruct" a scientific language "from scratch," as it were; *Methodisches Denken* (Frankfurt: Suhrkamp, 1968) pp. 41 ff., 26 ff. Also Wilhelm Kamlah and Paul Lorenzen, *Logische Propädeutik* (Mannheim: Bibliographisches Institut, 1967) pp. 15 ff.

[25] *Encyclopaedia*, § 87.

[26] *Logic* I, p. 90.

[27] *Logic* II, 346–7.

soul, world – there comes a time when its understanding of the sentences discussing these totalities is "checked in its course" and "suffers a counterthrust,"[28] so that the ordinary sentence is "exploded." The presumably stable and quiescent subject of the sentence, to which accidents are juxtaposed in the predication, is brought into movement. For example, in the sentence "God is One," "One" no longer expresses an accident but the very essence of God. In such a case, the subject of the sentence "dissolves" into the substantial meaning of the predicate. In thus losing the subject, thinking loses its solid ground and begins to "waver." For the predicate has now become the subject – and yet the old subject is still present in this predicate, so that thinking is at the same time "thrown back" on it.[29] The ordinarily linear movement of predication, coming to full stop with the period, is cancelled and sublated into the dialectical circle of conceptual manifestation. Accordingly, a single sentence is inadequate to express the whole truth of the concept: "the judgment is through its form one-sided and to that extent false."[30] The oppositional movement of the speculative sentence thereby generates an entire system of propositions and counter-positions in order to express the comprehensiveness of the con-cept, in which each individual sentence finds its place. The exposition of this overall structure is the task of the *Logic*.

It is precisely this speculative-dialectical movement that Gadamer in his hermeneutic seeks *mutatis mutandis* to transfer to the "living metaphoric" of language itself, in its "inner dimension of multipli-cation."[31] For Gadamer, Hegel's doctrine of the speculative sentence is already a step toward overcoming the hypostatized metaphysical-logical-grammatical structure of language and one suggestion toward the new possibilities in the essence of language that Heidegger seeks. There are even suggestions in Hegel that this movement of the specu-lative "method" is not entirely under human control but a "doing of the subject matter itself."[32] But Hegel's assumption of the absolute self-transparency of knowing here encounters the phenomenological *sine qua non*, the affirmation of the insuperable finitude of human experience. Whence the phenomenological reversal of perspectives countering all of classical metaphysics, the re-duction that calls for

[28] *Phenomenology of Mind*, p. 119.
[29] *Ibid.*, p. 121.
[30] *Encyclopaedia*, § 31.
[31] Hans-Georg Gadamer, *Wahrheit und Methode: Grundzüge einer philosophischen Herme-neutik*, 2nd ed. (Tübingen: Mohr, 1965) pp. 409, 434.
[32] *Ibid.*, p. 439.

going "back to the things themselves," in order to consider experience in its own right and not only in terms of its end in Science. Thus, in contrast to Hegel's progress of spirit in a universal history, Heidegger sees his own endeavor as a regressive backtrack into its secret ground. In the same vein, the locus of dialectic for Gadamer is not in a knowledge moving toward its culmination in Science, but in a linguistically situated experience which is ever subject to the negative through an always possible encounter with the new and unexpected. And the motor as well as the medium of the dialectic is now language itself, the condition of possibility of any experience that warrants being called human experience. The "doing of the subject matter itself," which Hegel situates in the self-reflection of spirit, now manifests itself in *and through* language, in a speculative movement that constitutes an inexhaustible "play on words," a self-propelled language game, "the play of language itself which speaks to us, strikes forth and draws back, questions and in the answer fulfills itself."[33] The "concept formation" is accordingly first situated in the historicity of language itself, or better, of the topic which manifests itself in language, a movement which then shows itself in e.g. the bridging that the interpreter must execute when he confronts from his present situation a text inherited from the past. And just as the speculative sentence is no longer a simple assertion that states something about something, but rather overflows into a whole system of sentences in order to express the comprehensive unity of the concept,[34] so every word is not simply a fixed and given being but rather mirrors the whole of language as its suggestive unsaid. Whence the finitude of human discourse, which brings into play a totality of meaning without being able to say it totally. Against the self-transparency of a language which merely serves to express the results of the thought of a clairvoyant spirit, what emerges here in the said/unsaid structure of language is a regard for the finitude of the human situation open to the future and the unexpectedly new. A de-absolutized reading of Hegel precisely on this level is likewise emphasized by Findlay: "The main contemporary importance of Hegel lies in his recognition of the 'open texture,' the unclear corners of all living notions, the fact that they imply more than they clearly cover, and in the further fact that it is natural for them to move or develop in certain ways as soon as they are subjected to unwonted pressures."[35]

---

[33] *Ibid.*, p. 464.
[34] *Ibid.*, p. 442.
[35] J. N. Findlay, *Hegel: A Re-Examination* (New York: Collier, 1962) pp. 22–3.

THE DIREMPTIONS OF HISTORY

While language is again and again driven to the periphery of Hegel's philosophy, history certainly is not, and it is precisely his reflections on this theme that attract contemporary hermeneutical philosophers to him, and even warrant calling Hegel himself a hermeneutical philosopher. Gadamer testifies that the confrontation with Hegel is of central significance for the hermeneutical problem, inasmuch as Hegel has already thought through the historical dimension in which the problem of hermeneutics finds its roots, namely, the mediation of the historical tradition with the present which occurs when an interpreter reads an inherited text.[36] We have already seen that Gadamer attempts to de-absolutize this mediation between past and present by situating it in language instead of in absolute reflection (or a variant thereof like "universal history").[37]

The hermeneutical problem arises when a text, an artwork or some other human creation strike us as strange and incomprehensible and therefore evoke the task of understanding. Most commonly, such estrangement occurs through the passage of time, whereby the art and literature are transmitted to us as torn out of their original context and accordingly obscured in their original meaning. How does one go about to overcome this alienation from the tradition? Basically, two models serve to define the extreme procedural possibilities: Hegel's mediating integration of the past with the present and Schleiermacher's restoration and reconstruction of the past.[38] Gadamer argues against the predominance of the latter in favor of the former, and accordingly interjects Hegel as a corrective into a tradition of hermeneutical philosophy which has emphasized the goal of "objective" understanding, which means the attempt to establish what the author really intended, to reproduce the original production (e.g. of a play), to restore the original state and even to recreate the original contest of a bygone world and lifestyle within which an artwork first found its meaning. Such anti-quarian extremes ultimately only serve to communicate a dead meaning, though a moderate application of these endeavors no doubt has its place in hermeneutical procedure.

Hegel was undoubtedly aware of the absurdity of such restorative

---

[36] *Wahrheit und Methode*, p. 328.
[37] Cf. Wolfhart Pannenberg, "Hermeneutics and Universal History" in Robert W. Funk (ed.) *History and Hermeneutic* (New York: Harper & Row, 1967) pp. 122–152, esp. p. 140n.
[38] *Wahrheit und Methode*, p. 158.

excesses, for example, the recreation of pastoral settings at the height of 18th century romanticism, and his own attitude is clearly manifested in his rejection of Rousseauism and the romantic poetization of the original "state of nature," his struggles with the political Restoration of his times, and his rebuff of exhortations to an advanced society that it return to the ways prevalent in the "wilds of the North American woods" or to the "religion of Melchisedek."[39] In a poignant passage in the *Phenomenology of Spirit* describing the transition from the Greek religion of art to the Christian religion of revelation, he graphically portrays the death of a world gone by ("God is dead") i.e. the hermeneutical predicament, the first superficial attempts to restore it and the more integrative response that he himself pursues. The power of the passage[40] with its still contemporary overtones warrants citing it in its entirety, here divided, in a good Hegelian tradition, into its three phases:

Trust in the eternal laws of the gods is silenced, just as the oracles are dumb, who pretended to know what to do in particular cases. The statues are now corpses in stone whence the animating soul has flown, while the hymns of praise are words from which all belief is gone. The tables of the gods are bereft of spiritual food and drink. and from his games and feasts man no longer receives the joyful sense of his unity with the divine Being. The works of the muse lack the force and energy of the spirit which derived the certainty and assurance of itself from the crushing ruin of gods and men. They are themselves now just what they are for us – beautiful fruit broken off the tree. A kindly fate has passed on these works to us, as a maiden might offer such fruit off a tree. Their actual life as they exist is no longer there, not the tree that bore them, not the earth and the elements which constituted their substance, nor the climate that determined their character, nor the change of seasons which controlled the process of their growth. So too it is not their living world that fate preserves and transmits to us with those works of ancient art, not the spring and summer in which they bloomed and ripened, but only the veiled memory of this reality.

And so when we enjoy this fruit, our action is not that of a spiritual character, through which our conscious life might attain its complete truth and be satisfied to the full: our action is external; it consists of wiping off a drop of rain or speck of dust from this fruit. In place of the inner elements of the actuality of the ethical life, the actuality that environed, created and inspired these works, we erect in prolix detail the scaffolding of the dead elements of their outward

---

[39] *Einleitung in die Geschichte der Philosophie*, ed. Johannes Hoffmeister, Philosophische Bibliothek vol. 166 (Hamburg: Meiner, 1966) p. 74. Citations from this text will be from the German original, since the English translation constitutes a patchwork of the several different versions of this Introduction, with important deletions of this hermeneutically significant text. For what follows, the first half of the English translation of the Introduction may in particular be consulted. See *Hegel's Lectures on the History of Philosophy*, vol. I, pp. 1–55.

[40] *Phenomenology of Mind*, pp. 753–4. Both Gadamer (*Wahrheit und Methode*, pp. 160–1) and Ricoeur (in his 1970 lectures at the University of Chicago on Hegel and hermeneutics) have pointed to the hermeneutical pregnance of this passage.

existence: language, historical circumstances, etc. All this we do, not in order to enter into their very life, but only to represent them in themselves.

But just as the maiden who hands us the plucked fruits is more than their nature displayed in their conditions and elements: the tree, air, light, etc. – the nature that offered them in their immediacy – since she recapitulates all of this in a higher way in the scope of her self-conscious eye and the sweep of her offering gesture, so too the spirit which transmits these works of art to us, is more than the ethical life and actuality of that nation. For this spirit is the *interiorizing* recollection (*Er-Innerung*) of a spirit which is still *externalized* in them; it is the spirit of the tragic fate which gathers all those individual gods and attributes of the substance into the one Pantheon, into the spirit which is itself conscious of itself as spirit.

The passage describes the hermeneutical movement of integrating the Greek into the Christian world, and even more explicitly, the assimilation of the Greek religion of *spiritual* art, i.e. *linguistic* works like Homer's epic poems, Sophocles' tragedies and Aristophanes' comedies. As such, it overlaps with the transition between the two major epochs of Hegel's history of philosophy, the transition from Greek to "Christian-Germanic" philosophy, as well as the hermeneutical problems of the numerous lesser transitions within this more encompassing one. The text therefore can be discussed from the vantage point of the philosophical experience, for Hegel the most "inner" experience.

The first phase. A time no longer speaks to us, a soul has left its body, a unity is broken, a *Zeitgeist* vitiated, words emptied of meaning, a world has passed its zenith and declined, like overripe fruit fallen from a tree, a shape of life has grown old, dusk has fallen: the metaphors mix and cross, but they all move in the same Hegelian direction: alienation. And diremption (*Entzweiung*), Hegel tells us, is the source of the need for philosophy. [41] "When the power of unification disappears from the life of men and the oppositions have lost their living relation and interaction and win independence, then the need for philosophy arises." [42] When a way of life is disrupted, "when the powerful bond between the outer and the inner existence has been torn asunder," [43] the time has come for the Owl of Minerva to spread its wings, not in order to rejuvenate this old way of life but to understand it. From its

[41] Just as for Gadamer the "temporal distance" between present and past is the positive source of the need for hermeneutic.

[42] *Differenz des Fichte'schen und Schelling'schen Systems der Philosophie*, Philosophische Bibliothek vol. 62a. (Hamburg: Meiner, 1962), p. 14.

[43] *Einleitung in die Geschichte der Philosophie*, p. 153; also p. 286. On p. 151, Hegel himself alludes to the familiar "Owl of Minerva" passage from the Preface to the *Philosophy of Right:* "Philosophy begins with the decline of a real world. When philosophy arises and – painting gray in gray – propagates its abstractions, the fresh color of youth and vitality is already past and gone. It then brings about a reconciliation, but only in the world of thought and not in the earthly world."

very beginning, philosophy has had its heyday in times of decline and revolution, in fact serving to speed up this decay. When outer reality is no longer satisfying, the spirit withdraws into the ideal world of thought to work out a new reality. The maiden suggests Dame Wisdom, who offered the consolation of philosophy to Boethius.

And she brings with her *living* "beautiful fruit." The old reality is not all gone – its fruits are still there, "the veiled memory of this reality," and it is with these that philosophy begins anew. The fruit unites within itself all the stages that led to its production: the tree, earth, elements, climate, and moreover, contains within itself the seed for the new.[44] The veiled memory of the fruit awaits the new and higher re-collection potential in the seed. The fruit must die as fruit for the sake of the new life in the seed. But the genus (in more non-metaphorical terms, the thought or idea) remains, indestructible, eternal, and it is on this level of universality that philosophy finds its element, which moths cannot corrupt nor thieves take away, where the formal thought articulates itself and "grows together" into the concrete concept. For the universal is always present, never past. Its particularities may fall away, the artists and philosophers who discovered it pass away, but the universal content of artworks and philosophies remain. It is because of this that an artwort continues to "work" and assumes the perenniality of a "classic."[45] "An artwork presupposes genius, but everyone recognizes it. The individual who creates it does not explicitly show his genius in it, but simply represents the subject matter (*Sache*). Thus all particularity in the artwork is already lost in the objective."[46] This applies even more so to philosophy, the standpoint of the wholly universal, the element of pure thought. The history of philosophy never deals with the past but with the present, and in fact with the "most living present,"[47] the ever-present.

The second phase. And yet, at first sight, the works of the past strike us as exotic fruit with alien origins, so that our attempts to assimilate them tend to be external, i.e. "objective." We resort to the strategies of abstract analysis (*Verstand*) instead of concrete comprehension

[44] *Ibid.*, pp. 131, 108–9, which show how deeply Hegel's concept of development is rooted in the metaphor of fruit and seed. The word here is always *Frucht* and not *Obst*.

[45] *Ibid.*, p. 71. In a similar vein, Gadamer speaks of the capacity of an artwork to be "contemporary for every present." (*Wahrheit und Methode*, p. 115).

[46] *Ibid.*, p. 282. Also striking here is the fact that Hegel sides with Gadamer against Schleiermacher in stressing the *Sache* rather than the *psyche* as the centerline of interpretation.

[47] *Ibid.*, p. 280. One is reminded of Husserl's *lebendige Gegenwart*.

(*Vernunft*). We "represent them in themselves" rather than "enter into their very life," which is the life of their concept at its present stage and not as it was in its earlier embodiment. The objective methods of aloofness and the subjective methods of empathy are at one here in their quest for *wie es gewesen ist*. Both pure impartiality and simple restoration are inadequate approaches to the problem of reconciliation with history.

The stance of impartiality and disinterest seeks to establish the facts of history and opinions of others without prejudice and distortion, to describe what is given without seeking its own system in the account. Such an approach is useful in authenticating facts and texts, "in wiping off a drop of rain or speck of dust from this fruit," but in its extreme it is only an external history, a chronicle with no more structure than that of temporal sequence. To be without party or interest is to be without order or context, and the result is a failure to understand the issue. "In reality only he who understands nothing of the issue (*Sache*) and merely has historical bits of information acts impartially." [48] The writer of history must be partial to his subject matter, must desire to understand it, must in other words be interested in it. Interest in the topic is the one necessary partiality. In the history of philosophy, the historian must be a party to philosophy. To be without interest in a topic is to deal with alien things which are themselves without interest, fit matter for only the driest of pedants. The best advice here: let the dead bury the dead and follow the living, the interesting, the present. And history, especially that of philosophy, is not the becoming of alien things, but our own becoming, something very much present, "which for our thinking spirit is necessarily interesting." [49] "What it comes down to is whether we hold ourselves worthy to have all that has been thought as our own thought," [50] and in fact in such a way that we "know it better than all earlier thinkers." [51] The mighty battle of reason and not the tiny forays of analysis!

Biblical exegesis, to take another example, has had a tradition which strove for the literal interpretation of the text, which "receives the written word, interprets it and purports to advance only the understanding of the word, to wish to remain true to it." But mere word clarification does not really advance understanding; the gram-

[48] *Ibid.*, p. 261.
[49] *Ibid.*, p. 134.
[50] *Ibid.*, p. 281.
[51] *Ibid.*, p. 280.

matical sense of a word is not its speculative sense. "The letter kills, but the spirit giveth life." Extrinsic clarification is merely propaedeutic to intrinsic understanding. In fact, when we look more closely, we discover that even biblical exegesis does more than it purports. "Commentaries on the Bible do not so much make us acquainted with the content of the Scriptures as with the manner in which things were conceived in the age in which they were written." The interpreter spontaneously brings his own world into play in the interpretation:[52]

> Thought expressly contains determinations, principles, presuppositions which must make their influence felt in the work of interpretation. If interpretation is not to be mere clarification of words but explanation of sense, the thoughts of the interpreter must necessarily be put into the words which constitute the foundation. Mere word interpretation can only amount to this, that for one word another coextensive in meaning is substituted; but in the course of explanation further determinations of thought are combined with it. ... It is indeed the sense contained in the words which is presumed to be given. But the giving of meaning means to bring the meaning to consciousness, into the realm of ideas; and these ideas, which get determinate character elsewhere, then assert their influence in the exposition of the meaning presumed to be contained in the words.

"To know it better than all earlier thinkers" – Hegel's ambition sounds much like Schleiermacher's hermeneutical dictum "to understand the author better than he understood himself."[53] This is so, but since in dealing with the thoughts of past philosophers we are not treating these thoughts as past, but rethinking them in terms of our present, "in which *a deeper, more determinate concept* now *lives*," it is not a matter of a simple revival of the old philosophies as they were. "For this reason there can be no more Platonists, Aristotelians, Stoics and Epicureans today. To revive these, to wish to reverse the spirit which is now more developed and entered more deeply into itself would be as impossible and foolish as the wish of a man to be a youth again, or the youth a boy or child, although the man, youth and child are one and the same individual."[54] Such a nostalgia for the past betrays the longing for a fixed starting point, but this is to be found in the spirit

---

[52] *Hegel's Lectures on the Philosophy of Religion*, trans. Rev. E. B. Speirs and J. Burdon Sanderson (London: Routledge and Kegan Paul, 1962) vol. I, p. 28–29.

[53] The dictum is already in Kant: *Critique of Pure Reason*, Transcendental Dialectic, B 370. For the background of the discussion of this dictum prior to Hegel, see Lutz Geldsetzer, *Die Philosophie der Philosophiegeschichte im 19.Jahrhundert* (Meisenheim am Glan: Hain, 1968) pp. 202–5, 195. Here Hegel is explicitly considered to be a hermeneutical philosopher.

[54] *Einleitung in die Geschichte der Philosophie*, pp. 72–3. Cf. W. H. Walsh, "Hegel on the History of Philosophy," in John Passmore (ed.) *The Historiography of the History of Philosophy*, Beiheft 5, *History and Theory* (s-Gravenhage: Mouton, 1965) pp. 67–82.

and not in the "authority" of tradition. And the spirit has since become rich. The rehash of old philosophies would only manifest their obsolescence even more blatantly in a time when the problems are different, and the needs "higher" ("deeper") than those that initiated these philosophies. At best, learning a past philosophy by heart (*auswendig*), if not a rote exercise in a dead language or a mechanical submission to authority, might be an initial but temporary "scaffolding" of externals in which the more original work of getting it into one's mind, i.e. spirit (*inwendig*) [55] can eventually take place, and this means to integrate it into the present life of spirit, to situate it in the context of the tasks of the present need for philosophy. Philosophical ideas, to stay alive, must be *aufgehoben* into the present.

The third phase. The fruit does not come directly from the tree but is brought by a messenger (Hermes), who is compared with "the spirit of fate, the spirit which transmits." And the maiden (the spirit of historical transmission) is "more than" their nature; she recapitulates in a "higher" way. Likewise we of the present generation, in relation to our past, "we belong to a richer spirit, which has concretely in itself recapitulated the wealth of all earlier philosophies. This deeper principle lives in us without being conscious of itself. The spirit poses tasks for itself which were not yet tasks of an older philosophy." [56] The earliest philosophies are the most indigent, simplest, most abstract, poorest in determination and content, in relation to which the latest philosophies are the more concrete and articulated. And nothing is ever lost or thrown away. Fundamentally, no earlier philosophy is ever refuted; what is refuted and becomes passé is merely its position as highest; its position is now altered, but its philosophical principle is retained in what follows. The newest philosophy is necessarily a developed system that contains all the earlier as branches of its organization, but now sublated in their onesidedness, just as the elementary capacity of writing, which was the chief concern in boyhood learning, is still retained in the man but now as part of a larger culture. The older ideas, to stay alive, must be superseded, integrated into the newer spirit of the times. [57]

But the spirit of history is not only integrating but also internalizing (*Er-innerung*). The maiden is Mnemosyne whose gesture invites us into the temple of Memory, "the one Pantheon," but now as a more

[55] *Phenomenology of Mind*, p. 100.
[56] *Einleitung in die Geschichte der Philosophie*, p. 145.
[57] *Ibid.*, pp. 66, 74, 125–7, 141–5, 279.

comprehensive "self-conscious" *Zeitgeist* that beckons us to new tasks. For "deeper ideas slumber in the spirit of the newer time."[58] The times are pregnant with a new content, but this *Zeitgeist* is still only "substantial," i.e. in-itself, external, and is yet to be internalized by us, made into a for-itself. The course of history is "not the becoming of alien things but our becoming,"[59] but we have yet to undergo through thought the inner transformation that the times demand of us, a demand experienced here in the need to overcome the diremption from our past. The end result of internalizing recollection is the intimacy of "Being at home with itself in otherness." This homecoming occurs particularly in the stage of "Christian philosophy," where spirit "is itself conscious of itself as spirit." "Here the principle, the object of interest is immediately the inner itself, the concrete interiority, the concrete world of spirit, the concrete intelligible world, the reconciled world."[60]

It is thus that philosophy becomes "the consciousness of the substantial of its time,"[61] at home with the spirit of its time. In being identical with its time, philosophy does not stand above time but remains a child of its time. "No one can escape the substantial of his time, as little as he can climb out of his own skin."[62] In explicitly bringing forth the implicit rational content of its time through thought, "philosophy is its time apprehended in thoughts." This timeliness of philosophy is both its wealth and its poverty: every philosophy is for its time, responding to its problems, but it is only for its time.

However, insofar as it is the *knowledge* of the substantial of its time, philosophy in its form stands above time; "it is the inner birthplace of the spirit that later emerges as reality."[63] As Hegel once asserted in a letter to Niethammer:[64] "Day by day, I am more and more convinced that theoretical work brings about more in the world than the practical. If the realm of ideas is revolutionized, reality does not hold out."

Insofar as philosophy reflects the world of its day and interprets the signs of its time, it can be called a hermeneutical philosophy, in the sense that Marx's reflections on the Industrial Revolution and,

[58] *Ibid.*, p. 75.
[59] *Ibid.*, p. 14.
[60] *Ibid.*, p. 301.
[61] *Ibid.*, p. 149.
[62] *Ibid.*, p. 149.
[63] *Ibid.*, p. 150.
[64] *Briefe von und an Hegel*, ed. Johannes Hoffmeister, Philosophische Bibliothek vol. 235 (Hamburg: Meiner, 1952) p. 253. Written in Bamberg, October 28, 1808.

more self-consciously so, Heidegger's reflections on the present nuclear-space-automated age of technology are hermeneutical philosophies.[65] According to Joachim Ritter, Hegel stands at the fountainhead of such philosophies, as the first philosopher who equated metaphysics with "politics," in the broadest sense of reflection on the sense of the contemporary world. For Hegel, "philosophy *as* knowledge of Being is *at once* 'its time apprehended in thoughts,'"[66] and can remain a knowledge of Being only as long as it is at once a knowledge of its time.

Hegel's time was marked by the diremption between the opposing spirits of revolution and restoration. The spirit of the French Revolution posited a negative or abstract freedom that set itself uncompromisingly against all historically established institutions, which naturally evoked the reaction of restoration, with its romantic denial of the new epoch in order to save the historical substance of man. Both therefore belong together in their diremption, so that the breach in history thus brought about poses the problem, not of choosing one or the other, which would be a denial of history, but of reconciling the two in a higher unity, a tensile unity far removed from a monotonous uniformity free from contradiction. The tension of diremption thus remains throughout, from initial provocation of the "need of philosophy" to interpret a world torn asunder to the final reconciliation of the tenses of past and future, of the historical heritage (*Herkunft*) and the forthcoming society (*Zukunft*). Diremption thus manifests itself as the positive and rational ground of the movement of history.[67]

Ritter explicitly identifies this process of reconciliation of past and future as a hermeneutics,[68] and proceeds to exemplify[69] how such an

[65] Rüdiger Bubner points out that two intertwined but distinguishable attitudes are possible from the Hegelian dictum that "philosophy is its time apprehended in thoughts": the critical attitude, which directs itself against its time, and the hermeneutical attitude, which enters thoughtfully into its time; which is why both ideology critique from Marx to the present and hermeneutics are possible out of Hegel and why both continually dovetail into one another. Ricoeur, for example, considers ideology critique as a hermeneutics in its demystifying movement. Cf. Rüdiger Bubner, "Philosophie ist ihre Zeit, in Gedanken erfasst," in *Hermeneutik und Dialektik*, edited by R. Bubner, K. Cramer and R. Wiehl (Tübingen: Mohr, 1970) vol. I, p. 325. These two volumes are in fact a *Festschrift* to Gadamer on the occasion of his 70th birthday.

[66] Joachim Ritter, *Metaphysik und Politik: Studien zu Aristoteles und Hegel* (Frankfurt: Suhrkamp, 1969) p. 189. I wish to thank Otto Pöggeler for calling my attention to the significance of this book for a Hegelian hermeneutics, and for granting me access to the facilities of the Hegel-Archiv in the preparation of this essay.

[67] *Ibid.*, pp. 206–252. The essay here is Ritter's famous "Hegel und die französische Revolution."

[68] *Ibid.*, p. 266n. Similarly, the hermeneutical process for Gadamer culminates in the fusion of the horizons of present and past.

[69] Especially in the last two essays of this collection entitled "Europäisierung als europäisches Problem" and "Die grosse Stadt."

Hegelian hermeneutic can be applied to the present world situation, whose major diremption is particularly visible and dramatic in the sudden onslaught of technology upon the tradition-bound lands of the East. The new principle of technology appears as a sharp break with the past, the old and the new separate, heritage and future are without relation. The extreme responses to this situation, on the one hand the futurist theories of progress in their revolutionary denial of heritage, on the other the theories of decadence, the romantic reaction against technology and the glorification of little-trodden "forest trails" in "primeval woods" leading to the "distant summits," have one thing in common: they both try to do away with the necessity of diremption by seeking to abolish one or the other side of the dilemma. The Hegelian response to the problem of historical discontinuity is the evocation of the positive power of mediation in order to overcome the negative relation of progress to heritage and of the past to the future. For there is no history without a future and no future without a history.

CONCLUSION: HEGEL AND HEIDEGGER

One may recognize in the above the overtones of a critique of Heidegger. And since Heidegger in our time has developed a hermeneutic of our historical world that seeks to uncover the most subliminal presuppositions of today's technological world, a comparison of Hegel with Heidegger almost appears inevitable at this point. Such a comparison, often invoked nowadays, will serve not only to summarize some of the issues discussed above but also to accentuate from a somewhat different slant some further critical points at issue between Hegel and the contemporary hermeneutical scene.

To say that Heidegger puts a premium on its presuppositions in his confrontation of the historical world already suggests that his approach to history is more "regressive" than Hegel's. Thus he tells us that in relation to Hegel's *Aufhebung*, the character of his own dialogue with the history of philosophy is that of a backtrack, "the step back." [70] We have already seen that Hegel's progressivist scheme calls for a step forward that reconciles all that has gone before with the present stage of spirit in the movement of interiorizing recollection, *Er-innerung*. Nothing is ever lost or thrown away, all past achievements of thought find their place as parts in the present consummation

---

[70] *Identity and Difference*, trans. Joan Stambaugh (New York: Harper & Row, 1969) p. 49.

of spirit. Nothing therefore remains fundamentally concealed or mysterious. We understand past thinkers better than they understood themselves, as subordinate phases of a more complete system. It can therefore be said that we understand them better by understanding them differently.

Heidegger instead speaks of a forgetting, a *Seinsvergessenheit*, an oblivion of Being that demands a rethinking of the concealed foundations of what has already been thought in order to draw from its unthought what is yet to be thought. Metaphysics is therefore to be "destroyed" and "overcome" rather than "elevated" and "consummated." If Heidegger calls for a return to the concealed beginnings of philosophy, it is with a conviction that is the direct opposite to Hegel's: This beginning is no longer the poorest and most abstract, but the richest and most concrete, the source of perpetual novelty. Being is not an empty word, but rather "inexhaustible wealth," an "abyss" with infinite "give." Even more basic than the history that we remember and relate is the history that we forget, which at any time can break in on what we do relate with an unexpected surprise from the charge of its unthought. In Heidegger's terms, even more basic than the *Geistesgeschichte* is the *Seinsgeschick*, the message that we *receive*, coming as it were from the "outside," from the situation in which we find ourselves, to which we must be receptive and open, rather than from the active spirit within. History then is not the immanent reconciliation of the unfolding of an ultimately self-transparent spirit, but rather the epochal articulation of a Being that essentially conceals itself in its revelations. The last word is not the recollection of spirit but the retreat of Being.[71] Accordingly, the centerline for the dialogue with the history of philosophy is not to be found in what has already been thought by past thinkers, but in something that has not been thought *in them*.[72] Therefore it is not a matter of understanding these thinkers better than they understood themselves, but of understanding them differently. In his own place, each great thinker understands himself the best; but from another vantage point, something unthought can disclose itself in what he has thought. In the process of disclosing this new aspect of thought, some of what has already been thought may sink back into the unthought, and what is disclosed tends to conceal the undisclosed as such. Ac-

[71] As Heidegger puts it, the topic of thinking for Hegel is Being as it is thought, while for himself it is Being as difference. *Ibid.*, p. 46.
[72] *Ibid.*, p. 48.

cordingly, there may well be losses as well as gains and the movement of history is more "erratic" than continuous, in keeping with its radical finitude. For the source of the "need of philosophy" now resides in the unthought rather than in diremption. And the movement of history is no longer ultimately determined by the healing *Er-innerung* of the diremption (*Entzweiung*) between present and past, but by the receiving (*Ent-sprechung*) of the "appropriation" (*Er-eignis*) that responds to one's own time, which may even demand a breach with the past. The emphasis falls not on the totalizing of all that has gone before, but on appropriating the possibilities proper for one's own time, which first demands a retrieving re-vision of the facticity of its presuppositions. The German prefixes are telling here: For Heidegger, the brunt of the alienation (*Ent-*) falls on man and not on the times, while the initiative and consummation (*Er-*) of the process, its alpha and omega, its center of gravity, is located in the historical situation rather than in the human spirit. Accordingly, in the human response to history, the stress is no longer on the interiorizing of spirit but on the ecstatic stance to that which always exceeds man. It is this ecstasis of time which for Heidegger is the principal unthought factor of the metaphysical tradition that emphasized the *nunc stans* and the translucence of light, which found its most consummate expression in Hegel.

Instead of the tradition of light metaphysics, Heidegger, especially in his emphasis on a receptivity to an unsaid and even unsayable dimension, finds much of his inspiration in the German tradition of "logos mysticism" from Eckhardt to Boehme, which Hegel in his lifelong argument with romanticism, with Jacobi and Schelling, for example, considered to have overcome. How far removed Heidegger is from the spirit of Hegel can be divined from some telling remarks against Reinhold which Hegel articulated quite early in his career.[73] According to Reinhold, following Jacobi, what philosophy must first assume as absolute, at least provisionally in order to begin, is the primordially true (*Urwahres*) "which is the inconceivable, unexplainable and unnameable pure and simple." But such an absolute is not an active work of reason but rather the "already in and for itself," in relation to which any act of reason would alter its primordially true character and therefore produce error. Thinking would accordingly have to be reduced from a passive receptivity to an already finished

---

[73] *Differenz-Schrift*, pp. 103–5.

truth. With an inconceivable primeval truth, philosophy cannot leave its starting point; it acquires a point of departure only with conceivable truths, with concepts, even if these be at first "inconceivable concepts." "Philosophy must in fact begin, proceed and end with concepts, but with inconceivable concepts; for in the confinement of a concept the inconceivable, instead of merely being proclaimed, is *aufgehoben*."

APPENDIX

Reason and Religious Truth: Hegel's Foreword to H. Fr. W.
Hinrichs' *Die Religion im inneren Verhältnisse zur Wissenschaft* (1822),
translated from the German by A. V. Miller, with an Introduction by
Merold Westphal

INTRODUCTION

This foreword is the most lucid and succinct statement of Hegel's
mature position on the question of faith and reason insofar as that
position begins with a negative critique of prevailing approaches to
the problem. Sometimes, as here and in *Glauben und Wissen* (1802),
that critique is allowed to stand alone. But it is never omitted from
its role as the dialectical point of departure whenever Hegel presents
his own positive proposals. Thus this obscure foreword is a valuable
introduction to the *Phenomenology, Encyclopaedia, Logic, Philosophy
of Religion,* and the 1829 *Lectures on the Proofs of the Existence of God,*
since all of these are, in their most fundamental intention, attempts
to reconcile faith and reason.

Like Hegel's foreword, Herman Friedrich Wilhelm Hinrichs himself
is of more interest than his book. He was a young scholar whom Hegel
had known at Heidelberg. Hegel's boost for his book had happy
consequences for both of them. Hinrichs got a position as Lecturer at
Breslau that very year, 1822, and as the first to teach Hegelian
philosophy apart from Hegel himself, he became the founder of the
Hegelian school. He was later identified with the so-called right wing
Hegelians.

In referring above to Hegel's essay as obscure it is our own perspective
that is invoked. In its own time it was not at all unnoticed, though it

attracted attention in an ironical way. Designed to lead the way to an authentic peace between faith and reason, it was decisive in effecting an irreparable breach between Hegel, the leading philosopher of the day, and Schleiermacher, the leading theologian. The two had been colleagues since the beginning of Hegel's tenure as Fichte's successor at Berlin in 1818. In fact, it was Schleiermacher, in his capacity as University President, who had presented Hegel's nomination by the University Senate to the government for appointment. But from the first there was an intense personal rivalry between the two, aided by theoretical differences. Its expression from time to time was not free from either bitterness or pettiness.

It is true that after one public confrontation between them Schleiermacher began his letter of apology by supplying Hegel with the address of a wine merchant which he had requested. And it is reported they they once took a tobaggan ride together at the Tivoli. But this was about the extent of their ability to work together. Just before Hegel wrote his foreword for Hinrichs' book Schleiermacher's systematic theology, *The Christian Faith*, appeared. Since he defined religion there as the feeling of absolute dependence, Hegel was unable to treat *Speeches on Religion* (1799) and its defense of feeling as the essence of religion as merely the expression of a youthful romanticism. Schleiermacher's mature stance could only be conceived as the theology of feeling.

In this context the sustained polemic against the theology of feeling, especially the assault on the "third universal prejudice" of the day, "that feeling is the true and even the sole form in which the religious spirit preserves its genuineness," is an undisguised attack on Schleiermacher. There can be no question whom Hegel has in mind when he says that "a dog would be the best Christian for it possesses [the feeling of its dependence] in the highest degree and lives mainly in feeling. The dog also has feelings of deliverance when its hunger is satisfied by a bone."

The main thrust of Hegel's case against allowing feeling to be normative needs no comment. But two related matters should be noted. First, as Hegel sees it, the issue is not just a theological one. The soil in which this sort of theological subjectivism can grow will also nourish the kind of ethical and social subjectivism which might be called romantic anarchism, a phenomenon no stranger to our time than to Hegel's. Thus it is not just a matter of religion but of morality, or right and duty, and of the "ethical form of social life, both in the family and in the State." In fact, the confrontation with Schleiermacher mentioned above was grounded precisely in Hegel's concern that the reign of feeling would become the reign of terror.

"From the begining," Hegel writes, "philosophy has been in conflict with sophistry." By applying this label to the "evil of the present time" Hegel assigns to his own philosophy a Platonic-Aristotelian task. This leads to the second point, namely that the cult of feeling is not the sole component of the sophistry he had to deal with. "This evil, the fortuitousness and caprice of subjective feeling and its opinions associated with the culture of reflective thought which has proved to its own satisfaction that spirit is incapable of knowing the truth, has from ancient times been called sophistry." It is subjectivism in conjunction with scepticism which constitutes sophistry.

Between the two of them the components of sophistry can bring about a reconciliation between faith and reason. In fact, one of the things most attractive about grounding faith in feeling is that this form "seems to offer no aspect which could be dialectically attacked by thought." But Hegel finds this to be a "superficial, barren peace." He says any peace between faith and reason would be unsatisfactory "if, on the one hand, faith had lost all substantial meaning, only the empty husk of subjective conviction remaining, or, on the other hand, reason had renounced all claim to a knowledge of the Truth, the human spirit being left with only appearances and feelings for its sustenance." But this is precisely the kind of peace which sophistry can negotiate. A genuine peace presupposes the overcoming of sophistry.

It is Hegel's thesis here as elsewhere that its two elements, subjectivism and scepticism, are not equally fundamental. Subjectivism is seen to be the natural outgrowth of scepticism, which thus assumes the more basic position. The scepticism Hegel has in mind is one which on its theological side is called Enlightenment and on its philosophical side Kantianism. He is concerned with both its character and its origin.

As to the former this scepticism is to be described as the Understanding. Hegel uses this name as a technical term for finite thinking, or more specifically, that thought which directs itself to finite objects and is properly equipped for just this task. In the following passage Hegel uses the term secular as a synonym for the Understanding. "The aim of secular science is a knowledge of finite objects; the goal to which it aspires in its efforts to penetrate to their interior is a knowledge of causes and grounds. But these causes and grounds are essentially analogous to what is to be explained and for that reason the forces which come within its purview are likewise only finite." If this passage has a Kantian ring, it is no accident.

Now it is clear that the Understanding can only express itself as scepticism with reference to what is Absolute or Infinite. The form this takes in Kant is familiar. Hegel links to this the deism and materialsim of the Enlightenment. In both cases the Understanding, directed toward the question of what is Absolute or Infinite, was only able to be negative and critical. It "has emptied Truth of all content whatever so that nothing remains for it except, on the one hand, the pure negative, the *caput mortuum* of a merely abstract Being, and on the other hand, a finite material."

But if the Understanding is taken for reason as such it follows that man cannot know the divine, except perhaps, as some lifeless abstraction. And if he should find that he cannot abandon the project of some sort of intercourse with God, what is left for him but romantic yearning and a resort to feeling as the vehicle of contact? In this way the second component of sophistry arises from the first.

But this first component Hegel distinguishes as "the other mischief" from "the first mischief," leading us back to a still earlier stage in the story he is telling. As we regress to its point of departure that story increasingly resembles Plato's account of the decline of the state. In this case the starting point or "the first mischief" turns out to be the theological orthodoxy which was the Enlightenment's opponent. This is presented as a theology of the Understanding, reminding us that the Understanding is not only not inherently opposed to faith, but first appears in its service. But since its proper subject matter is finite, the result is that it confuses the finite content to which it is suited with the Eternal Truth which is its goal. Hegel gives special attention to its concern for historical matters, since in the eighteenth century much of the conflict between orthodoxy and Enlightenment was rooted in the question of biblical criticism. An example of the sort of confusion Hegel has in mind would be the way in which the conflict over biblical criticism led orthodoxy often to treat, e.g., the Mosaic authorship of the Pentateuch as an article of faith.

Hegel believes this kind of theology bears the seeds of its own destruction, that the Understanding will see the error of its ways and turn on itself in a "switching round of reflection – unexpected by reflection itself – into an activity hostile to its own work, a switching round which equally is only the spontaneous determination of reflection itself." In view of Kant's discovery of the inherently antinomic character of the Understanding, we should not be too surprised to find such apparent opposites rooted in one and the same finite mode of thought. This is how we must understand Hegel's claim that it is theological orthodoxy which gives rise to the theological negativity of the Enlightenment. He anticipates Rudolf Otto's suggestion that orthodoxy is the mother of rationalism, but he goes on to add that rationalism is the mother of scepticism, which in turn begets subjectivism and anarchy. And none of the children are bastards.

After telling this tragic story of the fall of the house of Truth, Hegel sketchily indicates his alternative proposal for reconciling faith with reason. He tells us that his models are Plato and Aristotle, on the one hand, and the scholastics on the other. This latter is surprising, since he usually dismisses their work as the theology and metaphysics of the Understanding. But here he speaks of their "sublime aim" in contrast to "a very inferior type of theology that places its scientific difference from general religious doctrine in the historical element . . ." Once again Hegel's position on the historical becomes central. He has already indicated that distinguishing the finite from the infinite, the inessential from the essential, involves separating "finite and external narratives," i.e., temporal history, from eternal history and eternal Truth. This requirement, as his praise of the scholastics reminds us, is central to the Reason which he will oppose to Understanding in order to reconcile it to faith.

But faith, for Hegel in this essay, is not just the form of subjective certainty and personal appropriation. It includes the content, "the *credo*, the church's confession." Since Hegel is talking about the Christian faith in particular, this would have to refer primarily to the canonical confessions of faith which constitute the Bible, and secondarily to the creeds of Christendom. But in these documents, instead of the flight to eternal history and eternal truth, great prominence is given to historical events as part of the content of faith. To be sure, one does not find the church confessing its faith in the Mosaic authorship of the Pentateuch. But just as Israel confesses its faith by acknowledging the mighty acts of God in history, the call of Abraham, the deliverance from Egypt, the covenant with David, the exile as God's judgment and the return of the remnant as God's faithfulness, so in the New Testament the faithful confess the incarnation and atonement, not as eternal truths or events in an eternal history, but as the presence of God himself in a particular part of our history.

The problem then is this. Hegel knows that between faith and reason there can be a "superficial, barren peace. In such a peace it may seem that what offends has been eliminated whereas it has only been put on one side." Since the historical, except as the inessential, the frame which adorns the picture of eternal history, is what offends in this case, the question is whether anything but this superficial and barren peace can be negotiated between the Christian faith and Hegelian reason. Hegel knows that the church's teaching can be opposed "by a creed of man's own making" and that there is a difference between merely human thought and that thought which "though human, is also divine." The question is whether from the perspective of faith (which is being asked to sign the peace treaty) Hegel's standpoint of eternal history can be seen as anything but a creed of man's own making, the product of merely human thought. Nor will it suffice to respond that Hegel's standpoint is not that of the Understanding but of Reason, for Hegel himself, by referring to the former as "so-called reason," reminds us that the claim to be reason is neither infallible nor self-authenticating – not everyone who says "Reason! Reason!" will enter the kingdom.

But are we to include among those who merely *say* "Reason" the author of the *Science of Logic* and the *Encyclopedia*? Hegel, as it turns out, is not hostile to the historical *as such;* but he does insist that a clear distinction be made between the absolute Truth and the external phenomena associated with its manifestation. The "reason" which is simply offended by the historical element as such in religion is the "reason" of the Enlightenment. By contrast Hegel stresses the historicity of Jesus in his *Philosophy of Religion* (*Begriff d. Religion*, p. III, Lasson's ed.). After saying that we accept Homer's stories of Jupiter and the other gods without treating them as historical, he goes on to say: "Yet there is also a history that is a divine history which, moreover, is meant to be history in the strict sense of the word: the *history of Jesus*. This counts not as a mere myth but as something perfectly historical."

As early as 1802 in the first paragraph of *Glauben und Wissen*, Hegel sought to get beyond the way reason and faith had struggled over the historical during the eighteenth century. "The glorious victory won by the reason of the Enlightenment [rationalism] over faith – or rather over that faith which the Enlightenment with its very limited religious comprehension regarded as opposed to it – is seen, on closer inspection, to be nothing else than this: that the positive element [in religion] against which reason set out to do battle no longer remained religion, nor did the victorious reason remain reason; and the offspring of reason and faith which hovers triumphantly over these corpses as the child of peace uniting them both, has within it as little of reason as it has of genuine faith."

What we may take to be Hegel's final word on this topic comes in the introduction to his Berlin lectures on the *History of Philosophy* (Hoffmeister's ed., p. 192) "Philosophy, as a thinking that *comprehends* this content [the dogma of the Church] has the advantage over the picture-thinking of religion that it understands both; for it understands religion and can do justice to it; it also understands rationalism and supernaturalism; and also it understands itself. But the converse is not true; religion as such, since its standpoint is that of picture-thinking, recognizes itself only in such thinking, not in philosophy, i.e., in Notions, in universal determinations of thought. Often, a philosophy is rightly reproached for its opposition to religion; but often, too, the reproach is unmerited, viz. when it emanates from the religious standpoint; just because religion does not understand philosophy."

Hegel's Foreword to H. Fr. W. Hinrichs' *Die Religion im inneren Verhältnisse zur Wissenschaft* (1822)

The opposition between faith and reason which for centuries has been not only of academic, but also of popular, interest may seem nowadays to have lost some of its importance, indeed almost to have vanished. If this were indeed so, our age might perhaps be congratulated on it. For the nature of that opposition is such that the human spirit cannot turn its back on either faith or reason; each shows itself to be so deeply rooted in man's innermost self-consciousness that when they come into conflict, he is shaken to the depths of his being and his inner disharmony makes his condition one of utter wretchedness. But even if the conflict between faith and reason had vanished and given place to a reconciliation, it would depend essentially on the nature of the reconciliation whether it would be a matter for congratulation or not.

For there is also a peace that is indifferent to the depths of the spirit, a superficial, barren peace. In such a peace it may seem that what offends has been eliminated whereas it has only been put on one side; but what is only overlooked or despised is for that very reason not overcome. On the contrary, if the reconciliation has not brought satisfaction to the deepest, true needs of the spirit, if the sanctuary of the spirit has not received its due, the disharmony will in principle remain and the hostility will continue to fester all the more deeply beneath the surface; the harm, unsuspected and unperceived, will be all the more dangerous.

It would be an unsatisfactory peace if, on the one hand, faith had lost all substantial meaning, only the empty husk of subjective conviction remaining, or, on the other hand, reason had renounced all claim to a knowledge of the Truth, the human spirit being left with only appearances and feelings for its sustenance. How could there still be any great cleavage between faith and reason when neither any longer possessed an objective content, anything, therefore, about which there could be any dispute?

For I understand by faith neither the merely subjective state of belief which is restricted to the form of certainty, leaving untouched the nature of the content, if any, of the belief, nor on the other hand only the *credo*, the church's confession of faith which can be recited and learnt by rote without communicating itself to man's innermost self, without being identified with the certainty which a man has of himself, with his consciousness of himself. I hold that faith, in the true, ancient sense of the word, is a unity of both these meanings, including the one no less than the other. They are fortunate times for the church when the opposition between faith and reason is limited simply to the formal distinction referred to above and the church's teaching is not opposed by a creed of man's own making, nor has changed into something external, untouched by the Holy Spirit. The church's work in relation to its members will consist primarily in educating them to the stage where the Truth, which at first could be communicated to them only in the form of something to be learnt by rote, has developed into an interior possession which touches their hearts so deeply that in that Truth alone do they find their own fulfilment and their essential, permanent being. It is implicit in this perpetual process of education that the unity of these two aspects of faith is not present to begin with, nor is the union continuous and fixed: that between the certainty of self and the genuine content of faith there is a separation. Self-certainty is at first feeling and will in their natural state and the subjective opinions and idle thoughts that go with them. The true content of faith, however, comes to the spirit at first externally as words understood literally; and religious education produces the twofold result that the power of the natural feelings is subdued and the letter of the Truth is quickened and appropriated by man's own spirit.

This process of transforming and appropriating the externally given material is from the beginning involved in a struggle, its antagonist being the "natural" man. This latter is a necessary presupposition, because what is to be produced is the free spirit, not a natural life, and the free spirit exists only as twice-born. This natural enemy has, however, been vanquished in its origin and the free spirit liberated by the divine Idea. The struggle with the "natural" man is, therefore, only the manifestation in the finite individual. But still another enemy proceeds from the individual, an enemy which does not originate in man's natural being but, on the contrary, in his supersensible nature, in his *thinking*, in the pure form of man's inwardness, in that which signalizes his divine origin and distinguishes him from the animal and which alone is the source of his greatness as also of his degradation, for the animal is incapable of either. With the threat to faith by such independent thinking there ensues a struggle more stubborn and on a higher level than that other struggle in which only the natural will and the naive consciousness that has not yet asserted its independence are involved. This thinking, then, is what is called human thought, one's own understanding, finite reason; and this is properly distinguished from that thinking which, though human, is also divine, which seeks not its own interest but the universal, from that Reason which knows and contemplates the infinite and eternal as that which alone has affirmative being.

However, this finite thinking need not be immediately opposed to religious doctrine. On the contrary, its efforts will at first be directed to the supposed advantage of religion by adorning, supporting and glorifying it with the products of its own invention, curiosity and acumen. As a result of these efforts, a host of inferences, presuppositions, grounds and ends, all of them with a finite content, become associated with religious doctrine. But because they appear in the immediate context of eternal Truth they easily become endowed with the same worth, importance and validity as the Truth itself; and since they have only a finite import and are therefore exposed to contradiction and counter-arguments, they naturally require to be defended by external authority and so become a field for impassioned dispute. Having been produced in the interest of what is finite, they lack the testimony of the Holy Spirit and can be supported only by finite interests.

But with its manifestation, the absolute Truth itself assumes a temporal shape with the external conditions, relationships and circumstances associated with it. In so doing it surrounds itself with a complex of local, historical and other positive material. Because the Truth *is*, it must manifest itself, and its manifestation must be an accomplished fact. Truth's self-manifestation is an inseparable part of its own eternal nature, so much so that if it did not manifest itself it would cease to be, that is to say, its content would be reduced to an empty abstraction. But a clear distinction must be made between the eternal manifestation which is inherent in the nature of Truth and the transient, local, external phenomena of its inessential side, else the finite will be confused with the infinite, the inessential with the essential. This phenomenal side of Truth opens up to the activities of the Understanding a fresh field of finite material in the context of which it finds a direct inducement to elevate these inessential particulars to the dignity of the truly divine, to ascribe to the frame the same worth as to the picture it surrounds, in order to demand for finite narratives, events, circumstances and imagery the same reverence, the same faith, as for that which is absolute Being and is eternal history.

These then are the aspects of Truth where the *formal* meaning of faith begins to make its appearance, the meaning that it is simply a *subjective belief* that something is true regardless of its inner nature. It is the same subjective belief that is appropriate in the ordinary affairs of everyday life or in connection with the phenomena of Nature. If the outer sense of sight or inner, immediate feeling, the testimony of others and confidence in them, and so forth, are the criteria for belief in such things, then of course a distinction can be made between a conviction, a belief based on *grounds* that something is true, and belief as such. But this is too trivial a distinction to support any alleged superiority of such a conviction over mere belief; for the so-called grounds are none other than the sources just indicated of what is here called belief.

With respect to this general subjective belief that a thing is true, there is a distinction of another kind, one which refers to the material and especially to the use made of the material. For since those finite and external narratives and circumstances which lie within the sphere of religious belief enter into the context of the eternal history, the pious mind draws on this material for much of its inspiration, edification and instruction about mundane affairs, individual destinies and situations, and finds its imagery and the whole range of its culture mostly or wholly linked up with that sphere of narrative and doctrine which surrounds the eternal Truth. In any case, that sphere from which, as from a "people's book," mankind has developed its consciousness of all the wider bearings of its mental and spiritual life, which indeed is also the medium through which it raises its actual world to the religious standpoint, that sphere deserves at least the greatest respect and a reverent treatment.

Now it is one thing when such narratives and doctrines are taken and used, just as they stand, by simple piety for its own purposes; but it is a different matter when they are grasped by the Understanding in a way which gives them a fixed, settled meaning with the aim of establishing them as canons of belief for others: for this implies that the understanding of these others shall be subjected only to that Understanding and this subjection is demanded in the name of divine Truth.

In point of fact, this demand does the very opposite of what it pretends to do: the demand for the subjection of the ordinary understanding comes not from the divine spirit of faith but from the Understanding itself which thus is directly authorized to speak with authority on divine matters. Over against this content of literalism and the barren learning of orthodoxy the better mind has a divine right. And so it happens that the more this finite wisdom encroaches on the sphere of divine things and the more it stresses the importance of the external historical element and the products of its own acumen, the more it is working against divine Truth and against itself. It has produced and recognized the principle that is opposite to divine Truth, has opened up and prepared an entirely different realm for cognition; in this realm, the boundless energy which is immanent in the principle of cognition and which contains the deeper possibility of its eventual reconciliation with genuine faith, will turn against its confinement within that finite sphere of the Understanding and will destroy its claims to be the kingdom of heaven.

It is the better mind that, indignant at the contradiction of such presumption which lets finite and external things be acknowledged and reverenced as divine, and armed with the weapon of finite thinking has, as the Enlightenment, on the one hand, restored and asserted the *freedom of the spirit*, the principle of a spiritual religion, yet, on the other hand, as only an abstract thinking, *has not known how to distinguish* between the characteristics of a merely finite content and those of *Truth* itself. Consequently, this abstract Understanding has turned against all determinateness, has emptied Truth of all content whatever so that nothing remains for it except, on the one hand, the pure negative, the *caput mortuum* of a merely abstract *Being*, and, on the other hand, a finite material. Part of the latter is, by its nature, finite and external and the rest, which it has procured for itself from the divine content, has itself been reduced to the externality of merely ordinary historical events, to local opinions and particular contemporary views. But Thought simply cannot be inactive. From such a God, in Him, there is nothing to be had for He has already been emptied of all content. He is the Unknowable, for knowledge has to do with a determinate content, with movement; but the void lacks a content, is indeterminate and possesses no immanent life and action. The doctrine of Truth is wholly and solely this, the revelation of what God is, of His nature and works. But the Understanding, having dissipated all this content, has again veiled God from human knowledge and reduced Him to the status of something merely yearned for, something unknown. Consequently, all that remains as material for thought is the finite material already mentioned, only with the *consciousness* that it is merely temporal and finite in character; it is to such material that thinking is restricted and it must find its satisfaction in the vain elaboration in various ways of a subject-matter lacking any substantial import and in procuring for itself in scholarly fashion a vast mass of such material.

But to the spirit that cannot endure this vanity only yearning is left; for that in which it would satisfy itself is a Beyond, without shape, content or definite character. Yet it is only through shape, content and a determinate nature that anything can exist for spirit, can exist as Reason, actuality, life, can possess an intrinsic being of its own. This finite material is, however, merely subjective and is incapable of yielding a substantial filling for the empty Eternal. The need therefore of the spirit which again seeks religion, what that spirit really demands, is a substantial content that is independent and self-subsistent, a Truth that is not a matter of opinion and intellectual conceit but which is *objective*. The only way now in which this need can still be satisfied is for spirit to fall back on *feelings*. Feeling is the sole mode in which religion can still exist for spirit; in the higher forms of its existence, in the representation of a content and in the belief that the content is true, reflection always plays a part and reflection has gone to the length of negating every objective determination.

These, in short, are the main features of the course taken by formal reflection in religion. The system of hair-splitting, metaphysical, casuistic distinctions and determinations into which the Understanding split up the substantial content of religion and to which it gave the same authority as to eternal Truth, is the first mischief which begins within religion itself. But the other mischief, much as it may seem at first to be the opposite, is already established in this first standpoint and is only a further development of it; it is the mischief that thought appears as autonomous, and armed with the formal weapons to which that mass of arid insignificant determinations owes its origin and which thought itself owes to its first activity, turns against them and finds its ultimate principle in pure abstraction itself, the characterless supreme Being. From a philosophical point of view it is interesting to observe this switching round of reflection – unexpected by reflection itself – into an activity hostile to its own work, a switching round which equally is only the spontaneous determination of reflection itself.

It follows from what we have said that the nature of the mischief done to religion and theology by the Enlightenment is that they no longer possess a truth that is *known*, an *objective content*, a *doctrinal* theology: although, strictly speaking, it is only religion of which this can be said, for where there is no such content there can be no theology. It is reduced to historical erudition augmented by the meagre exposition of some subjective feelings. The stated result is, however, what religion on its part has done towards reconciling faith and reason. It now remains to be mentioned that philosophy on its part has also offered a hand to achieve a settlement and that, too, in the same manner.

For the defect from which philosophy now suffers proves to be likewise a lack of *objective content*. It is the science of thinking Reason, just as religious faith is the consciousness and the absolute conviction of the truth of Reason presented in the form of picture-thinking, and for this science the subject-matter has become just as attenuated as it has for faith.

The philosophy from which the standpoint of general intellectual culture in recent times has primarily been derived and which rightly calls itself the *critical* philosophy, has done nothing else but reduce the work of the Enlightenment, which was in the first instance directed to concrete conceptions and objects, to its simple formula; this philosophy has no other content and result than what has been produced by the ratiocinative intellect. It is true that the *critical* or *Kantian* philosophy, like the Enlightenment, is outmoded so far as the *name* is concerned, and nowadays one would meet with a cool reception from those writers who regard themselves as philosophers and, too, from professional writers on theological, religious and moral topics, as well as from those who write on politics, law, and constitutional matters, if one described such philosophy as there might seem to be in their writings as Kantian philosophy; just as one would meet with an equally cool reception from ratiocinative theologians and still more from those who base religion on subjective feelings, if one associated them with the Enlightenment.

Who has not refuted or improved upon the Kantian philosophy and who will not even now win his spurs, so to speak, on the Kantian field? But if one examines the works of all these writers, philosophical, moral and theological – the last-named often protesting most vehemently against any desire to be philosophical – one immediately recognizes only the same principles and results; but here they already appear as *presuppositions* and *acknowledged truths*. "By their fruits ye shall know them." The fact that this self-satisfied conceit floats only on the stream of current popular ideas and prejudices does not prevent it from fancying that the trivialities it has scooped up from the general stream are entirely original views and fresh discoveries in the intellectual and scientific fields.

What is in and for itself and what is finite and temporal – these are the two fundamental determinations which must be present in a theory of truth, and the particular import of such a theory depends on how these two sides are apprehended and fixed and what our attitude to them is supposed to be. Let us apply these criteria to the truths of contemporary philosophy, truths which are accorded such general recognition that there is no need to waste a word on them!

One of the absolute presuppositions in the culture of our time is that man *has no knowledge of the Truth*. The mentality of the Enlightenment has not so much become conscious of this its result and enunciated it as that it has led up to it. As already mentioned, that mentality started out to liberate thought from those fetters of the other mentality which wanted to plant its own finite determinations in the soil of the divine doctrine itself and which wanted to use the absolute, divine authority for its own rank weeds; it also wanted to restore the freedom which had been won by the religion of Truth and in which it had made its home. Thus its intention at first was to attack error and superstition and, indeed, what it truly succeeded in destroying was not religion, but that pharisaical mentality which had applied the wisdom of this world to the things of another world and fancied that its sophistries could also be called religious doctrine. It wanted to remove error solely to make room for the Truth; it sought eternal Truths and acknowledged them and still placed the worth and dignity of man in the fact that *such truths are for him* and for him alone, not for the animal. In this view, these truths are meant to be firmly established and objective in character in contrast to subjective opinions and the impulses of mere feeling, and opinions, like feelings, are to have their justification in being in conformity with the insight of reason, subject to it and led by it.

However, the *consistent* and *independent* development of the principle of the Understanding leads to the stage where all definite character and with it all content receive a finite significance, thus destroying the specific form and character of the Divine. Through this development, the objective truth which was supposed to be the goal has been attenuated to such an abstraction that all that the Kantian philosophy needed to do was to bring it before consciousness and to declare that it constituted the goal of Reason. Accordingly, this philosophy pronounced the *identity of the Understanding* to be the supreme principle, the ultimate result both for cognition itself and also for its object – the *void* of the atomistic philosophy, God deprived of all definite character, predicates and properties, lifted into a *beyond* where we cannot know Him, or rather reduced to an abstraction void of all content. This philosophy has given the Understanding a correct awareness of itself, namely, that it is incapable of apprehending the Truth. But in holding spirit to be *only* the Understanding, Kantianism has given currency to the general proposition that man can have no knowledge of God and – as if apart from God there could be absolute objects and a Truth at all – in general, that man can have no knowledge of what possesses *intrinsic Being*. If religion declares that man's glory and salvation lie in his knowing God and that religion's service to man consists in having imparted to him this knowledge and in having revealed the unknown nature of God, then this philosophy forms the most monstrous antithesis to religion for in it spirit has fallen to the lowliness of the animal as its highest destiny, only that, unhappily, spirit has the advantage of still being conscious of its ignorance; whereas the animal in fact possesses the much purer, truer, namely, the completely natural, humility of ignorance. This result may well be regarded as having become, except in a few instances, the universal prejudice of our culture. To have refuted the Kantian philosophy or to despise it is of no avail; the advances, or imagined advances beyond it, may in their way have accomplished much in other directions, but they are only the same secular wisdom as the Kantian result, for they deny to spirit the capacity and the vocation to know the objective truth.

The other principle directly bound up with this wisdom is that spirit, although conceded a cognitive faculty, is denied a knowledge of the Truth and therefore can have commerce only with phenomena and finite objects. The church and pious minds have often held the secular sciences to be suspect and dangerous, indeed to be hostile to religion and have regarded them as leading to atheism. A famous astronomer is supposed to have said that he had scanned the whole sky and could find no God in it. In point of fact, the aim of secular science is a knowledge of *finite* objects; the goal to which it aspires in its efforts to penetrate to their interior is a knowledge of causes and grounds. But these causes and grounds are essentially analogous to what is to be explained and for that reason the forces which come within its purview are likewise only finite. Now although these sciences do not conduct their knowledge over into the region of the Eternal – which is more than a merely supersensible being, for those causes and forces, that inner realm which is generated by the Understanding and apprehended after its own fashion, this too is not sensible – since it is not their business to bring about this result, there is nothing to prevent the finite sciences from conceding a divine sphere. In face of such higher sphere it seems quite natural to recognize those objects of consciousness deriving from the senses and from intellectual reflection as an intrinsically null content, as only appearance. But once knowledge of Truth as such is renounced, then knowledge has only one basis, that of appearance. From this standpoint, even a doctrine recognized as divine cannot itself as such be the object of enquiry, but only the facts and circumstances surrounding it. The doctrine itself remains outside the interest of intellectual activity and because its content is assumed to be unattainable, it is idle to seek an insight into the doctrine, a belief in it and a conviction of its truth. Accordingly, intelligence in occupying itself with religious doctrines must confine itself to their phenomenal aspects, must concern itself with the outer circumstances, and the interest becomes a matter of history where spirit has to do with things past, with something it has left behind it, in which spirit is *not itself present*. The products of the earnest efforts of scholarship, of industry, of acumen, etc., are likewise called truth, and an ocean of such truths is brought to light and propagated; but these are not the sort of truths which the earnest religious spirit demands for its satisfaction.

Now if what is *present* and *actual* for spirit is only this wide realm of empty appearances, while substantial, absolute Being is removed to an empty Beyond, where can the human spirit still find a place where it could meet with substantial, absolute Being, where the Eternal could approach it and it could attain to union with the Eternal, to the certainty and enjoyment of it? In the region of feeling alone can the spirit take refuge in its quest for Truth. Consciousness can endure substantial Being, that which can withstand the onslaughts of reflective thought, only in the veiled form of feeling. This form lacks the objectivity and definiteness which knowledge and an awakened faith demand but which the Understanding has learned to destroy; and it is just for this reason that the religious spirit which fears this danger withdraws into this veiled form which seems to offer no aspect which could be dialectically attacked by thought. In such religiosity, when it springs from a genuine need, the soul will find the peace it demands, for it will strive to make good by intensity and inwardness what its faith has lost in definite character and extension.

There still remains to be mentioned as the third universal prejudice, the opinion that feeling is the true and even the sole form in which the religious spirit preserves its genuineness.

In the first place, this religious spirit is no longer simple and unreflecting. Spirit, because it is spirit, demands in general that what is in feeling must also be in representation and imagination; that corresponding to feeling there must be something felt; that the spontaneity of feeling must not remain an inert concentration, but must at the same time be concerned with objective truths followed, as occurs in the cultus, by an expansion into acts which proclaim the community of spirits in religion and, like the concern with truths, nourish religious feeling, preserving it in the truth and procuring for it the enjoyment of truth. But such an expansion into a cultus and into a body of doctrinal beliefs is no longer compatible with the form of feeling; on the contrary, religiosity in the form considered here, has fled from any development and objectivity to feeling, which it has challengingly declared to be the exclusive and predominant form.

Here then is where the danger of this standpoint originates, the danger that it will turn round into the opposite of what the religious spirit seeks in it. This is a point of the greatest importance which can be touched on only briefly here and I must refer to it only in the most general terms without being able to go further into the nature of feeling. It cannot be doubted that feeling is a form which, itself indeterminate, embraces matter of the most diverse and opposite kinds. Feeling, by itself, is the natural subjectivity which is equally capable of being good as evil, pious as ungodly. When, now, the seat of authority in matters of belief and conduct is transferred from so-called reason (but it is really the finite Understanding and its way of reasoning) to feeling, there has vanished even the semblance of objectivity which is at least implied in the principle of the Understanding. For according to this, what is to be valid for me must rest on a universally valid ground, on something which is in its own self true. But more definitely still, what is truly divine, eternal and reasonable in every religion and in every ethical form of social life, both in the family and in the State, is re-cognized as an *objective law* and, as thus objective, is recognized as a *prius*. It is from this alone that feeling gets its support, its true direction. The natural feelings are meant to be shaped, corrected, purified by the teachings and practice of religion and by the established principles of morality and only then ought feeling to be made the form for a content which will constitute a proper, *religious* and *moral feeling*.

"*The natural man* perceiveth not the things of the spirit of God and cannot know them for they must be spiritually discerned." But the natural man is man in his natural feelings, and according to the doctrine of subjectivity, though such a man is not supposed to know anything, it is he alone who, as natural man, is supposed to perceive the spirit of God. Of course, included among the feelings of the natural man is *also* a feeling of the divine; however, a natural feeling of the divine and the spirit of God are two quite different things. And what other feelings besides cannot be found in the human heart? That the natural feeling just mentioned is a feeling of the divine, even this is not implied in the feeling as natural; the divine is only in and for the spirit and, as we have already said, the life of the spirit is not from Nature but is twice-born. When feeling is said to constitute the fundamental character of man's nature, then he is put on the same level as the animal, for the peculiarity of the animal is to have its determination in feeling and to live in accordance with feeling. If religion in man is based only on a feeling, then the nature of that feeling can be none other than the *feeling of his dependence,* and so a dog would be the best Christian for it possesses this in the highest degree and lives mainly in this feeling. The dog also has feelings of deliverance when its hunger is satisfied by a bone. The human spirit on the contrary has its liberation and the feeling of its divine freedom in religion; only the free spirit has religion and can have religion; what is brought into subjection in religion is the natural feeling of the heart, the particularity of subjectivity, and what becomes free in it and precisely in this freedom comes to be, is spirit. Even in the worst religions – those that is in which servitude, and with it superstition, is most powerful – it is when man lifts himself up to God that he feels, intuits and enjoys his freedom, his infinitude and universality, that is, his higher nature, and this does not originate in feeling as such but in the spirit.

In speaking of religious, ethical and other feelings of this kind we must, of course, admit that these are genuine feelings; and if then we go further and regard thought with mistrust or rather with contempt and hatred – the misology of which Plato already speaks – it is an obvious step to place in the feelings the source of what is genuine and divine. Certainly it would not be necessary to see only a choice between intellect and feeling for the source of religion and truth, especially in connection with the Christian religion. In fact one must have already utterly discounted the higher, divine revelation which Christianity declares to be its source if one is faced with such a restricted choice and if, after rejecting not only the Understanding but thought in general, one seeks to establish Christian doctrine on the basis of feelings.

However, in making feeling the seat and the source of the True it is overlooked that the essential nature of feeling as such is to be a *mere form*, indeterminate on its own account and capable of holding any content whatever. There is nothing which cannot be felt, and is felt. God, Truth, duty are felt and so too are evil, falsehood, wrong; every human condition and relationship is felt; every conception of man's relationship to spiritual and natural things becomes a feeling. Who would attempt to name and count all the feelings from those of religious feeling, duty, compassion, etc., to envy, hatred, pride, vanity, etc., joy, pain, sadness, and so on. The very fact of the diversity of feelings, not to mention the opposition and contradiction between them, makes it possible even for ordinary thinking to draw the correct conclusion that feeling is something merely formal and cannot be a principle for truly determining a content. Further, it is equally correct to infer that if feeling is made into a principle that determines a content, all that has to be done is to leave it to the individual *which* feelings he will have; it is an absolute indefiniteness that constitutes the standard and authority, i.e. the caprice and inclination of the individual, to be and to do what pleases him and to make himself the oracle for what shall be accepted as true as regards religion, duty, right, and what is fine and noble.

Religion, like duty and right, also becomes and should become a matter of feeling and dwell in one's heart, just as freedom in general also sinks into feeling and becomes in man a feeling of freedom. Only, it is quite another matter whether such a content as God, Truth, freedom, as simply felt, is supposed to have its warrant in feeling, or whether on the contrary such an objective content possesses its own inherent validity before it enters into one's heart and feeling, so that the character, the correction and the warrant of feeling derive from that content. Everything turns on *this difference of attitude*. On this rests the separation of the rectitude and faith of former days, of the genuine religious and ethical spirit which puts God, Truth and duty *first*, from the perversity, the conceit and absolute egotism prevalent in our time which makes self-will, one's own opinions and inclinations the rule for what is religious and right. Obedience, discipline, faith in the old sense of the word, reverence for God and for Truth, these are the feelings which go together with the first attitude and proceed from it; vanity, conceit, shallowness and pride are the feelings which proceed from the second attitude, or rather these are the feelings of the merely natural man in whom this attitude has its origin.

The foregoing remarks could provide suitable material for a lengthy exposition, but I have already dealt with some aspects of this material elsewhere and moreover this is not the place for it. They may serve only as reminders of the points of view touched on in order to characterize more precisely what constitutes the evil of the *present time* and so, too, what the *need of the time* is. This evil, the *fortuitousness* and *caprice* of *subjective* feeling and its opinions associated with the *culture of reflective thought* which has proved to its own satisfaction that spirit is *incapable of knowing the Truth*, has from ancient times been called *sophistry*. This it is that merits the nickname of "worldly wisdom" which Friedrich von Schlegel has raked up again; for it is a wisdom concerned with what is usually called the *world*, of things that are contingent, untrue and temporal; it is the conceit that elevates the vanity, the fortuitousness of feeling and the pleasing of one's fancy to the absolute principle for determining what right and duty, faith and truth, are. Certainly, one often hears expositions of these sophistries called philosophy; yet this doctrine itself contradicts the use of the name of philosophy for them, for it is a commonplace with it to declare *that there is nothing in philosophy*. It is right in wanting to know nothing of philosophy; it thereby consciously asserts what it actually wants and is. From the beginning, philosophy has been in conflict with sophistry. All that the latter can take from philosophy is the formal weapon, the culture of reflective thought; but it has nothing in common with the content of philosophy since it is characteristic of it to shun completely the objective aspect of truth. Nor can sophistry in its effort to acquire a content have recourse to the other source of truth, that is, of truth in the form of religion as revealed in Holy Writ; for this doctrine recognizes no other ground but its own conceited opinions and discoveries.

But as regards what is *needed* at the present time, the need common to religion and philosophy is a *substantial, objective content for Truth*. An enquiry on the part of religion into the way in which it is again to procure respect, reverence and authority for its doctrines in face of mere arbitrary opinions and to create for itself a bond of objective faith, doctrine and cultus, such an enquiry which by itself is far-reaching in scope would also have to take fully into account the various tendencies in contemporary thought and opinion. Consequently, such an enquiry would not only be out of place here, but also it would definitely have to be other than purely philosophical in kind. However, in one part of the enquiry the two spheres of religion and philosophy coincide. For this at least can be mentioned, that the spirit of the time has developed to a stage where *thinking* and the way of looking at things which goes together with thinking, has become for consciousness an *imperative condition* of what it shall admit and recognize as true. It is not a matter of interest here to determine whether only a part of the religious community might no longer be able to exist spiritually without freedom of thought, or rather whether there are whole communities in which this higher principle has manifested itself, for which the form of thought in some stage or other of development is from now on an essential requirement of its faith. There can be very many stages in the development of thought and the return to first principles; for, popularly expressed, thinking means tracing back particular instances, propositions, etc, to an *immanent general principle* which relatively is the *fundamental principle* for the material made dependent on it in consciousness. Thus what at one stage in the development of thought is a fundamental principle, an ultimate basis, requires at another stage to be traced further back to still more general, profounder principles. But the principles are a content of which consciousness is firmly convinced, a content attested by spirit and which is now unseparated from thinking and from the nature of one's own self. If such principles are exposed to the formal reasoning of ordinary reflective thought then the way is opened to the error already mentioned of substituting subjective opinion and caprice for principles, and the reasoning finally becomes sophistry.

But conviction in religion can remain in the form of what is properly called *faith*, only it must not be forgotten that faith, too, should not be conceived as something external, something to be mechanically imparted; on the contrary, if it is to be vital and not servile, it essentially requires the testimony of the indwelling spirit of truth and must be implanted in one's heart. But if principles have penetrated into this religious requirement, then that requirement is no longer separate from the necessity and the activity of thought, and religion demands from this side a *science* of religion – a theology. What in theology is more than – or what in theology deserves to be more than – the general knowledge of religion possessed by every adherent of religion of whatever culture, that knowledge theology has in common with philosophy. Thus the Middle Ages saw the rise of scholastic theology, a science which cultivated religion from the side of thought and reason and strove to grasp intellectually the profoundest doctrines of revealed religion. In comparison with the sublime aim of such a science, it is a very inferior type of theology that places its scientific difference from general religious doctrine in the historical element, the whole compass of which in its endless detail it tacks on to religion. The absolute content of religion is essentially *here* and *now* for spirit. Consequently, it is not in the external accretion of the products of historical erudition, but only in the speculative knowledge of that content that the spirit which requires something more than simple faith can find a truth that is freely accessible to it here and now and which alone is capable of satisfying its eternal need, namely, to think, and so to endow the infinite content of religion with the infinite form.

The prejudice which a philosophical treatment has to contend with nowadays, namely, that the divine cannot be *comprehended*, that, on the contrary, the Notion and a knowledge in terms of the Notion reduces God and the divine attributes to the status of finite objects and precisely in so doing destroys them, with this prejudice the scholastic theology fortunately did not have to contend; to such a level the glory and dignity of conceptual knowledge had not sunk but, on the contrary, was left unimpugned and unspoiled. It has been left to the philosophy of the modern age to misunderstand so badly its own element, the Notion, and to bring it into this discredit. It has not grasped the infinitude of the Notion and has confused it with finite reflection, with Understanding; so much so that only Understanding is supposed capable of thought, whereas reason is capable only of immediate knowledge, i.e. capable only of feeling and intuition and hence only of knowledge in the medium of sense.

The conception of divine justice in the ancient Greek poets depicts the gods as hostile to those who rise above mediocrity, or are happy or who excel, and as bringing about their downfall. This conception was dispelled by the purer thought of the Divine. Plato and Aristotle teach that God is *not envious* and does not withhold from mankind knowledge of himself and of Truth. For what else would it be but *envy* if God denied to man a knowledge of God; in doing so he would also have denied to man all Truth, for God alone is the True; what else is true, yet may not seem to have a divine import, is true only in so far as it is grounded in God and is known as coming from him; all else in it is transient appearance. According to Plato and Aristotle, just as according to Christian teaching, it is the knowledge of God, of Truth, that alone raises man above the animal, that gives him his distinctive character and is the source of his happiness or rather blessedness.

It is the quite peculiar phenomenon of this age at the peak of its culture to revert to that ancient conception of God as not communicating himself and not revealing himself to the human spirit. This assertion that God is envious must, within the bounds of the Christian religion, all the more astonish since this religion is and claims to be nothing else but the *revelation* of what God is, and the Christian community is supposed to be none other than the community into which the spirit of God has been sent and in which that spirit leads the members into the *knowledge of God* just because it is spirit and the divine, holy spirit, not sensation and feeling, not a picture-thinking of sensuous things. And without this knowledge what would the Christian community be? What is a theology without a knowledge of God? Precisely what a philosophy is without that knowledge, sounding brass and a tinkling cymbal!

When my friend desired me to write a foreword to this, his first published work, I had in the first place to visualize how an attempt at a speculative treatment of religion would fare in the climate of current philosophical opinion. I felt obliged to remind the author in this foreword what kind of a reception and goodwill he could expect in a state of affairs where what goes by the name of philosophy and, indeed, always has Plato on its lips, no longer has even an inkling of the nature of speculative thought, of the contemplation of the Idea; where in philosophy as in theology, the *brutish ignorance of God* and the *sophistry of this ignorance* which puts individual feeling and subjective opinion in the place of religious doctrine and the principles of right and duty, have got the upper hand, and where the writings of Christian theologians like Daub and Marheineke which still preserve Christian doctrine and the right and the glory of thought, and writings in which the principles of reason and ethics are based on the Notion and defended against those doctrines destructive of the substantial ethical ties of mankind and the State and of religion, suffer the meanest disparagement at the hands of shallow and ill-disposed critics.

But my friend's purpose in writing his treatise can best be put in his own words; he wrote to me about it in a letter dated 25 January of this year as follows:

"My book has now acquired an entirely different shape from what it had and was capable of having in the manuscript I sent you, and it will now, I hope, be more to your liking. It really had its origin in my spiritual need. For from my youth up, religion (not an affected piety) had always been for me the highest and most sacred thing, and I held it to be true for the quite simple reason that the spirit of mankind cannot be deceived in this matter. Science, however, deprived me of the element of picture-thinking in which I had been accustomed to see the Truth, and what was more natural than that I should strive to overcome the extreme disharmony and extreme despair produced in me by science and so win a reconciliation in the element of knowledge. I then said to myself: if what is presented in Christianity as the absolute Truth cannot be comprehended by philosophy in the pure form of knowledge so that the Idea itself is this form, then I want to know nothing more about philosophy. – But then (I continued) science in its modern development as Christian philosophy must itself be the supreme product of Christianity. So it was that the enquiry carried out in this book became my problem and I have exerted myself to find a solution which would satisfy my need both for religious peace of mind and for the recognition of science."

Berlin, Easter 1822.   Hegel

CONTRIBUTORS

GEOFFREY REGINALD GILCHRIST MURE was educated at Merton College, Oxford, became Fellow and Tutor there in 1922, and served as Warden of Merton from 1947 to 1963. His books include a translation of Aristotle's *Posterior Analytics* (1925), *Aristotle* (1932), *An Introduction to Hegel* (1940), *A Study of Hegel's Logic* (1950), *Retreat from Truth* (1958), and *The Philosophy of Hegel* (1965).

MEROLD WESTPHAL studied at Wheaton College (Illinois) and Yale University, and has been on the Yale Faculty since 1966. He was a Woodrow Wilson Fellow in 1962–63, and was appointed a Danforth Associate in 1968. Professor Westphal's published articles include "Temporality and Finitism in Hartshorne's Theism" (1966), "In Defense of the Thing-in-Itself" (1968), "Theism and the Problem of Ethics" (1968), "Hegel, Tillich, and the Secular" (1972), "Hegel, Pannenberg, and Hermeneutics" (1974), and "Hegels Phänomenologie der Wahrnehmung" in *Materialien zu Hegels Phänomenologie des Geistes* (1973).

ALBERT HOFSTADTER is Professor of Philosophy at the University of California, Santa Cruz. He was previously Professor of Philosophy, and, for a time, Chairman of the Department of Art History at Columbia University. His books include *Philosophies of Art and Beauty* (with Richard Kuhns, 1964), *Truth and Art* (1965), and *Agony and Epitaph: Man, His Art, and His Poetry* (1970). Professor Hofstadter has translated Heidegger's *Poetry, Language, Thought* (1971), and his articles include "Art and Spiritual Validity" (1963), "Art: Death and Transfiguration. A Study in Hegel's Theory of Romanticism" (1970), and "The Aesthetic Impulse" (1973). Much of Professor Hofstadter's work has been done, as he puts it, "in encounter with" Hegel, and he is presently preparing for publication a book on Hegel's Philosophy of History with the aid of a grant from the National Endowment for the Humanities.

HENRY PAOLUCCI was educated at CCNY and Columbia University. He taught ancient Greek and Roman history for many years at both institutions, as well as at Brooklyn and Iona Colleges, and is now Professor of Government and Politics at St. John's University. Dr. Paolucci's books include *Hegel on Tragedy* (with Anne Paolucci, 1962), *The Political Writings of St. Augustine* (1962), *The Achievement of Galileo* (with Professor James Brophy, 1962), and *War, Peace, and the Presidency* (1968). He is the translator (with Anne Paolucci) of Machiavelli's *Mandragola* (1957), Beccaria's *On Crimes and Punishments* (1963), and has edited *The Enchiridion of St. Augustine* (1961). His "Hegel and the Celestial Mechanics of Newton and Einstein" was read at the HSA Boston Symposium on Hegel and the Sciences (1970), and his "The Poetics of Aristotle and Hegel" appeared in *Hegel in Comparative Literature* (1970).

ERROL E. HARRIS was born in South Africa and educated at Rhodes University College and later at Magdalen College, Oxford. He has been Hugh le May Research Fellow at Rhodes University (1949), Bollingen Research Fellow (1960–63), Ford Foundation Research Fellow in International Affairs (1964–65), and National Science Foundation Research Fellow (1968), He was the Terry Lecturer at Yale University in 1957, and has held university chairs at the University of Witwatersrand in Johannesburg, the University of Kansas, Edinburgh University, and is now Professor of Philosophy at Northwestern University, and a member of the Executive Council of the Hegel Society of America. His books include *The Survival of Political Man* (1950), *Revelation Through Reason* (1958), *Nature, Mind, and Modern Science* (1954), *The Foundations of Metaphysics in Science* (1965), *Annihilation and Utopia* (1966), *Fundamentals of Philosophy* (1969), and *Hypothesis and Perception* (1970). His many articles include "The Philosophy of Nature in Hegel's System" (1949), and "Dialectic and Scientific Method" (1973).

JOHN NIEMEYER FINDLAY has been at the forefront of Hegel scholarship for the past two decades. His *Hegel: A Re-examination* (1958) put the study of Hegel on a new footing in the English-speaking world.

Professor Findlay, a Fellow of the British Academy, has held university chairs at King's College, University of London, the University of Texas, Yale University, and Boston University, where he is now Distinguished Professor. He was President of the Aristotelian Society in 1955–56, when he first called to our attention "Some Merits of Hegelianism." His Gifford Lectures at the University of St. Andrews were published under the titles *The Discipline of the Cave* (1966) and *The Transcendence of the Cave* (1967). His other books include *Meinong's Theory of Objects and Values* (1933), *Values and Intentions* (1961), *Language, Mind and Value* (1963), and *Ascent to the Absolute* (1970). He has collaborated with A. V. Miller in the publication of the first English translation of Hegel's *Philosophy of Nature* (1970), and in the publication of a complete translation (with *Zusätze*) of the *Philosophy of Mind* (1971). Professor Findlay has translated Husserl's *Logical Investigations* (1970), and contributed papers at major Hegelian and other conferences both in this country and abroad.

QUENTIN LAUER, S. J. is Professor of Philosophy at Fordham University. His books include *La phénoménologie de Husserl* (1955), Edmund Husserl: *La phénoménologie comme science rigoureuse. Traduction, Introduction, et Commentaire* (1955), *The Triumph of Subjectivity* (1958), reprinted as *Phenomenology: Its Genesis and Prospect* (1965), *Phenomenology and the Crisis of Philosophy* (1965), *A Christian-Communist Dialogue* (with Roger Garaudy, 1968), and *Hegel's Idea of Philosophy* (1971). Among his published articles are "Hegel on the Proofs for the Existence of God" (1964), "Hegel on the Identity of Content in Religion and Philosophy" in *Hegel and the Philosophy of Religion* (1970), Hegel's Critique of Kant's Theology" in *God Knowable and Unknowable* (1972), and "Hegel as Historian of Philosophy" in *Hegel and the History of Philosophy* (1974). Father Lauer is currently at work on *A Reading of Hegel's Phenomenology of Spirit*, to be published by Fordham University Press.

THEODORE KISIEL was educated at the University of Pittsburgh and Duquesne University. He has been Visiting Professor at Northwestern University, and is presently Professor of Philosophy at Northern Illinois University. He has twice been awarded grants from the Alexander von Humboldt-Stiftung, the first in 1970–71, the second for 1974 to support research on his forthcoming study of Heidegger. Professor Kisiel's published works include *Phenomenology and the*

Natural Sciences: Essays and Translations (with Joseph J. Kockelmans, 1970), a translation of Werner Marx's *Heidegger and the Tradition* (1971), "The Happening of Tradition: The Hermeneutics of Gadamer and Heidegger" (1969), "The Dimensions of a Phenomenology of Science in Husserl and the Young Dr. Heidegger" (1973), and "Scientific Discovery: Logical, Psychological, or Hermeneutical?" (1971).

A. V. MILLER is best known for his highly praised translations of Hegel, which include Hegel's *Science of Logic* (1969), Hegel's *Philosophy of Nature* (1970), and Hegel's *Philosophy of Mind* (1971), which supplements William Wallace's existing translation of the third part of the *Encyclopaedia of the Philosophical Sciences* with a translation of the *Zusätze* in Boumann's text. In the words of Professor Findlay, Arnold Miller is "a dedicated Hegelian" whose "deep enthusiasm for, and passionate identification with the thought of Hegel has opened his eyes to the sense of many of the most difficult passages." Mr. Miller is presently collaborating with Professor Peter Fuss on a new translation of Hegel's *Phänomenologie des Geistes*.

FREDERICK G. WEISS was educated at Iona College and the University of Virginia, and has taught Philosophy at Purdue and Indiana Universities, Florida State University, and The Citadel. He is the editor of *The Owl of Minerva*, the quarterly publication of the Hegel Society of America. His books include *Hegel's Critique of Aristotle's Philosophy of Mind* (1969), *Hegel in Comparative Literature* (1970), and *Hegel: The Essential Writings* (1974). His "A Critical Survey of Hegel Scholarship in English, 1962–69" appeared in the *American Philosophical Quarterly* (1971), in Spanish translation in *Teorema* (1972), and was reprinted in *The Legacy of Hegel* (1973), together with his "Hegel: A Bibliography of Books in English, Arranged Chronologically." His "Cartesian Doubt and Hegelian Negation" is forthcoming in *Hegel and the History of Philosophy*, the proceedings of the 1972 HSA conference.